Speaking in Many Tongues

To W. H. Frederick
    D. J. Ross
    L. B. Rivers

Speaking in Many Tongues

Essays in foreign-language teaching

THIRD EDITION

Wilga M. Rivers

Harvard University

Cambridge University Press

Cambridge
London   New York   New Rochelle
Melbourne   Sydney

Published by the Press Syndicate of the University of Cambridge
The Pitt Building, Trumpington Street, Cambridge CB2 1RP
32 East 57th Street, New York, NY 10022, USA
296 Beaconsfield Parade, Middle Park, Melbourne 3206, Australia

First and second editions © Newbury House Publishers, Inc. 1972, 1976
Third edition © Cambridge University Press 1983

First published by Newbury House Publications, Inc. 1972,
second edition 1976
Third edition published by Cambridge University Press 1983

Printed in the United States of America

Library of Congress Cataloging in Publication Data
Rivers, Wilga M.
Speaking in many tongues.
Bibliography: p.
Includes index.
1. Language and languages – Study and teaching.
I. Title.
P51.R53   1983   418'.007   82-23657
ISBN 0 521 25402 7 hardcover
ISBN 0 521 27418 4 paperback

Contents

Preface

We often speak of language as a vehicle of expression – a metaphor that can illumine many aspects of our foreign-language teaching situation. Language is a vehicle of meaning that we do not even realize we are using; in other words, a vehicle that is transporting a person's message somewhere but is not itself the object of the trip. Before students can use such a vehicle for their purposes it must be constructed, and this construction requires a blueprint and various stages of production, with tryouts as the various sections and combinations are assembled – tryouts during which what has been assembled to date is used, if only momentarily, for its ultimate purpose. With our language vehicle this ultimate purpose is expression: people revealing themselves to, or disguising or hiding themselves from, other people. Expression involves all the problems of interpersonal relations. For this reason it is frequently less painful for teachers and students to continue working on the construction of the vehicle than to try it out for level of performance.

In a model of foreign-language teaching and learning processes that is now quite well known,[1] I have distinguished *skill-getting*, represented by both cognition and production (or pseudo-communication), from *skill-using* in interaction, which involves both reception and expression and is dependent on motivation to communicate.

The construction of our vehicle presupposes a design. Some particularly talented individuals can put the design into effect without the help of the blueprint; they appear to move directly from the prototype to production, which means that they develop their own internal representation from acquaintance with the prototype. These are the exceptions, however. Most need help in developing a series of blueprints of increasing complexity as a basis for production. Some prefer lessons in drafting blueprints, whereas others can draw them up from experience with a prototype of the vehicle. These blueprints represent the system underlying both reception and expression. Our students depend on their blueprints as they put the parts together in production so that the vehicle will function. Sometimes students try merely to copy someone else's assembly. This may work for a time but leaves the student bewildered as the assembly becomes more complicated. At this stage only those with comprehensive blueprints, or internal representations, are able to make the mechanism operate as they would like. Construction is not, however, the use of the vehicle: This is represented by the trying out that continually takes place as the assembly takes form. It is only through such tryouts that the operation of the vehicle can be smoothly integrated, the faults corrected, and the user gain confidence in handling it.

No analogy should be pushed too far. I have given attention to the differences between the blueprint, the assembly of the vehicle, and its trying out in use in Chapter 3 of this book, "From Skill Acquisition to Language Control," where I have emphasized that mere production of itself is not sufficient. In every lesson it must be regarded as preliminary to actually trying out what is being learned so that from the earliest stages all learning activities lead to some form of real communication rather than remaining at the level of pseudo-communication through imposed utterances.

Interaction has always been the most neglected part of the language activities in which we engage in the classroom. This situation will not improve unless definite steps are taken to include substantial interaction activities in each lesson. Because "real" communication for our students takes place in the native language, it is not surprising that they need some stimulus to use the foreign language for natural purposes. Interaction does not take place in a void. It is not enough to put several people together; there must also be some situational element that naturally elicits an interchange. Interaction is a purposeful person-to-person affair in speech and in most kinds of writing. This interpersonal character of interaction explains why so much of foreign-language teaching and learning remains at the production or pseudo-communication level.

In most classrooms there is very little reason or opportunity for students or teachers to reveal themselves to each other: The relationship is a formal and formalized one for which conventionalities suffice. The teacher is there to teach; the students are there to learn what the teacher or the administration thinks they should learn. The usual greetings are exchanged, conventional questions are asked about material presented aurally or graphically, and conventional answers arising from the material are expected. Common remarks that may be heard are: "Come to the point, Johnny. We're not interested in your personal history"; "Don't ask silly questions"; "That's nothing to do with it. Didn't you hear the question?" John Holt describes the mechanisms students employ to defend themselves in class and protect their real selves from the humiliation and embarrassment that could result if they ventured to express themselves in an uncertain, often hostile environment[2] (and this in their native language). The emotional needs of the individual that must be understood by the teacher if the students are to realize their full potential are discussed in Chapter 7, "Motivating through Classroom Techniques."

G. I. Brown points out that "attempts at communication solely on a rational level are bound to fail when the issues involved have personal relevance for the participants. Personal relevance connotes an affective dimension, people feel and value as well as think about the position they hold. Denying or ignoring the existence of feelings in communication is like building a house without a foundation or framework."[3] No wonder it is more comfortable for student and teacher in the foreign-language class to remain at the level of pseudo-communication. Those who advocate that foreign-language instruction should begin with spontaneous communication and free interaction with no preparation with structured materials are ignoring this affective element.

Spontaneous communication and free interaction are possible in any language only when teachers and their students have built up a warm, uninhibited, confident, sympathetic relationship and when such a relationship also exists among the students themselves. In the first lessons no such state of affairs exists as yet. The teacher's efforts from the beginning should be devoted to building up such relationships through enjoyable, successful experiences in using interesting and amusing segments of language in a multiplicity of ways so that students begin to feel that they can express real concerns through this new medium and that it is exhilarating to do so. This confident attitude, so essential to development of future speaking skill, is very fragile and can be stifled quite early by a situation where the teacher has the advantage of fluency and is inevitably right while the student is uncertain, groping, and for the most part wrong. Early interaction practice calls for self-restraint and tact on the part of the teacher. Once the students understand the rules of the game – that you do the most you can with the little you have in some meaningful activity shared with others in the group, and that the teacher is there not to condemn but to give a helping hand, a gentle reminder, and much encouragement – confident self-expression is possible even at a very early stage. In Chapter 10, "Testing and Student Learning," I consider how this approach affects our testing procedures, particularly for effective evaluation of macro-language use as opposed to micro-language learning.

It is because of this fundamental interpersonal factor that methods and techniques imposed on the teacher, efficient as they might have seemed in the abstract in terms of language-learning theory, have always proved successful for some people working with some classes but not for all. (For a survey of the major approaches, see Chapter 1, "The View on the Way Up: A Wider Perspective"; for trends in language learning and teaching, see Chapter 9, "Understanding the Learner in the Language Laboratory.") The interaction of teacher personality, multiple student personalities, and what each brings into the classroom from the outside can be observed only in unique situations. Take one student away from the group or add one student and you immediately have a new mix. Change the teacher and the situation is no longer the same. All teachers are conscious of this fact, which has been the bane of large-scale investigations and experimentation in teaching methods.

Is methodology then futile? Not at all. Methodology should be based on what we know about language (what it is and how it operates – still a matter of controversy); what we know about human beings (how they learn and how they learn language and whether these are different processes or merely different manifestations of the same process, another question still under investigation); and what we know about people in interaction (a prolific area of psychological study). It is inevitable, then, that methodological recommendations will change as our knowledge of these three factors evolves, with earlier postulates being rejected and new premises accepted. Teachers should keep in touch with findings in these areas and share the excitement of a developing and progressing discipline. "If Only I Could Remember It All! Facts and Fiction about Memory in Language Learning," "Linguistic and Psychological Factors in Speech Perception and Their Implications for Listening and Reading Materials," and "Reading Fluently: Extracting Meaning for Pleasure and Profit" (Chapters 4, 5, and 6, respectively) will supply teachers with much new information, particularly in the psychology of perception and cognitive processing.

At this point the teacher takes over as a professional and as an individual with his or her own gifts, insights, and preferences. First, teachers must know themselves and their strengths and weaknesses in interpersonal relations. Then they must know their students: who they are, what their aspirations are, how they learn as individuals. The teacher will find that the general attitudes of students fluctuate, not only from generation to generation or from decade to decade, but also, in a period of rapid change, almost from year to year. Senior high school and college students may still accept what their younger brothers and sisters are already rejecting. In an earlier period, for instance, with a more docile student population, it seemed possible to subordinate individual students to the efficient system for their own good, as seen by their teachers; now the efficient system must be subordinated to individual learning preferences if there is to be a high quality of learning. This is a period of plurality of objectives and diversity of learning approaches, a subject I discuss in Chapters 11 and 12, "From the Pyramid to the Commune: The Evolution of the Foreign-Language Department" and "The Revolution Now: Revitalizing the University Language Departments."

Teachers in this volatile period must understand how teaching and learning relate to each other and interact fruitfully, realizing that either can exist without the other. They must learn to teach in such a way that they do not interpose themselves between the learner and what is to be learned. They must accept and encourage a variety of learning styles allowing for differences in individuals. Some people learn more by the ear than the eye, others learn from printed texts; some learn from abstract reflection, some from concrete manipulation; some learn more slowly than others; some prefer to learn by themselves, whereas others prefer help, even direction, and need the stimulation of a group if they are to realize their potential. Foreign-language teachers for this generation must consider carefully how they can devise learning programs for types of students they did not ordinarily meet in their classes in an earlier period. These and related matters are examined in Chapter 8, "Teacher–Student Relations: Coercion or Cooperation?" and Chapter 13, "Conservation and Innovation: Foreign Languages in Two-Year Undergraduate Institutions."

By this time my teacher-readers may find their heads spinning. They have listened, they have studied, they have read. None of this is sufficient. Truly successful teachers are highly idiosyncratic. From this plethora of information and recommendations, they select. They take from the new what suits their own personality and their teaching style and what is appropriate for the personalities and aspirations of their own students, thus forming their own approach. They are not afraid to innovate, to rearrange, to redesign their courses, because continual reflection and appropriate adjustment and readjustment keep them professionally alive, making them more interesting to their students. Above all, they do not remain caught up in their own discipline but see it in relation to the total educational experience. They see themselves contributing, along with their colleagues in mathematics, in social studies, in guidance, to the maturation process of young minds and personalities. They remain in step with changing approaches to the whole curriculum and view their subject in that perspective. In step? Why should they not be in the vanguard in meeting new challenges and seeking new opportunities? How they can lead while remaining true to the essence of their own discipline is discussed in Chapter 2, "Educational Goals: The Foreign-Language Teacher's Response." Such an approach requires flexibility of mind and sensitivity to professional winds of change. The directions of change that seem to be shaping up at present and the important matter of preparing future teachers who can fit into new patterns are developed in Chapter 14, "Students, Teachers, and the Future."

So we move, let us hope, as a profession into an era of tolerance and acceptance of difference – the era of the commune, where divisive and acrimonious competition to draw teachers in one direction and then in another will appear irrelevant, and the word "best" will be recognized for the subjective and relative term it is. Let us look forward to a period of "many flowers blooming, day lilies perhaps, but each in its day and hour bringing fragrance to the experience of some."[4] Invite me to visit your garden at that stage so that I can see what your skill and care have brought into being.

Speaking in Many Tongues is intended primarily for teachers of foreign languages in high schools and undergraduate institutions, although teachers of second languages (where the language being taught is in general use in the surrounding community) will find much of interest and importance to them, especially in Chapters 1–10 and 14. The book will be enlightening and helpful to teachers and prospective teachers in preservice methods courses and inservice training, in institutes and courses for updating knowledge of the field, or for general reading. In this preface I have drawn together the main themes to show how they reflect a coherent view of language learning. The American Council on the Teaching of Foreign Languages has adopted as programmatic priorities Curriculum and Materials Development, Public Awareness, Foreign Language Proficiency (for students and teachers), Research, and Teacher Education.[5] Each of these is treated in considerable detail in the various chapters of this book. Because the chapters contain revised versions of articles written over a span of years for a number of special meetings, conferences, or publications in different places, the reader will find a certain reiteration of major emphases: the centrality of the learners (their needs, wants, inner motivation, and innate or acquired learning styles and language-using processes); the understanding and empathetic role of the teacher; the importance of relating educational programs (and these include language-teaching programs) to the requirements of the local situation; and the necessity for a broad approach to language learning, going beyond the development of language control to interactional competence and the acceptance and appreciation of the ways of thinking, the values, and the reactions of speakers of other languages. These are the messages of the book.

The questions in the *Let's discuss* section at the end of each chapter are intended to be used. It is in thinking through the material and developing one's own viewpoint that one makes ideas one's own.

Extra readings are suggested in the Notes. The Bibliography comprises only books; references to articles can be found by looking for the author's name in the Index. The Notes are placed at the end of the book to provide easier reference to these materials than is provided by footnotes on individual pages. For those seeking a more thorough study of subjects raised, cross-references are given to *Communicating Naturally in a Second Language: Theory and Practice in Language Teaching* (Rivers, 1983); *Teaching Foreign-Language Skills*, 2d ed. (Rivers, 1981); and the *Practical Guides to the Teaching of French, German, Spanish, English as a Second or Foreign Language, and Hebrew* (Rivers, 1975, and Rivers et al., 1975, 1976, 1978, and in press).

Finally, I would like to express my unbounded gratitude to Ann Julie Boruvka for her devoted and untiring support in the preparation of the manuscript and to Reed Woodhouse for his expert and cheerful typing and retyping of the materials.

Wilga M. Rivers

Harvard University
Cambridge, Massachusetts
August, 1982

1   The view on the way up: a wider perspective

We often talk about *cycles in language teaching* or even swings of the pendulum. I prefer a different metaphor. Imagine you are climbing a cathedral tower in Europe. Your muscles ache and you pause, out of breath, on narrow landings. Each time you rest on the way up, you glimpse the landscape through narrow slits, until finally you see it spread out before you as you reach the top.

As we come to the first slit in the wall, we peer out and we see a school with some children playing in the yard. At the next slit, we are looking out over a farm. A young boy is bringing some cows into the yard. As we go around, there is another slit, through which we see glinting the water of a small river. Next we look out at the sea, with the small waves breaking on the sandy shore. As we continue past the landing to the next flight of stairs, we discover that the school is out in the fields. A track leads to a wood. Then the farm comes back into view, and we see the farmer on his tractor gathering bales of hay. He is going out of sight. In a few moments, we see him again as he reaches the fence by the river. At the next chink, we see that the river flows into the sea farther along the shore. As we go around and up, we find the track through the woods comes out behind the farmhouse, and on the far bank of the river is a village with a road running down to a small cove where fishing smacks are at anchor.

As we mount, then, we see wider and wider perspectives. *Each time around, as we see different parts of the landscape in greater depth, individual elements begin to form comprehensible relationships*, and one part is seen to be interdependent with another.

Isn't this what we have been experiencing in language teaching – changing perspectives of what is basically the same landscape? The school, the farm, the village, the sea – how, we wonder, are they related? Why are they in such close proximity? Is there a deeper, underlying rationale we have not yet perceived at the level we have reached?

Revised version of an article published in W. C. Born, ed., *The Foreign Language Learner in Today's Classroom Environment* (Middlebury, Vt.: NEC, 1979), pp. 11–18.

For purposes of discussion, I shall call the four sides of our tower *the Why, the What, the How, and the Who of language teaching.* The *Why* will refer to both rationale and objectives. For what reasons are we teaching languages in this day and age, and toward what objectives are we directing our efforts? These, we will find, are as closely related as the sea and the fishing smacks at anchor. The *What* refers to the nature of language (the substance of our teaching), as well as to the content of our courses. Here again there is a close relationship like that of the fields and the hay. The *How* refers to the way language is acquired, and this determines approach, method, techniques, and materials (the teacher's contribution to language learning). The *Who* refers to our clientele: the language learners. Who are they? What are their needs and wants, their aspirations, their learning styles, and their aptitudes?

Let us look now at some of the early stages of our progress up the language-teaching tower, what we thought we were seeing, and the importance we placed on our partial insights.

Grammar-translation emphasis

We will come in at the grammar-translation landing. There was no doubt about the *Why* in those days! When the method was first developed and swept Europe like wildfire, modern languages were trying to establish themselves as a respectable study for intelligent students, as a study that made a real contribution to mental training and intellectual development. Clearly, the aim of modern languages was to prepare students *to read and appreciate great literature and philosophy*, a goal that was to be reached by serious mental effort in language study.

For the *What*, consequently, there was much study of structure, understanding of grammar rules and applying these, particularly through translation, and much memorizing of long vocabulary lists. As soon as possible one was reading and translating difficult descriptive and expository passages, studying sixteenth-century poetry, seventeenth-century plays, and eighteenth-century philosophical treatises. This was the period when it was quite acceptable to pronounce *b-o-i-s* in French as *boys*. After all, as one Oxford professor is said to have remarked, "My concierge speaks French fluently, but I wouldn't employ her in my department."

The *How* was the deductive presentation of rules and explaining of structure, followed by exercises and translation of passages of prose, and sometimes poetry, to make students conscious of the contribution of each word or syntactic structure.

Who, then, were the students? Clearly they were an elite. Only the intellectual, abstract thinker was welcome. Those who could not reach the required standards were expected to drop out early in the sequence. As one of my colleagues who was addicted to this teaching approach used to say, "I can only teach the 'A' students!" The *Why* at this period led logically to the *What*; the *What* led to the *How*; and these determined the *Who*, that is, the type of student who might want such a course and who had any possibility of completing it successfully.

Audiolingual or aural-oral approach

Next came the audiolingual period. To the question "*Why* teach foreign languages?" the answer was clear. Apart from its intrinsic values, still undisputed within the profession, the *national interest* demanded it. From the needs of the armed forces to the post-Sputnik trauma, it was clear that Americans needed to understand and be understood. How could peace be built if peoples of different cultures and different languages did not understand each other? And this included people of very different cultures: Not only were French, German, and Spanish important, but Chinese, Russian, and Ewe as well.

So the concentration was on the *What* and the *How*. What was language basically and how was it acquired? Clearly, according to the structuralist principles of the time, language for communication was *primarily spoken*, although reading the written language would also be important for some. It was generally believed that language was "a system of arbitrary vocal symbols by means of which the members of a society interact in terms of their total culture."[1] Language and culture were intertwined. *How* then was language acquired? The accepted answer was that our knowledge of and ability to use the language reflected *a set of habits built in by reinforcement or reward*, that is, by confirmation of their efficacy.[2] Mastery of a language to a level of near-native performance, primarily in listening and speaking, became the goal, and this required a long sequence of study. This mastery would be achieved by building in habits of language use, through the memorization of building blocks of communicative language material and by drilling in the use of structural frameworks. I shall not dwell in detail on how this was to be done, since the approach is now well known.[3] Common expectations were quick-fire response; active participation of students as frequently as possible through choral and individual response and in language laboratory work; avoidance of possible error through the structuring of the materials; immediate confirmation of the right response; language practice before analysis; and the use of near-authentic materials and native speed of speech.

Who then were the clientele? Those who could stay the course, for the most part. Aptitude tests were developed to detect the weaker candidates, and there was a process of natural selection by attrition. Teachers tried to reach a broader clientele, but near-native mastery is only an attainable goal for the few in most conventional programs. The *Why* seemed self-evident, so emphasis fell on the *What* and the *How*.

Cognitive approaches

At the second landing, we begin another round of the tower. This leads us to the so-called cognitive approach. I say "so-called" because it was based on a very limited view of what is "cognitive." All processes that involve the mind are cognitive. Perceiving a sound or word, imitating a sound or phrase, analyzing an utterance into functional components, categorizing components, constructing a similar utterance by analogy, inferencing, repeating accurately what someone else has said, adapting this to a new context – all of these involve cognitive processes.[4] Let us be clear on what we are talking about when we use technical vocabulary.

The cognitive approach broke with audiolingualism over the *What* and the *How*: *What* is language and *how* is it acquired? Here language teachers were dragged somewhat bewildered into squabbles among linguists, at a time when even linguists could not agree on the application, if any, of their theories.[5] Language was not "a system of arbitrary vocal symbols" linguistically, or "a system of habits" psychologically, we were told. Instead, in accordance with Chomskyan theory, it seems that human beings come into the world with *innate language-learning abilities*, a language acquisition device (LAD) that proceeds by *hypothesis testing*. Children make hypotheses about the form of the grammar to which they are attending and compare this with their innate knowledge of the grammar of a possible language that is congruent with the abstract principles of universal grammar. This grammar is capable of generating the many surface variations of the specific language to which the child is attending.[6] In this way the individual's competence, or internalized knowledge of the grammar

4

of the first language, is built up. Language use, or performance, is thus *rule-governed behavior* that enables the speakers to create new utterances that conform to the rules they have internalized.[7]

This theory led in two directions: the first was up a set of steps into the bell ringer's room. This room had a restricted view, rather like that from the first level (the grammar-translation level), because of an obscuring gargoyle. The other direction was up to the next level. We'll follow the deviation to the bell ringer's room first.

Seizing on the idea of rule-governed behavior, *a cognitive code-learning method* was proposed that developed from a point of view rather similar to that of the grammar-translation method: a "modified grammar-translation approach," it was acknowledged to be.[8] Basically, it recommended explaining grammar rules, practicing their use through exercises, and then seeing them in action in the context of reading (or listening) materials. This is a process of language analysis, then application, then synthesis. It is a deductive approach: from rule to application. Students were to acquire "competence" first, before being asked to "perform."[9] The *What* and the *How* predominate here. We hear little about the *Why* or the *Who*.

Taking the other direction from the same Chomskyan theory, we arrive at level three: *natural language learning*. If this sounds familiar, "natural" methods have been with us for a long time. They were the focus of much controversy in the United States in the middle of the nineteenth century and were referred to by Sweet in 1899.[10] Language teachers have always been fascinated by the experience of little children learning their first language. It seems so effortless, so enjoyable, and so successful, in contrast to most classroom language learning, that we feel we should be able to reproduce it.

Starting from the *How* of first-language learning, which I have just discussed, natural language learning builds on the premise that human beings have an innate language-learning capacity that proceeds by hypothesis testing. Second-language learners, then, are perceived as proceeding through a series of approximate *interim grammars, or interlanguages*, as they gradually acquire the full grammar of the language. These partial grammars are an essential stage in the learning process, as learners test out hypotheses as to the real nature of the grammar of the new language. These hypotheses are borne out or refuted as the individuals try to communicate and are, or are not, successful in conveying their meaning.[11]

The *Who* now enters the picture. Who are our language learners? They are individuals who have already learned one language by a natural process. They retain a certain capacity, according to the theory, for acquiring language naturally through communication and interaction in the language, as well as for learning it in a more structured fashion. The stage is set so that the students decide when they will begin using the language. The *What* is social interaction, which constitutes essentially the course content. As students hear and use the language they acquire structure – a clearly inductive procedure. *Why* make this effort? Because people have a natural desire to communicate and this we can build on. (Curran's Community Language Learning fits into this paradigm, as learners attempt to communicate from the beginning with the help of counselors, who supply the new words and structures for what the learners want to say.[12])

The more orthodox supporters of natural language learning, however, have learned something on the way up. In the nineteenth century, proponents of the natural method rejected all grammars and dictionaries and all visual representations of the language for long periods of time. This time around, by contrast, systematic study of the grammar is retained. Grammar is studied by the students out of class, so that class time can be devoted to focused communication and *interaction activities*. With these activities, language may be acquired in a natural way through use. This means skill-using in class and skill-getting as preparation out of class.[13] Vocabulary becomes important again. To facilitate understanding and use of the language to express their own meaning, students are encouraged to broaden their vocabulary.

Now we proceed out on to the platform at the top of the tower to view the whole landscape and gather the various parts into perspective. (In case anyone should think we have reached the top of the spiral, I may add that plans are already underway to raise the level of the tower, so that it will not be overlooked by those of St. Scientia, St. Mathematicus, and St. Aesthetica.)

What does our wider perspective on language teaching bring to our notice? We have had the *Why, What, How,* and *Who* priorities of the grammar-translation approach; the *What, How,* and *Who* emphasis of the audiolingual approach; and the competing *What* and *How* of the cognitive-code learning approach. Natural language learning began with *How* and brought *Who* to the fore, these providing the rationale for the *What* and the *Why*.

What about our students?

Now, in the fresh spring air at the top, we see that the *Who*, which has been rising through our various experiences, now becomes the pervasive factor that interrelates the other elements in our programs. The individualization emphasis of the seventies was the view down

6

the light well that made us aware of the centrality of the *Who*. It cast light on our efforts at all levels. Once the *Why* and the *What* were established, individualization provided a way of adapting the *How* to the *Who*.

From our viewpoint at the top, we ask the basic question, *Who* are our students? – with its corollary, *What* are their needs and wants? As educators as well as foreign-language teachers, we then have to strike a balance between these two – our students' needs and wants.

How do we find out who our students really are and what they are seeking in language learning? The most direct approach is to ask them. Instead of looking at neighboring schools, or trends in the profession, or trends in textbooks for guidance, we look at our own students. (Questionnaires for this purpose have been published at various times.[14] Teachers should use these as a guide to devising one suited to their own situation.) I would not presume to tell you who your students are, and who mine are is irrelevant to you.

Starting from *Who* leads to a different *Why* or rather *Whys*. Why would *my* students want to learn another language? In my situation what are the community priorities that are influencing their choices?

Inevitably, beginning with *Who* leads to *multiple objectives*. Some want to be able to communicate with people of other tongues; some want to be able to read, whether it be comics, science fiction, poetry, road signs, technical information, novels, or newspapers; some want to understand films or radio; some want to be able to sing the songs of another culture. Our students hope to use the skills they are acquiring in *diverse occupations*. A University of Illinois investigation in 1973 unearthed the following aspirations: Students expected to use their knowledge of a language in science, anthropology, philosophy, music, journalism, business, aviation, law, inner-city medicine, linguistics, engineering, social work at home, social, military, or religious service abroad, diplomacy, international law, interpreting, library science, advertising, speech therapy, archaeology, and astrophysics, among others.[15] A decade later, we would certainly wish to add to this list government, banking, and international business operations.[16]

Our answer to these expressions of interests has to be a reexamination of the *What*. Whatever our view of language, what should be the content of our courses? Clearly the twenty-six areas of interest I have listed cannot demand of us twenty-six different courses. The demands of many of these are basically similar: *to be able to communicate effectively*. Our students want to be able to understand and be understood, to be able to operate in another culture without offensiveness, and to know and be comfortable with the basics of a language, so that they will have a firm foundation on which to build as future need requires. The very variety of their needs, however, requires us to make *broad interdisciplinary contacts*. It implies broadening our horizons to the interpenetration of language in many areas. It demands of our future teachers a much broader general culture than in the past, so that they may be prepared intellectually to seize opportunities, and create opportunities, for the integration of language with other disciplinary approaches.[17]

Many more students are interested in what we have to offer than we allow ourselves to believe, but we must listen to their voices. They want more than bits and pieces that lead to no real knowledge or skill; they want more than a carefully crafted elementary competency. They want to be able to use what they have learned in real acts of communication, but they are not willing to accept the humiliation of being laughed at because they sound so odd.

As examples of the adaptation of a program step-by-step to a particular student body, I would like to cite our own experience in Romance languages at Harvard and a similar approach to a very different student body at Northeastern University in Boston, which has a unique work-study approach to higher education.

To begin with *Harvard*, a period of sensitization to Harvard students makes it clear that most students do not see themselves as future foreign-language teachers, so the number of potential concentrators of the traditional kind is limited. For instance, of 950 semester enrollments in French language classes in 1980–1, barely 4 percent were concentrators, although 36 percent of these students were studying at postrequirement level. Furthermore, I do not view our role as essentially to provide compensatory instruction in elementary and intermediate language, although we do this well and those who need a requirement course pass through it quickly and enjoyably for the most part.[18]

Of 455 elementary-level students in Romance languages in the first semester of 1979–80, only 28 percent were there specifically to meet a requirement (about 127 students), and of 302 intermediate-level students, only 32 percent were specifically requirement students (about 95 in all). Who were all the others (535 out of 757)? What was their uncoerced interest in learning another language? Of students in Romance languages, 75 percent at the elementary level and 49 percent at the intermediate level were studying a third or fourth language. Thus, language learning cannot be antipathetic to them.

This is not the situation just at Harvard. To keep to institutions I know, at the *University of Illinois*, a typical Midwest state institution, in 1973 only 38 percent of the students at the advanced level were majors or concentrators. At the advanced level, 62 percent were there just because they were interested in going further with the language. The Illinois situation has been confirmed at Harvard where, after three days of testing to select thirty out of sixty applicants for our most advanced French language course, our *cours de perfectionnement*, the course instructor found that only two of the thirty accepted were concentrators. The others were heading for fields as diverse as those I quoted earlier. Many of these advanced students are motivated to seek language study at such a high level because their enthusiasm was fired by excellent high school teaching. (Of those accepted, 72 percent had studied French at junior and senior high school for five or more years.)

Our enrollments in languages at Harvard, as at many other institutions, are steadily increasing (by 66 percent between 1974 and 1981). Where is this increase coming from? It does not come from an increase in the requirement groups, which remain approximately at the same level from year to year. (Each year about 20 percent of new students have to undertake language study to fulfill the undergraduate graduation requirement.) We have, however, been creating postrequirement language courses to an advanced level that are innovative and exciting, using literature, film, poetry, folklore, documents of contemporary culture, active communication, authentic listening materials, translation as a craft, and case studies for business students. These are the courses that are constantly expanding. Students may now continue their language study at fifteen different entry levels, which supply varied content from which to choose.

At the fourth semester postrequirement level (upper intermediate), we have our "Oral Survival" courses in French and Spanish, which meet the needs of many students for confident, active use of language for oral communication. The French oral survival course expanded from one to five sections within three years of its establishment, and we expect a similar development in Spanish. We have special intensive beginning courses in French, Spanish, and Italian for students who have already been successful in another language and have strong reasons for needing or wanting this additional language. Because these courses may not be used to meet the language requirement, only good language learners enroll. Consequently, the courses move very fast, and students achieve considerable fluency and language control within one semester.

We have created a first semester – second semester – fourth semester literature survey or advanced language route for our own beginners, because they learn too much to keep them marking time unnecessarily with weaker second-year entering students. We have paralleled the usual advanced language courses with more communication-oriented courses, which emphasize contemporary culture, and have had to add new ones. Enthusiasm spreads over the grapevine. We have initiated a French for Business course (*Le Français des*

Affaires), based on case studies from French enterprises, and this has the support of senior faculty in the Harvard Business School. Portuguese will soon follow.

In case some should object that Harvard is different, I will relate experiences at *Northeastern University* in Boston, a school noted for its *integrated work-study programs for professional training*. The language departments at Northeastern have been experimenting with innovative courses directed at the "many thousands of students in majors such as Criminal Justice, Human Services, Recreation, Nursing, Pharmacy and Allied Health, Rehabilitation, Business, and Engineering whose effectiveness in their chosen professions could be vastly enhanced by a knowledge of a foreign language."[19] Beginning with German for Business (with a reading emphasis) and Spanish for Criminal Justice and Human Services (with an oral communication orientation), the language departments have substantially increased enrollments and are constantly looking for new openings to establish a useful complementary role for foreign language in the university's distinctive cooperative education program, which places students in internships both in this country and abroad.

I am sure many other institutions could tell similar stories. I am quoting our own experience and that of Northeastern to counter the unnecessarily gloomy attitude that has been in fashion for a few years. There is no need for languages to languish and wither. We have much to give, and we must not let new opportunities pass us by. By way of digression, I offer a caption from one of Winston Churchill's books: "How the great democracies triumphed and so were able to resume the follies which had so nearly cost them their life." The future will depend on our following through.

Let us move on from the *What* to the *How*. With a diversified *Who*, *Why*, and *What*, we must expect various approaches to the *How*. A great diversity of students results in multiple objectives, a multiplicity of possible content, and therefore a great variety of techniques from which to choose. One caveat is in order: Once the *Who* becomes central, the *affective* aspect of language teaching becomes very important. The different personalities of the students, the different ways they react and express themselves, and their different modes of learning must remain in the forefront of our thinking and planning.[20]

You may have observed that there is a Yale Plan and a Dartmouth Model. In the past there was a University of Chicago Method. But, for foreign languages, there is no Harvard Plan, Model, or Method. Perhaps that is because our chief concern is with good teaching. We are strong on *individual initiative* and *imaginative course development*, with approaches that are compatible with teacher personality and preference. In this way, the teacher reacts as a person with

10

students as persons in particular associations; both teacher and student can thus be very much at ease in class and feel free to develop a unique style of interaction for that particular course. We subscribe to Palmer's view, expressed in 1921: "We use each and every method, process, exercise, drill, or device which may further us in our immediate purpose and bring us nearer to our ultimate goal; we adopt every good idea and leave the door open for all future developments; we reject nothing except useless and harmful forms of work. . . [selecting] judiciously and without prejudice all that is likely to help us in our work."[21]

Interrelationships

To return then to our original view from the tower. From our higher perspective we see that the school is there because there are children at the farm. The farm is there to feed the people in the village. The village is there because there are fish in the sea. Without the sea, the others lose their purpose and relationship.

From the higher level of experience we achieve a wider perspective and perceive new interrelationships and dependencies. *We* are here because we have students. Students determine our course objectives. Our course objectives determine our content. Our techniques are selected and developed to enable us to teach that content more effectively, so that we may enable our students to realize *their* objectives.

With a changing climate at the present time, I feel we, as foreign-language teachers, are about to have a new chance to show what we can contribute to the general education of all students. I shall finish, then, with a warning from James Russell Lowell (a New England voice from a century ago): "There is a tide in the affairs of men, but there is no gulf-stream setting forever in one direction."

Let's discuss

1 By what method or approach did you learn a foreign language? What actually took place in the classroom? How did you personally react to this type of teaching? What proposals would you like to have made to your teacher to improve the instruction?
2 Who are *your* students? Describe their background, age, interests in language learning, special problems, and so on. What types of courses would be of most interest to them?

3 Do you personally prefer an inductive or a deductive approach to language learning? What are the pros and cons of each approach? (Inductive learning moves from examples to rule, deductive from rules to example.)
4 Set out a rationale for teaching other languages in your situation. Discuss this question with others in your class group. (Choose one to act as devil's advocate and point out the flaws in your argument.)
5 What seem to you to be the characteristics of "natural" language learning? How can these be provided for in the classroom?

2 Educational goals: the foreign-language teacher's response

A continually changing educational environment that is responding to social pressures, political demands, and rapid changes in career opportunities, as new knowledge transforms old practices, requires each section of the educational profession to review its objectives from time to time with great care. Such a review must precede plans for future development. The ultimate aim of such a review will be to bring educational practice into line with these demands in a way that is consistent with its own intrinsic aims, namely, to provide optimal opportunities for students to develop their potential as individuals and as productive citizens.

As educators, we innovate and we conserve. We try to pass on the best of what humanity has experienced and learned. As we study the present in the special light thrown upon it by the past, we seek to understand and prepare for the demands the future will make upon us and the graduates of our programs.

In a modern pluralist society there are many clashing voices. These force on schools short-term pressures that are often contradictory. *The profession must continually weigh the value of what it does and what it has learned through past experience, against what society, or sections of society, would have it do.* Innovation must build on strengths, correct weaknesses, and eliminate what is no longer useful or compatible with firm directions of change. A continual swinging to and fro, hither and yon, in order to be in the forefront of particular movements, is not only dizzying, but also leads to dispersed efforts, which produce unspectacular results as two or three directions are scouted at the same time. Then, when a continuing direction of change does appear, the would-be leader in innovation is often left high and dry on a sandbar.

Before we decide what our objectives in language teaching should be at any particular time in any specific place we need to consider carefully where our society is headed, and the demands this future will make on our students. These factors are fundamental to the

Revised version of an article originally published in W. C. Born, ed., *The Foreign Language Learner in Today's Classroom Environment* (Middlebury, Vt.: NEC, 1979), pp. 19–51.

major educational emphases that are shaping the total curriculum, of which foreign-language study is an integral part. Ten such emphases have come to the fore more recently, and it is worth discussing carefully ways in which foreign-language study may contribute to each of these trends. As a particular emphasis is selected as an educational priority by a district, state, or nation, or is forced on schools by a crucial social or political circumstance, administrators will expect teachers to present a rationale for the continuing role of foreign language as an essential element in the educational enterprise. We can do this under pressure if we have devoted time beforehand to a careful analysis of what we can reasonably offer in each set of circumstances.

A rationale is not of itself sufficient. We must also show that we have the flexibility, the courage, and the imagination to adapt our content and approach, in order to bring what we can offer in line with what society is demanding of us and what others also are willing to contribute.

Trends in educational objectives

The short-term and long-term objectives I have identified can be broadly subsumed under two educative approaches, both valid and both centering on the needs of students of diverse aptitudes, personalities, and ambitions. Two questions the students need to ask will serve as headings for these two approaches: *What can I do with it in practical domains?* and *What can it do for me as a person and as a citizen?*

These questions reflect the pragmatic, utilitarian approach, on the one hand, and the humanistic, individual development, preparation for life approach, on the other. Not surprisingly, several of the trends to be discussed straddle these categories. Education, in practice, cannot be boxed in this neat, schematic fashion. The attribution to categories in these cases is a subjective decision of the author's.

A. *What can I do with it in practical domains?*
1   Accountability, competency-based education, minimal competency testing, thorough teaching of the basics
2   Career education
3   Equality of educational opportunity and mainstreaming
4   Lifelong learning and community education

B. *What can it do for me as a person and as a citizen?*
5   Self-actualization, personality development, self-enhancement, humanistic education

14

6   Interpersonal relations and communication
7   Multicultural education, values clarification, understanding and appreciation of one's own cultural heritage and that of others
8   Development of an international or global perspective
9   Developing the full potential of the gifted
10 Revived emphasis on the value of a liberal education and the role of the humanities

A. What can I do with it in practical domains?

A.1. ACCOUNTABILITY, COMPETENCY-BASED EDUCATION, MINIMAL COMPETENCY TESTING, THOROUGH TEACHING OF THE BASICS

If standardized test scores are going down, if students are leaving schools unable to read, write, or calculate sufficiently well to perform what is required of them in employment or in further education, taxpayers will hold accountable educators who are spending their dollars for not producing what these taxpayers think they are paying for. Not unreasonably then, the taxpayer-parent is now demanding that schools set out clearly what their objectives are, describe the means by which these objectives are to be achieved, and provide evidence of the degree to which they have been achieved. Explanations that the educational situation is more complex than this simple, direct approach would indicate, or that the body of students presenting for standardized tests is much more heterogeneous than it was when the tests were instituted, will not satisfy those who wish to call the schools to account for many deteriorating situations in society. What must be the response of foreign-language teachers as educators in this situation?

Before setting off blindly after the bellwethers of this trend, we should ask ourselves some penetrating questions.

a) In an educational undertaking, *what are the basic skills* a student should be able to demonstrate? At what age?

b) *How "basic" is basic*? A reductio ad absurdum would eliminate reading, writing, and arithmetic from the curriculum, as well as history, algebra, music, literature, foreign language, physical education, and the sciences. After all, students will watch television, use telephones, tapes, and eventually computers for messages and have easy access to sophisticated calculators.

c) Can we be satisfied with an education that produces a *minimal* competency or should we aim rather for an *optimal competency*: the best possible competency for each student as an individual in as many areas of personal development as a full and useful life will require?

15

d) Once the "basic" basics are assured, what comes next? We will need to move beyond mere instruction to education – *educating future citizens* of the local district, the state, nation, and world. This involves cognitive, affective, and social education. Knowledge of how languages work, ability to communicate with others beyond our immediate community and culture, and an appreciation of the viewpoints and values of these others in a plural society and in an increasingly interdependent world are part of this essential learning.

e) *How can we list all the competencies an educated citizen will need*? Is it more important to be able to read the instructions on a bottle or to be able to separate the logic of an argument from the persuasive devices by which it is disguised? Is it more important to be able to check the unit prices in a supermarket or to explain to a non-English-speaking neighbor cultural differences in the public behavior of young people? Each is a valuable skill, yet in some situations one will be more important than the other. Reading instructions on a bottle may save lives; being able to recognize when one is being manipulated may decide who is elected. Similarly, checking the values in a supermarket may mean money will be saved, whereas being able to explain culturally determined behavior may mean the avoidance of serious misunderstanding or even violence. All are competencies that enrich the life of the citizen.

Clearly, the foreign-language teacher needs to take seriously the discontent expressed by movements such as the demand for accountability, while refusing to be coerced into any form of teaching, or organization of teaching, that violates the spirit of the language-learning undertaking as an element in the education of future citizens. Management-by-objectives (deciding precisely what you are aiming for and then using personnel and resources to achieve these ends most efficiently) may be the most viable approach to the sale of gaskets and wrenches, without necessarily being directly applicable to an enterprise that seeks to facilitate, to the varying degrees individual differences allow, the mental, emotional, and social growth of human beings.

The degree to which what we have to teach in a language course can be reduced to simple, objective statements that can serve as a check on achievement depends on what we think we are teaching. If we are teaching the morphology of a verb paradigm, items of vocabulary to be memorized, or the production of strange sounds, we can certainly set out objective and measurable aims: "The student shall know the endings for each person of the verb in the present tense for the regular first conjugation and shall demonstrate this knowledge by correctly assigning personal endings for a previously unknown verb of this conjugation in nine cases out of ten."[1]

If, on the other hand, we are talking about communication, then we must revert to statements like those in the Interagency Language Roundtable (ILR) definitions of oral proficiency, established for personnel in federal agencies, such as the Foreign Service Institute and Defense Language Institutes.

Elementary Proficiency

S-1 Able to satisfy routine travel needs and minimum courtesy requirements. Can ask and answer questions on very familiar topics; within the scope of very limited language experience can understand simple questions and statements, allowing for slowed speech, repetition or paraphrase; speaking vocabulary inadequate to express anything but the most elementary needs; errors in pronunciation and grammar are frequent, but can be understood by a native speaker used to dealing with foreigners attempting to speak the language... Should be able to order a simple meal, ask for shelter or lodging, ask and give simple directions, make purchases, and tell time.

In the ILR guidelines descriptions such as these are developed, for both speaking and reading, through six levels (S-0 to S-5 and R-0 to R-5), from no practical proficiency (0) through elementary proficiency (1), limited working proficiency (2), professional proficiency (3), and distinguished proficiency (4), to native or bilingual proficiency (5). Assessing the attainment of these types of competencies can never be purely objective and requires the judgment of trained and experienced examiners.[2]

The American Council on the Teaching of Foreign Languages (ACTFL), in association with Educational Testing Services (ETS), has drawn up guidelines of this type for secondary school and undergraduate foreign-language students, which parallel the levels of the ILR scale, using the designations *novice* (low, mid, high), *intermediate* (low, mid, high), *advanced, advanced plus*, and *superior*. Detailed descriptions have been written for the competencies to be attained in speaking, listening, reading, writing, and culturally acceptable interaction. (See Appendix to this book.[3])

It is possible and desirable for us to analyze what we wish our students to achieve in language use for precise purposes in terms like these, if we know *for what purposes the students will need to use the language.* This has been the approach of the Council for Cultural Cooperation (CCC) of the Council of Europe in its analysis of the language needs of adults for forty-four specific occupations.[4] First, the contexts in which learners will want or need to express themselves in

17

the new language are established and then the linguistic resources they will need to communicate in these contexts are identified and can be taught.

The CCC approach presumes the need for a *threshold level or basic course*. This threshold level specifies in detail exactly what students with minimum requirements will know and be able to do in particular situations. These *situations* are analyzed into the social and psychological roles the speakers will need to play, the settings in which they will operate, and the topics within those settings they will need to be able to handle. The *communicative functions* they will need to fulfill are also specified, and the semantic and syntactic features required for each are listed. Finally, the concepts or *notions* people use in oral communication have been identified and the linguistic items needed for expressing these notions (for example, such concepts as spatial and temporal properties and relations, size, shape, and texture) are elaborated. The *lexicon* for the threshold level has been set at 1,000 words for production and reception and another 500 words purely for recognition purposes.[5] This "systems approach" is the most detailed so far to appear in the foreign-language field.

The 1978 New York State Curriculum guide, *Modern Languages for Everyone*, also recommends a basic course that will fulfill a diagnostic function as well as provide a "ground-floor" level. The objectives of this basic course are stated in terms of exposure rather than performance, because it provides the students with the opportunity to develop fundamental language skills while identifying their individual strengths, interests, and needs in language learning. The basic course is to be followed by a series of options that capitalize on these strengths and interests: a four-skill sequence, a listening-speaking sequence, a reading sequence, a reading-writing sequence, and special-interest courses. These options form a framework for lifelong learning and a basis for further course options at the advanced level. The instructional objectives for courses beyond the basic course are expressed in terms of students' performance. In individual language sections of the guide the objectives for each of the four communication skills are "arranged according to learning taxonomies, beginning in each case with the simplest tasks and leading in a succession of steps to the more complex."[6] Projects such as these are fundamental if foreign-language study is to be considered a full partner in the development of career education, which is discussed in the next section.

Students should learn "basics" of language and "tools" for further study. (Idaho, high school, French, German)*

*Quotations in italics are from questionnaires described later in this chapter.

Le but de l'étudiant en langue étrangère doit être d'acquérir une base à partir de laquelle il pourra élargir ses connaissances suivant ses besoins. (France, Collège d'Enseignement Secondaire, English)

A.2. CAREER EDUCATION

Properly understood, career education is not vocational education: It provides opportunities for students to investigate possible careers with their demands and satisfactions, and what successful pursuit of a particular career will require in the way of further education and additional skills.

That knowledge of a foreign language is a useful adjunct in the preparation for many different careers is becoming more and more evident. In 1978, Huebener found that 2,317 jobs requiring competence in a foreign language were advertised in the Sunday *New York Times* for the first six months of that year. In order of frequency, the languages required were Spanish, French, German, and Italian, but Portuguese, Russian, Japanese, and Arabic were also cited.[7] In the last few years articles have appeared frequently in professional journals (particularly the *ADFL Bulletin*)[8] giving information on careers in the business world; in law, medicine, and social work; in banking and finance; and in journalism or in international agencies.

Teachers in schools should gather such information and use it to inform not only career and guidance counselors, but also the administration, parents, district officials, and their own students. If our area of study is neglected because of lack of information about its potential usefulness, the fault lies with ourselves for lack of persistent effort in *dissemination of available information*. We must not delude our students, or ourselves, however, into believing that knowledge of a foreign language alone will open doors to exciting careers for them. We must work out programs within the schools that provide opportunities for students interested in these careers to continue study of particular foreign languages that will be useful to them in those fields. We must also encourage those gifted in languages to seek out career areas where they can combine their first love with more clearly vocational preparation.

Foreign-language teachers should work with career counselors, not only by providing information about the wider opportunities in many fields for those with competence in another language, but also by suggesting possible *work experiences* where the language can be used. Students in work-study programs may be encouraged to help with social work in areas where there are concentrations of persons who speak the language they are learning, or act as interpreters in hospitals, tax information centers, or welfare agencies. They may help local businesses with international correspondence or translate brochures and instruction sheets. They can help the local library catalogue foreign-language books. Students interested in teaching can help with foreign-language instruction in elementary schools or give introductory lessons to groups of children in after-school clubs. They can also help children who speak other languages who are having problems with instruction in English.

Participation in career education endeavors must be accompanied by a close look at the orientation and content of the language courses. Do they provide the type of language experiences these career-oriented students need? An investigation of students' needs and interests of the type proposed in the section on Research for Development will give direction to the rethinking of the curriculum.

Many career-oriented courses have been described in our professional journals during the last few years: courses for inner-city firefighters and police officers, for business majors, secretaries, social workers, and health science workers, among others. Special courses for those needing to be able to read in a special field have been available in colleges and universities for a long time. The direct thrust toward the goal in these existing courses can, of course, be strengthened.

At high school level, *language courses for specific purposes* should normally come after the basic course. For adults already engaged in a particular occupation, a course more directly oriented to their needs in that sphere of work may often be appropriate from the beginning. These adults will be able to help the teacher design the type of course and course content they need and can then use the material learned immediately in their next day's activities. The course will be as long or as intensive as the particular needs of the working group require. An analysis of the actual degree to which students will need to understand, speak, read, or write in their occupation will be revelatory, and a few hours of on-the-spot observation of actual working situations will reveal the type of vocabulary and structures day-to-day operations demand.[9]

> *The most important goals...are (1) to find well-paid jobs, (2) to secure promotions, (3) to lead a highly materialistic life.* (Hong Kong, technical education, English)

> *To develop the ability to converse with others; to translate current documents into English; and to prepare oneself for an exciting, rewarding career using foreign language as a tool.* (Texas, college, Russian)

A.3. EQUALITY OF EDUCATIONAL OPPORTUNITY AND MAINSTREAMING

If students of different cultures, socioeconomic backgrounds, aptitudes, abilities, disabilities, preferred modalities of learning, and career aspirations are to have equal access to a full and rounded educational experience, then *foreign-language study must be available and accessible to all.*

No longer can foreign-language teachers limit their efforts to preparing an elite group of students for entrance to undergraduate programs or for advanced placement. This fact has been brought home to teachers rather forcefully in recent years, as some institutions have dropped foreign-language entrance or graduation requirements, a move that has forced teachers to reexamine their course objectives and their teaching style. Languages can be taught to all kinds of students. Courses can be created to suit a variety of temperaments, interests, and learning preferences. There is no one way to approach a language, and there is a multiplicity of activities and of possible course contents from which to draw to help different students reach a variety of levels and objectives.

This educational trend demands from teachers in all subject areas flexibility, imagination, and the courage to innovate. Foreign-language teachers cannot claim special exemption. Once again, professional journals, reports, and association bulletins are full of imaginative suggestions from innovative teachers for course development, and these should be studied.

Foreign-language teachers can also learn to teach students with all kinds of learning disabilities and physical limitations. Language learning should be open to them as well. Their motivation to share a full education with others can be channeled by the teacher into many successful learning experiences. For the visually impaired, courses can be primarily aural-oral; for those with severe hearing deficits, the emphasis may be on the visual-graphic, although many hearing-impaired persons learn to lip-read a foreign language almost as well as their native language. The content of language courses can be reduced or expanded; language can be learned through active oral use in concrete situations by students who find abstract manipulation a problem. Few other subjects in the school curriculum are as adaptable to all types of learners.

Where the need in the school is for *bilingual programs for minority-language students or special instruction in English as a second language,* the foreign-language teacher should be the first to offer support and help in identifying the appropriate objectives of the program in the specific situation, in helping design courses to suit the needs of the types of students involved, and in disseminating information and building support for the program in the school and in the wider community.

Language teachers should encourage language students to mingle as friends with bilingual and ESL special-need groups to help them

21

feel part of the social and intellectual life of the school. Where possible, teachers should involve these groups in joint activities with their foreign-language students, using them as aides and resource persons in cases where their native language is one of those being studied. In this way, their self-esteem and pride in their ethnic origin will be built up, and foreign-language students will be able to learn first hand about the culture and traditions of these new friends.

Where *magnet schools* are proposed, foreign-language teachers' associations should work actively to convince decision makers that at least one such school should provide special language-learning opportunities for those with particular aptitude and the motivation for learning several languages. They should prepare the necessary information on the particular values and usefulness of such a concentration of opportunities, with concrete proposals for its implementation. (Such language-oriented schools are sometimes called International High Schools.[10])

> *Our goals are...survival skills for a new culture and then the literacy skills which will enable them to function near grade level with their peers as quickly as possible.* (New York State, English-Spanish bilingual education)

A.4. LIFELONG LEARNING AND COMMUNITY EDUCATION

Students who have begun a language at school frequently experience the desire to make their knowledge active at some later stage in life, especially if their initial experience has been pleasurable. Others wish to experience foreign-language learning for the first time or to take up the learning of a second or third foreign language. Still others find that their developing careers or a move to a new location require them to use a different language. Some businesses are sending their employees to community education programs to learn a language needed for the expansion of their operations. There are parents who wish to learn a language their children are studying or one spoken by their neighbors. More and more descendants of non-English-speaking immigrants are becoming curious about the language and culture of their grandparents, and yet others wish to be able to communicate with their non-English-speaking in-laws. As a result, enrollments in language-learning classes for adults have been steadily rising.

Foreign-language teachers should encourage their communities to include languages in all educational programs for adults and should be willing to cooperate fully in developing courses appropriate to the specific needs of local adult students. The high motivation and determination of adult students make them a great pleasure to teach and can imbue weary high school teachers with a new enthusiasm and respect for their subject. Just transferring the textbook and the course content from the elementary-level high school class, however, is not enough and may well kill the program in its early stages.

Teachers in all nontraditional learning programs (adult education, inservice, retraining, and career development programs, courses for leisure-time interests and retirement, and other forms of continuing education) need to be flexible and democratic in developing the type of course the student needs. This frequently involves adaptation of materials or development of new types of materials. *Adult students should be fully involved in decisions on what and how they will learn.* If their previous school experience has not made them autonomous, self-directed learners, they should be learning now how to learn without assistance, except when a real need for guidance arises. The use of small groups or pairs who prepare and present material to the class, and who use the language for purposeful interaction, should be encouraged. Communication-oriented language classes are particularly appropriate for this type of activity.

In all community language-learning endeavors (as within the school, moreover) language teachers should avoid the defensive promotion of a particular language they have been trained to teach. They should realize that all successful language learning in the community has beneficial effects for the language programs in educational institutions at all levels by developing favorable attitudes toward language learning in general among those who ultimately pay for the cost of education.

> These skills [*speaking fluently and reading with pleasure*], *if preserved through use, will be an intellectual and personal asset throughout a lifetime, no matter what career a student pursues.* (Massachusetts, college, Spanish)

B. What can it do for me as a person and as a citizen?

B.5. SELF-ACTUALIZATION, PERSONALITY DEVELOPMENT, SELF-ENHANCEMENT, HUMANISTIC EDUCATION

Here we come to a trend that has provided a ground swell in American education for many years. A humanistic approach came to the fore during the era of progressive education under the leadership of John Dewey. In the individualization movement of the 1970s, humanistic education continued its struggle for recognition of the primacy of the individual personality against deterministic behaviorist emphases. Personal learning styles and strategies rose in importance as opposed to narrowly conceived behavioral or performance objectives. Growing emphasis on awareness of individual identity and on personal choice, and a renewed interest in humanistic psychology, have brought this aspect of education once more into prominence.

In an affective or humanistic approach, students are encouraged *to talk about themselves, to be open with others, and to express their feelings.* Humanistic techniques help both teacher and student to drop their masks, to be themselves, and to accept and esteem both themselves and others. Clearly, such techniques are needed and have a rightful place in foreign-language classes. Some of the major hindrances to learning to use a language are the anxiety, tension, and face-saving silence that pervade many classrooms. Genuine communication, which is the major goal of language learning, whether through the oral or graphic medium, is impossible where teacher and students are not at ease with each other, and student is wary of fellow student.

Students can learn about themselves and others, and can experience sharing with less risk in the foreign-language class, because much of the activity can be *role playing* and *simulation.* The students can express themselves from behind a mask, a puppet, or an assumed identity, until they achieve the confidence to accept themselves and reveal themselves to each other. This kind of rock-bottom interaction can only take place when the teacher also is willing to be an equal partner rather than a director.

Content is not neglected in a class that uses humanistic techniques, because everything one is learning about the structure of a language, lexical choice to express specific meanings, levels of language for different situations, and the phonology of language in context is immediately useful in communicative interaction.

The *expressive arts* are also an integral part of a foreign-language class that aims at personality development. Language has been learned very successfully through the cooperative activity of producing a play, and through the incorporation of music and song as stimulants to the free flow of imagination and self-expression. Dance, along with music and song, helps the student to penetrate to the "soul" of another culture. These elements draw out many students whose richest gifts lie in domains other than the cognitive.

The humanistic approach underscores the essential difference of the foreign-language class in that it can provide a new beginning for students defeated by years of cumulative failure in other areas of study. With a new beginning and the development of a new self-confidence, such students can find some area of a diversified language program that meets their needs. If learning another language is viewed as part of the general educative thrust of the school, and not merely as absorption of content, then varying levels of achievement become less important than what a successful language-learning experience has contributed to a particular student's development into a mature and balanced person. One either knows or does not know the atomic weight of a particular element. One can express oneself in another language with varying degrees of flexibility and accuracy and yet be understood and accepted.

> *To become free in their expression, so as to be able to talk and write about things they love. To become able to pursue their personal curiosities, reading any written material of their taste in the language being learned.* (Italy/Massachusetts, college, Italian)

B.6. INTERPERSONAL RELATIONS AND COMMUNICATION

If our students are to live happy, productive, and satisfying lives, they must *learn to live with others harmoniously and cooperatively.* For this they must understand the processes of communication: physical, cognitive, and affective.

Students need to study different ways of thinking, communicating, and acting in their relationships with others. They need to know how a message is expressed and understood; how language and thought are intertwined; how to express their meaning unambiguously and without offensiveness; and how to listen to what others are trying to communicate. They need to understand how language is used in relation to the structure of society and its patterns of inner and outer relationships, if they are to avoid clashes, misunderstandings, and hurt. They need to learn about nonverbal communication: the ways we express our real meaning in harmony with or even in contradiction to the words we use. They need to understand the subtle contributions to meaning of body movements and facial expressions, but also the implications of slight movements of the eyebrow, head, hand, and shoulders. They need to understand cultural differences in the distance we keep between ourselves and others; the ways we touch and avoid; the degree of eye contact we maintain; the effects of loudness of voice and emphasis and the uses of silence; as well as the subtle ways in which we impose our authority or convey disbelief, condescension, or support.

The processes of communication in our own language and culture become much clearer to us when we try to communicate in another language. We discover what a sentence really is when we find its form may be very different. We learn how words can indicate very slight differences in meaning, as well as the more obvious ones; how meanings are augmented or diminished by parts of words; how context, intonation, and stress modify and extend meaning. We begin to understand how we have been using language to assert our group

25

membership and keep others "in their place." These things become much clearer to us when we must first analyze what we really want to say before we decide how to express it to create the effect we desire. So much of the use of our native language is second nature to us that we are unaware of how we are using it until we study how another linguistic group uses theirs.

Similarly, the nonverbal aspects of communication become strikingly obvious to us when we see films, or even pictures, of people communicating in another language and relating to each other in another culture. Discussion of these observed differences can make us more sensitive to parallel aspects of behavior in our own environment.

Communication-oriented classes are fashionable. To be truly educational they must teach more than the ability to use the forms of another language to say what one could better convey in one's native idiom or, worse still, to express banalities, which are a waste of breath in any language. For foreign-language learning to become a full partner in the educational enterprise, we must seize the opportunities our field provides to teach *about* communication as well as indulge in it.

> Courses should be so designed that even the short-term learner grasps something about languages, and language, as interesting phenomena, interrelated and evolving, revealing both consistencies and inconsistencies, and reflecting different ways of living and thinking, so that he ceases to take language for granted, and tries to handle it with accuracy, pleasure, and respect. (New Zealand, college, French)

B.7. MULTICULTURAL EDUCATION, VALUES CLARIFICATION, UNDERSTANDING AND APPRECIATION OF ONE'S OWN CULTURAL HERITAGE AND THAT OF OTHERS

The emphasis of multicultural education is on the acceptance and appreciation of the cultural pluralism of our society. It opens eyes, minds, and hearts to different lifestyles, speech habits, traditions, and ways of interacting and enjoying life.

Multicultural education does not mean just learning about other cultural groups through listening to lectures and reading prepared materials. It means going into other cultural communities, sharing what they offer of their way of living, their pleasures and their griefs, and helping the community through friendship, support, and genuine caring for their contributions to community life. Foreign-language study with teachers who are themselves accepting of difference, and who understand and care for cultural diversity, can help students to overcome the fears and antipathies of their upbringing by providing explanations for the strange, the different, and the vaguely mysterious. If the language learned is that of a community in the neighbor-hood or nearby, it can act as a key to closer acquaintance and understanding, as students are encouraged to participate in activities of the community, make friends within the community, and help the community in its relations with the dominant language sector.

Of itself, *foreign-language study does not necessarily lead to appreciation of the values and viewpoints of those of another culture.* The cultural values of our students have not been consciously acquired and confrontation with other values can be a shocking experience: The new ways and viewpoints may seem "wrong," "bad," or "rude." This emotional revulsion to difference may be intensified by teaching materials that present stereotypes and caricatures of persons from the other culture, thus perpetuating the biases and prejudices of the students. Presenting only aspects of the other culture that are picturesque, quaint, or exotic can lead to a patronizing acceptance of these others as a lesser breed – harmless but in need of modernization and uplift to the level of the dominant culture. On the other hand, an uncritical presentation of the other culture as all that is admirable and inspiring can raise hostilities from students who feel their own culture is being denigrated.

Many of these problems can be overcome if the discussion of cultural differences is two-way. Teachers bring materials, students bring materials; both teachers and students raise questions; members of the other culture are involved in the discussions whenever feasible. Both the culture of the student and the target culture are investigated, examined, and analyzed. The students identify and discuss their own values as they consider those of others. The experience becomes one of self-discovery, as well as penetration of other values and viewpoints. A new dimension is added to our students' thinking as they find there are other ways of looking at things and other ways of expressing, cherishing, or rejecting them.

The sensitizing experience of bringing students to an appreciation and understanding of another culture creates for the foreign-language teacher another task within the school: that of *sharing this broader viewpoint with the teachers of other subjects.* The foreign-language class should not only foster an appreciation of one other culture, but also should awaken students to the great diversity and richness of the cultural heritage of a community. Other teachers of different ethnic backgrounds can be brought into the discussions, so that acceptance of multiculturalism, not just biculturalism, is encouraged.

Where cultural diversity within the community has led to the establishment of bilingual programs, these should not become little ghettos within the educational community. They should be, rather, living communities within which members of the dominant linguistic

27

group can interact with those of other cultural backgrounds and learn from them the many things their heritage has to offer. At the same time students of the majority culture will be introducing the bilingual students to aspects of the dominant culture with which they must learn to interact.

> To facilitate interaction and cooperation among diverse ethnic and linguistic groups, both intra-culturally and cross-culturally by learning to speak to each other and learning how misunderstandings occur, including value differences, verbal misunderstandings, and non-verbal misunderstandings. (Australia/California, all levels, FL and ESL)

B.8. DEVELOPMENT OF AN INTERNATIONAL OR GLOBAL PERSPECTIVE

In Section B.7, we discussed diversity of cultures in a pluralistic society. In this section, we move beyond the nation to the growing interdependence of a much more diverse world. The interdependence of nations and peoples is accelerating, in a way we could never have foreseen, through the active demands of young nations, many of which did not exist as entities even a decade ago. Future citizens will have to become aware of conditions, institutions, ideologies, historical circumstances, and different ways of thinking, communicating, and operating, if any meeting of the minds is to become a reality. We cannot expect all overtures and efforts to come from the other side. Third and Fourth World countries have much to do to reach even a minimally acceptable level of development without having to carry as well the total burden of international communication and understanding.

Learning about other peoples, other places, other institutions; learning another language for communication, so that we may hear representatives of other nations explain their viewpoint or read what they have to say to us and to each other; understanding their problems and the way these same problems affect us – these are essential elements for education today. We must reduce the bondage of our students to the familiar and the local. Foreign-language teachers should cooperate with teachers of the social studies and other subject areas in developing in their students the flexibility, resulting from informed understanding, that will be needed for *an open-minded and culturally detached collaboration with other nations in the solution of problems of planetary concern*. This awareness of global interdependence and the responsibilities it entails does not necessarily result from learning another language. The foreign-language program will need to be redesigned or reoriented to make this global perspective an acknowledged and achievable objective of the language study, as a segment of the overall school or district planning in this area. Furthermore, the teachers involved must be willing to broaden their own knowledge and accept retraining, where necessary, in order to make such a program effective.

Languages have moved beyond their countries of origin. English belongs as much to Alaska, Jamaica, or India as it does to the inhabitants of a small section of the British Isles. French serves as much for communication to a Haitian, a citizen of Montreal, or a Tahitian as it does to a Parisian. Spanish and Portuguese have for centuries been spoken by many more people out of their countries of origin than in them. Foreign-language teachers must demonstrate much more awareness of these languages as vehicles for widespread international communication, by broadening their own knowledge of areas where leading world languages are spoken and including the study of these peoples and their cultures in the materials from which their students learn. Foreign-language teachers must travel and encourage their students to travel. Even short periods of living in close contact with members of another linguistic and cultural group can change attitudes and develop greater understanding than the reading of many books. *Exchange programs*, where students from different nations live in each other's homes and share family life, should be expanded and multiplied. Foreign students should be welcomed into American homes and schools, so that there may be a sharing of information and viewpoints and a demonstrated caring for each other as friends.[11]

Magazines, newspapers, films, records, shortwave radio programs, videocassettes, correspondence by letter and tape – every means should be employed to see that today's students know and care about their neighbors in today's world. International days, fiestas, and national holidays of exchange students in the school make the concerns and ways of life of other nationals exciting, interesting, and attractive. Such activities should not be merely frills, however, but should provide opportunities to inform and to sensitize participating students and members of the community to the global diversity of ways of thinking, lifestyles, and concerns. Foreign-language teachers can do much, along with their colleagues in other disciplines, to combat parochial, chauvinistic, and ethnocentric attitudes among their students.

To create a feeling of belonging to a shrinking world. (Sweden, elementary and high schools, English)

B.9. DEVELOPING THE FULL POTENTIAL OF THE GIFTED

First of all, a distinction should be made between "good" students, who work and do as they are told, and the gifted: Gifted students will be superior achievers academically in most cases, but some may resist routine instruction, dodge homework, goof off, and refuse to conform to rules, regulations, and requirements. Tests of various types may help the teacher to identify superior ability in the latter cases, but even without such help the sensitive teacher should be able to detect superior ability and seek ways to involve and challenge such students with activities requiring originality, intellectual application, and leadership.

Gifted students are notable for their ability to evaluate facts critically, to distinguish new relationships, and to reason through complex problems. They usually demonstrate a high level of verbal and communicative skill. They are frequently, but not always, creative and original in their thinking. They may become bored with the laborious progression in thinking and learning their classmates require. The truly creative will take imaginative leaps and play around with ideas, but may be reluctant to perform purely routine operations for the sake of such extrinsic rewards as top grades.

If attempts are to be made to meet the specific needs of the gifted, care must be taken to identify all those with special gifts and talents, *without distinction of race, sex, ethnic origin, or socioeconomic background.* A different home language may obscure the gifts of some students. Above all, the "head start" gained by those privileged to grow up in an intellectually rich environment must not be confused with genuine intellectual and creative giftedness.

Once the gifted have been identified, the choice of program to advance them at their own pace has usually been between acceleration and enrichment. (Only in a limited number of schools are fully developed programs for the gifted available throughout their school career.) *Accelerated studies*, where students undertake advanced work beyond that of the majority of their age group, should be challenging and intellectually stimulating, rather than mere credit-grabbing busy work. The gifted are not well served by economizing on a year or two of schooling if this means remaining within narrow confines of study.

Enriched or advanced study should provide gifted students with full opportunity to explore new fields, develop their creative potential, and learn to be autonomous in their search for new knowledge. They should have "freedom to learn." Fortunately, such instructional innovations as individualization of instruction and independent research projects can provide gifted students with opportunities to range as far as their imagination and intellectual drive will permit. They should, however, have regular opportunities to report back to their classmates on things they have found out, so that they will not begin to feel isolated and ignored.

How should foreign-language teachers face the gifted student? First, they must realize that gifted students will grasp concepts rapidly and will not enjoy the large amounts of practice that some other students require. The foreign-language teacher must individualize much of the practice work, either through the use of the language-learning laboratory for as long or as short a time as the student needs, or through provision of achievement tests that allow students to move beyond specific units at their own pace. The gifted will often profit more from time spent in the library or in a nearby foreign-language community researching a topic to present to the class than in listening unwillingly to another exposition of a particular aspect of grammar that other students may still need. If they show the patience for it, they may be used as group leaders and as auxiliary aides in helping weaker students to learn.

By its nature, a language is something we are continually learning, and the gifted should be encouraged to move ahead of others in comprehension and production, through the provision of more advanced and challenging materials in areas of interest to them, both aural-oral and graphic. They can range widely in their reading, and yet be kept in touch with their fellows, by seeking out interesting articles or stories for the rest of the class or providing information on aspects of contemporary culture or current affairs that have caught their attention.

Certainly, the foreign-language teacher should be very alert to detect those with a particular gift for languages. These students should be encouraged to learn second and third foreign languages, including at least one of the less commonly taught languages. Where facilities in the school limit the choice of language, programmed self-teaching materials should be supplied or the resources of a nearby undergraduate program or extension course tapped.

Teachers should not be disconcerted by students who may be more gifted in certain areas than they are themselves. Truly gifted, nonproblem students will enjoy seeking out knowledge, and learning what interests them, without the tedious trammels of close supervision.

If all students are to be encouraged to study a foreign language, methodology and goals must be adapted to individual needs. (Maryland, elementary and high school, all languages)

B.10.   REVIVED EMPHASIS ON THE VALUE OF A LIBERAL EDUCATION AND THE ROLE OF THE HUMANITIES

There has been much soul-searching among all segments of the population concerned with education, as the nine trends already discussed clearly indicate. The claims of the marketplace must be carefully balanced with the need to educate the whole person. Students who receive a narrowly vocational preparation may well find their skills outdated quite soon after they begin to use them in working situations.

31

We cannot predict how our society and our world, interrelated as they are, will evolve, even in the immediate future. We do know that there will be men and that there will be women, and it will be for them to take the future – their present – boldly in their hands and live with what they can make of it. Basically human nature and human capabilities change little, or at least change slowly (although we can make more of the latter, as earlier sections have shown). It is people we must be concerned with, so that we can help them *develop their inner resources for whatever future they may encounter.*

So now, more than ever, we need to educate rather than instruct. It has become imperative for our young people to develop that flexibility of mind that will enable them to adapt to new circumstances and recognize new opportunities. They need to learn how to learn and be trained in various ways of approaching bodies of knowledge. They must learn how to assess facts, how to evaluate new knowledge, and how to put knowledge to use. Their education must encourage creative, heuristic thinking, boldness in application, and ability to function autonomously. They must have experience in cooperative planning and implementation of purposeful activity.

It seems apparent that, for many years to come, our students will have to live with uncertainty, variability, and ambiguity in practical and ethical domains. What decisions to make, what actions to take, and how to react and behave will not be obvious, as the many elements of a diverse population enter the mainstream and as encounters with persons of other countries and cultures increase. Our students will need to have confidence in and a clear understanding of the values and beliefs they themselves cherish in order to face this variability with equanimity and tolerance.

What contribution, then, can humane studies make to this type of education? Our students need a sense of history and of the diversity of mankind in the broadest sense of the ways of life, attitudes of mind, cherished institutions, environmental experiences, and slow but steady development of direction of many peoples in varied times and places: what they have written, what they have sung, what they have created, not just the wars they have fought and the leaders they have overthrown. They need to examine and discuss values, beliefs, and prejudices. They can share what has moved others emotionally, what has driven them to action and sacrifice, even to despair and decline, and what has drawn them close in cultural groups. A continually inlooking content, which studies and discusses only the students' own culture and history, fails to reveal to these students the full richness of their own heritage, or even of their contemporary culture. Because they have no basis for comparison, they miss the essential character of their own experience. It is because there is light that we know there is the dark, and various degrees of twilight. *Another culture, another literature, another history, seen through the prism of another language,* can make these distinctions more clear and obvious.

Our students need literature, poetry, music, and other artistic manifestations, not only of a literate elite, but also of the common people in oral traditions, folklore, the arts of the people, the history and stories that make small pockets of cultural identity unique. Through this content they can share the culture and the concerns of many times and many peoples, faraway and close at home. The preoccupations change and interweave, but societies and groups have had to face basically the same issues.

As they study the thoughts and actions of others, our students should be encouraged to reexamine critically and boldly what they themselves believe and hold dear and to relate this to the heritage of values and concerns of their own nation and people, distinguishing the good from the decadent and the tawdry. The educated person can see and understand the visions of others, while retaining a stable grasp on what he or she believes to be true, essential, and beautiful. A truly educated person is open to new ideas, open to trying the untried, yet not swept away by intermittent waves of fads and superficial enthusiasms, because there is an anchor of conviction that results from understanding beliefs one has made one's own.

Our students should be given the opportunity to develop broad interests and creative talents, which will continue to give them personal satisfaction whatever turns their life may take. This beginning in personal development, self-confidence, and personal satisfaction will give future citizens strength in combating an atmosphere of anonymity, dispensability, and powerlessness.

The foreign-language teacher is essentially a humanist and must believe in the contribution humane studies can make to the education of mind and spirit. None of these benefits will accrue automatically unless the planning and implementation of the language course are clearly directed toward the full involvement of the students in reliving and rethinking the content. *A liberal, humane education is a neverending process in which teacher learns with and from students* and kindles in them enthusiasms that will last far beyond the period of formal education. The real product of the endeavor is rarely seen by the instructor, but we can judge its impact by our own memories of those who influenced us most profoundly.

My first thrust would be to situate its value on the broadest possible level, as a basic structural part of a liberal education, not rationalized by concrete practical applications. (North Carolina, college, French)

Focused approaches and sets of objectives

With so many different pressures requiring the teacher to respond by emphasizing so many possible aspects of foreign-language learning, teachers may well feel bewildered. Should they emphasize communication, or cultural understanding, or language as a human activity? Should they be giving more time to opening students' eyes to the global implications of contacts with other peoples, or helping them learn to live with their neighbors (and themselves)? Or should they, as some suggest, just teach the four skills and leave it at that? What about the students' own interests and felt needs? Where do they come in?

Clearly, the teacher must select an approach that balances students' interests and the pressures of taxpayers and parents, while exercising a professional responsibility to design and implement a course that brings to both groups the best the subject area has to offer, within the general educational setting in which the teaching and learning are taking place. This requires very thoughtful consideration of possibilities and the realities of their implementation.

To add reality to what may appear to be merely an academic discussion, *I decided to draw on the collective wisdom of a worldwide profession, exercising its responsibilities in widely varying circumstances*, to clarify the relationship of foreign-language objectives to geographical, social, political, and human situations. To this end, I sent questionnaires to language teachers in many countries on widely separated continents and to all fifty states of the United States, asking which of twenty-one objectives frequently mentioned in the literature on foreign- or second-language teaching constituted the most important goals for language learners in their particular teaching situation. Respondents ranked seven of the items proposed, added extra items they did not find on the list, and wrote short statements, some of which have been quoted in this chapter. Approximately 500 questionnaires were sent out and 582 were returned, because a number of recipients passed the questionnaire on to colleagues or tried it out on teachers and teacher-trainees in summer institutes or orientation programs. Teachers from fifty countries,[12] and the fifty states of the United States, are represented in the sample. They teach twenty-one languages at all levels, from elementary school through graduate school and continuing education; some teach immigrants and minority-language students.

Before analyzing the data, I attempted to predict from the questionnaire *seven focused approaches to language teaching* that would be indicated by clustering choices of objectives. Such clusters were found in the data when certain key items as first choices were used as discriminators, but, interestingly, the clusters were not identical to those I had predicted.

For discussion purposes, I set out my own cluster predictions in the left-hand column of the following lists and the realities that emerged from the responses to the questionnaire in the right-hand column. The numbers do not represent rankings, but refer to the numbering of the items in the questionnaire at the end of this chapter. Beneath each approach, I cite the areas and countries for which the responses fell into the cluster indicated. These citations indicate averages of responses for that area and language as it appeared in my data, not the approach of any individual school. I leave it to the reader to reflect on the relationship between the needs of particular areas or countries listed and the categories into which the responses fall. (In the area citations, U = university; HS = high school; no designation = both.)

PREDICTIONS | REALITIES

I *Career orientation* (key discriminating item: 3)

PREDICTIONS	REALITIES
1 oral communication	1 oral communication
2 values and viewpoints	2 values and viewpoints
3 career tool	3 career tool
5 read technical literature	4 personal culture (literature)
9 for travel	5 read technical literature
14 [bilingual-bicultural where appropriate]	6 how language works
17 other places and times	13 another mode of learning
20 community structure	

The most important goal for learners is to get what they paid for... They have a right to expect some useable competency in the language from the program they participate in. (Wisconsin, college, eighty-five languages)

This orientation was reported for *EFL* in Western Europe, viz., Germany, Norway, Sweden, Holland, Belgium; India, Hong Kong, Thailand (omitting oral communication); Peru, Brazil, Chile; Eastern Europe: Rumania, Poland, Yugoslavia, the Soviet Union; Portugal (omitting oral communication). *ESL* in California, Midwest, Texas, Deep South; in Canada: Quebec, Ontario; in Australia, New Zealand. *French* in Southwest, Mid-Atlantic, Texas; Brazil. *French SL* in Canada: Quebec, Ontario. *German* in Sweden. *Oriental languages* in Northeast (with cultural understanding). *Portuguese* in Mid-Atlantic States (ethnic emphasis). *Russian* in California. *Spanish* in California, Midwest, Texas.

II *Cultural understanding* (key discriminating item: 2)

1	oral communication	1	oral communication
2	values and viewpoints	2	values and viewpoints
9	for travel	3	career tool
10	understand ethnic origin	4	personal culture (literature)
12	combat chauvinism	6	how language works
17	other places and times	7	intellectual development
18	different world perspective	12	combat chauvinism
20	community structure	13	another mode of learning
21	how meanings are expressed	18	different world perspective

The development of attitudes favorable to an harmonious and rewarding life in a multicultural society and world. (Australia, all levels, European and Asian languages)

EFL in Japan, Korea; Sweden HS; *French* in California U, Idaho HS, Mid-Atlantic U, Midwest U, Pacific Northwest, Southeast HS; Canada U; Australia, New Zealand; Germany U; Sweden HS; *German* in Idaho, Mid-Atlantic U, Midwest U, Pacific Northwest, Southeast; Ontario U; Denmark U; Rumania U; *Spanish* in Deep South HS, Midwest U, Northeast U, Southeast HS; Ontario.

III *International mindedness* (key discriminating item: 15)

1	oral communication	1	oral communication
2	values and viewpoints	2	values and viewpoints
9	for travel	3	career tool
11	meet other nations halfway	4	personal culture (literature)
12	combat chauvinism	5	reading technical literature
15	international community	7	intellectual development
17	other places and times	9	for travel
18	different world perspective	12	combat chauvinism
19	experience of another group	13	another mode of learning
20	community structure	15	international community
21	how meanings are expressed		

To open new doors through which the student can see and appreciate a vast and complicated world full of valid but differing attitudes, desires, and goals. (Illinois, junior college, French)

Chinese in California U. *EFL* in Sweden HS; Italy HS; France, Switzerland. *ESL* in Idaho, Mid-Atlantic; United Kingdom. *French* in Southeast U. *German* in Idaho U, Northeast U; Rumania U; Australia, New Zealand HS. *Italian* and *Portuguese* in Northeast (ethnic emphasis). *Japanese* in Australia. *Spanish* in Mid-Atlantic HS, Southeast HS.

IV *Self-enhancement and expression* (key discriminating item: 8)

1	[expressive] oral communication	1	oral communication
2	values and viewpoints	2	values and viewpoints
4	personal culture (literature)	3	career tool
8	express one's feelings	8	express one's feelings
10	understand ethnic origin	13	another mode of learning
16	for enjoyment	16	for enjoyment
19	experience of another group	19	experience of another group
		21	how meanings are expressed

> *Dare to use a foreign language you have learnt.* (Sweden, high school and college, English)

With *communication* as top priority: *ESL* in Ontario; Australia, New Zealand. *French* in United Kingdom. *German* in Midwest HS, California U; Holland and Belgium; United Kingdom.

V *Interpersonal relations/communication* (key discriminating items: 1, 19)

1	oral communication	1	oral communication
2	values and viewpoints	2	values and viewpoints
8	express one's feelings	3	career tool
9	for travel	6	how language works
11	meet other nations halfway	12	combat chauvinism
14	[bilingual-bicultural]	13	another mode of learning
19	experience of another group	19	experience of another group
21	how meanings are expressed		

> *To develop a sense of caring and responsibility for others…From this perspective…everything else falls into place.* (Ontario, short intensive courses, English)

ESL in Mid-Atlantic; Ontario. *French* in Deep South HS, Mid-Atlantic; Ontario U. *Spanish* in California U, Idaho HS, Mid-Atlantic U.

VI *Linguistic approach* (key discriminating item: 6)

1	oral communication	1	oral communication
2	values and viewpoints	2	values and viewpoints
6	how language works	3	career tool
7	develop intellectually	4	personal culture (literature)
13	another mode of learning	6	how language works
18	different world perspective	7	develop intellectually
21	how meanings are expressed	13	another mode of learning
		18	different world perspective
		19	experience of another group

> *To encounter language as an abstract object of study, as well as language as a medium of human communication.* (Pennsylvania, college, Spanish)

EFL in Italy. *ESL* in Pacific Northwest. *French* in Deep South, Midwest HS. *German* in Mid-Atlantic U, Deep South U; Ontario U. *Russian* in California U. *Spanish* in Pacific Northwest HS.

VII *As part of liberal education* (key discriminating items: three of 2, 4, 7, 17)

1	oral communication	1	oral communication
2	values and viewpoints	2	values and viewpoints
4	personal culture (literature)	3	career tool
6	how language works	4	personal culture (literature)
7	develop intellectually	6	how language works
10	understand ethnic origin	7	develop intellectually
12	combat chauvinism	12	combat chauvinism
13	another mode of learning	13	another mode of learning
16	for enjoyment	17	other places and times
17	other places and times	18	different world perspective
18	different world perspective		
21	how meanings are expressed		

> *To form a harmony between academic learning and professional training...as contributing to the goals of a liberal education.* (Thailand, college, English)

French in Northeast. *Hebrew* in Manitoba. *Latin* and *Greek* in Mid-Atlantic. *Russian* in Mid-Atlantic. *Spanish* in Idaho HS.

The realities, as opposed to the predictions, showed that most teachers, no matter what their approach, had realized that language learning needed to be related in some way to the career plans of their students. They also felt the need in the contemporary world for oral communication and for understanding the values and viewpoints of the speakers of other languages. They recognized the importance of understanding how language works. That they viewed their work as part of a general educational enterprise is shown by the high ranking of such objectives as intellectual development, broadening the educational experience of the students by introducing them to another mode of learning, and nourishing personal culture through acquaintance with literary works.

It may be objected that the form of the questionnaire directed choices toward 1, 2, and 3, but the personal statements showed that this was not the deciding factor. Many, in fact, did not give top rating to 1 or to 2, for what were clearly local reasons. Item 13 ranked higher than 4, and 19 was also highly rated.

Not surprisingly, many teachers proved to be eclectic, selecting from and combining orientations, according to the needs of their particular students. The statements showed that *most teachers were very sensitive to their students' personal and career interests*, as a perusal of the statements following the questionnaire at the end of this chapter will show. Of course, mere assertion of goals is not enough. The language teacher must be seen to be accomplishing the goals of the program, and the students must be experiencing success in the attainment of these objectives.

Varying objectives within the United States

Examination of the data from various areas and languages within the United States revealed no striking regional tendencies across languages. *Objectives seemed to be related rather to the situation for a specific language in a particular area* as, for instance, with the emphasis on interpersonal relations and communication for Spanish students in California and for French students in the Deep South, and the desire to understand one's ethnic origin among Italian and Portuguese students in the Northeast. Other traditional influences could be detected, like the strong liberal education tradition in French studies in the Northeast. On the other hand, Texans seemed to emphasize the career possibilities of French as well as Spanish. In the Deep South, German put a top priority on communication skills, but this was not so for Spanish in the Southeast, where students and teachers seemed to yearn more for cultural understanding. Midwest high school German gave strong priority to self-expression, whereas high school French in the Midwest emphasized knowledge of how languages work, and Midwest Spanish showed a career orientation. English as a Second Language everywhere was mainly geared toward career concerns, communication, and cultural understanding.

In *French*, there was a difference in emphasis between universities and high schools, irrespective of regions. High schools unanimously selected oral communication as their leading priority; universities varied in their emphases, some placing oral fluency first or second (California, Midwest, Northeast, Pacific Northwest, Texas), whereas others placed it last, or did not select it at all (Southeast, Deep South). All universities (except for the Pacific Northwest and Texas) rated the study of French literature as important; the rating for literature was lowest wherever the rating for oral communication was highest (except in the Northeast). Intellectual development rated highly with all. Except for some universities in the Deep South, French was considered a useful career adjunct by both high schools and colleges. Objectives related to international understanding were not highly rated for French (that is, items 11, 15, and 18), except for Texas, where seeing the world from a different perspective became important. Travel abroad did not seem to be a major concern of the French respondents. Universities rated cultural understanding more highly than high schools (except in the Pacific Northwest and Southeast). At both levels, the study of French was judged of educational value in introducing students to another mode of learning.

Respondents for *German* rated highly both oral communication and an understanding of how language works, at both high school and university levels, except in the Northeast, where another avenue of human knowledge and understanding the values and viewpoints of others were considered more important. Literature was less emphasized by German respondents than French respondents (except in the Pacific Northwest high schools and the universities in California and the Mid-Atlantic states). There was a fifty-fifty split on the value of German as a career tool. Very few of the respondents selected as an objective the reading of scientific or philosophical writings, and those who did gave it a low ranking. Most were more preoccupied with the breaking down of chauvinistic and ethnocentric attitudes. Only at university level was the question of travel abroad considered of urgent interest by the Germanists.

For *Spanish*, areas with strong concentrations of Spanish speakers (like Florida, Texas, New Mexico, and California) shared a common concern for developing the ability to communicate orally and to understand the values and viewpoints of their neighbors. They were also concerned about breaking down prejudices due to ethnocentric attitudes. In other areas, more emphasis was placed on intellectual development, a broader educational experience, a different view of the world, and the opportunity to read Spanish literature. Most teachers of Spanish saw the language as a useful career adjunct for their students. The goals for students of Spanish seemed to vary more from region to region than for French, for which the differences of viewpoint were greater between levels.

In California, the emphasis for the teaching of *Chinese* was on oral communication, understanding cultural differences, appreciation of one's ethnic origin, and increased opportunities for enjoyment of life, whereas in the Northeast (Chinese and *Japanese*) reading, understanding other cultures, and having opportunities to experience a new mode of learning received the highest rankings.

Idaho (fifteen responses in French, German, Spanish, and English SL) provides an interesting example of situational influences on language-learning goals. In all four languages, preference was shown for oral communication, understanding the values and viewpoints of others, and seeing the world from a different perspective. Spanish, however, put highest priority on experiencing another mode of learning, understanding another culture, and combating ethnocentric attitudes. Spanish teachers in Idaho put a lower priority on oral communication than did the French and German teachers. French respondents laid particular stress on oral communication, possibilities for travel, and the experience of another mode of learning. German respondents saw oral communication, cultural understanding, and seeing the world from a different perspective as most important. On the other hand, English SL teachers emphasized cultural understanding, oral communication, and the development of thought processes and comprehension of underlying meanings, the latter choice reflecting no doubt a realization that non-English speakers in high school and college need to learn to structure their intellectual products in a new way.

National differences in objectives

We shall now consider some very different situations in various parts of the world: Brazil, Thailand, various countries of the European Economic Community, the Far East, the Middle East, and Australasia.

Teachers in *Brazil* (English FL, French, German, and Spanish: twelve respondents) identified a strong need for language for career purposes, specifically the reading of technical literature, and for facility in oral communication. They also saw language study as providing an experience of another mode of learning. Teachers in *Thailand* (English FL: five respondents) also emphasized career uses and technical reading, but without the necessity for oral communication. The Thais also felt the need for their students to develop intellectually through the study of English, possibly because of the different thought patterns a noncognate language, from a radically different culture, requires. English, they felt, was necessary to give their students the feeling of belonging to an international community.

Sweden (English FL, French, German: forty-five respondents) has what one Swedish teacher described as a "peripheral language." It is a modern, industrialized country, deeply involved in social, political, and economic relations with other European countries. In Sweden, English is required at all levels and is essential for admission to a university. A strong effort is being made to internationalize higher education with exchanges of teachers and students. All languages in Sweden reported emphasis on oral communication, cultural understanding, language as a career tool (requiring particularly the ability to speak, read, and write the language, but with some emphasis on business skills and, to a lesser degree, on translating). The Swedes expected to travel and the students of English, particularly, saw the language as giving them a feeling of belonging to an international community.

Other countries in the *European Economic Community* – Belgium, France, Germany, Italy, Netherlands, United Kingdom (English FL, French, German: forty-three responses) – clearly cared a great deal about oral fluency in another language for career purposes (to a lesser degree for students of French and German in Britain). They also rated highly the ability to understand the values and viewpoints of others. They stressed the importance of knowing another language for international understanding (meeting other nations halfway, combating chauvinism, feeling that one belongs to an international community). Reading technical literature in another language was judged unimportant by most (except for ESL in Britain). This contrasts with the emphasis on this goal in less highly developed areas and in *Eastern Europe* (Poland, Rumania, the Soviet Union, Yugoslavia: seven respondents), where career goals and technical reading generally rated highly along with oral communication.

The goals of the learners of English in *Japan* (eight respondents) followed a similar pattern to that of the European Common Market countries, with the added emphasis on learning to express one's feelings more freely through a new medium. English teaching in *Israel* (six respondents) seemed more specifically career oriented, with stress on reading all kinds of material, technical and literary, but with a strong emphasis on how language works and on intellectual processes. The Israelis also saw English as a means of broadening their outlook.

The countries responding from the *Middle East* (Egypt, Iran, Iraq, Jordan, Kuwait, Saudi Arabia, Sudan, Turkey: seventeen respondents) all showed a strong interest in English for career purposes and technical reading. They looked forward to travel in other countries and broadened opportunities for enjoyment of life. They also considered language important educationally as another mode of learning. Kuwaitis, Iraqis, and Sudanese, in particular, showed a strong interest in understanding the values and viewpoints of the speakers of the language.

Australians and New Zealanders (English SL, French, German, Indonesian, Japanese: forty-three respondents) felt the need to see the world from a different perspective, and experience what it is like to belong to another linguistic group. They strongly emphasized oral communication, cultural understanding, and, for Japanese and English SL, the value of those languages as career tools (the English being mainly learned by immigrants and foreign students). Australians and New Zealanders also felt the need to combat ethnocentric attitudes in societies that have long been, at least psychologically, monolingual and monocultural, but that are now beginning to recognize their multilingual and multicultural character.

In *Canada* (English SL, French SL, German, Spanish: thirty-eight respondents), there was a common concern in all languages with oral fluency, understanding of the values and viewpoints of others, and the usefulness of another language as a career tool. There was also an emphasis on the need to break down ethnocentric attitudes. English-speaking respondents also stressed the need to experience what it feels like to be a member of another linguistic and cultural group. English-speaking Canadians emphasized the need for a bilingual and bicultural country more than French-speaking Canadians who preferred to work toward meeting others halfway.

Research for development

How can the teacher find out the type of program the situation demands?

The department head, in cooperation with the administration, teachers, counselors, parents, students, and school board, should investigate the needs and preferences of the community and of the school body in the area of language learning.

The following series of projects in research for development is proposed for the consideration of teachers. They move from simpler sensitizing activities, such as textbook and class observation, to fact finding at the classroom level. Much larger projects in the community itself may then be undertaken, and finally the experience gained should be shared with other teachers in other school systems.

1. Examine a textbook and establish the set of objectives it attempts to satisfy. Compare these with the focused approaches discussed in this report. How would you describe its basic orientation?

2. Observe a class. What objectives did the teacher promote, actively or implicitly? How would you classify this teacher's approach?

3. Fill in the questionnaire in the next section for your own approach to teaching a language to a particular class. Ask the students in this class to complete an adapted version of the questionnaire. Compare the results of your survey with your own profile of objectives. In what ways would you need to modify your teaching to bring it in line with your students' objectives? Do the students' objectives indicate a need for different types of courses from those being taught at present? How do you propose to meet this need?

4. Ask your parents' association and the school board to fill in the

questionnaire (appropriately adapted). Compare these results with your analysis of the students' objectives. How do the students' objectives differ from those of their parents? Do the parents' objectives differ from those of the school board? How does each of these relate to your teaching and your daily experience? Are there specific factors in your area that determine community views or student views? Do the discrepancies you observe indicate the need for some kind of information dissemination in the community? How will you go about this?

5. Ask all the teachers in the language department of your school to fill in the questionnaire. Are there differences in approach for different languages? Are there rational explanations for these? Are local factors influencing these differences? Are there local factors that should be influencing objectives? Do the profiles that emerge suggest that certain teachers would be most comfortable teaching courses with specific objectives? Can these orientations be accommodated in the course planning and teaching assignments for next year?

6. Ask the school counselors and administrative personnel to fill in an appropriately adapted form of the questionnaire. Do their views coincide with those of the students? of the parents? of the school board? of the teachers in your department? Write a short report for the counselors and the administrative personnel, giving them information on the views of the students, the parents, and the school board. Discuss this report in an inservice seminar with the teachers in your department. Where appropriate, plan changes in your present program.

7. Examine the course descriptions in the catalogue or curriculum guide of your school. To what degree do the descriptions reflect the objectives of the students, the parents, and the school board as you have identified them? To what degree do they reflect what actually takes place in the classrooms in your school? Discuss with the teachers in your department what changes should be made in the course descriptions and in actual classroom teaching.

8. Examine language-teaching journals and conference programs of the past year. Do they reflect the type of information you have uncovered for your school or school district? In what ways are the recommendations of experts different from those of practicing teachers describing their own programs? Prepare a conference paper or workshop to share your findings with others.

Professional implications

In the present atmosphere of competing pressures, with its consequent demand for careful decision making on the part of the teacher, the need for *flexible preservice and inservice training* becomes evident. Teachers need to have a thorough command of the language they are teaching and a wide knowledge of their professional field. They need to keep in touch with findings in the area of language learning. They should know how to design courses for the specific purposes of their students and how to select the techniques and materials that will enable their students to achieve these purposes in the most efficient and interesting way. They should not be tied to one approach or to one particular set of techniques, but be able to adapt and innovate. They should know where in the professional literature to find the kind of help and advice they need. They should help each other through the sharing of ideas.

Above all, our language teachers must be thoughtful professionals. Interest in languages, and in the phenomenon of language in operation in the communication of ideas and feelings, is always latent, ready to be sparked by stimulating programs. There may be a lull in one place at one time, while enthusiasm is rising in another. We must believe in the contributions we can make and are making to education worldwide as one profession. We can be encouraged by each other's successes and learn from each other's mistakes. Certainly, we have much to share with each other.[13]

In the final issue, however, it is individual teachers who must decide where their programs should be going and how they should be implemented. As Montaigne has expressed it:

L'archier doit premièrement sçavoir où il vise, et puis y accommoder la main, l'arc, la corde, la flesche et les mouvemens...Nul vent fait pour celuy qui n'a point de port destinè. (Essais II.i)

Questionnaire on foreign-language learners' goals*

Name:

Institution:

State or Country:

*This questionnaire should prove useful for stimulating discussion in methods classes, for inservice training, or for discussions on curriculum change and development. It is presented essentially as it was used in the study, except that "listening" and "as an adjunct skill in a career field" have been added to 3, "isolationism" has been changed to "ethnocentrism" in 12, "multilingual and multicultural" have been included in 14, and 22–24 have been added. All these additions and changes were suggested by respondents to the questionnaire. The author wishes to thank all who so willingly contributed to the study.

Main Language(s) Taught:

Level(s) of instruction to which my comments below refer:

Graduate	Elementary School
Undergraduate	Extension, Night, or Adult classes
Junior or Community College	Migrant or immigrant classes
Senior High School	Other (please specify)
Technical or Vocational School	

In the educational situation and social climate in which I work at the present time I consider the most important goals for foreign-language learners are the following (please write a concise statement):

In the present educational, national, and social climate I consider the most important goals for foreign-language learners in the situation in which I work are as marked below. (Please *rank in order of importance* about *seven* of the objectives given below, putting the numbers 1–7 in the squares at the left of the numbered objectives you have selected. Use 1 for the most important goal, 2 for the next most important, and continue to 7. If you rank two objectives as 1, the third selection will be 3, and so on. If some of the stated objectives seem to you patently inappropriate or unimportant today, write *NO* against the box. Leave the remaining squares blank.)

☐   1. To communicate orally with speakers of FL
☐   2. To understand viewpoints and values of speakers of FL
☐   3. To use FL as a tool for career purposes, particularly
     (check important boxes below)
     speaking FL ☐
     reading FL ☐
     writing FL ☐
     listening to FL ☐
     translating FL ☐
     business skills in FL ☐
     interpreting in FL ☐
     adjunct skill in a career field ☐
     other (specify) ☐
☐   4. To increase personal culture through reading literary works in FL
☐   5. To read technical literature (scientific, philosophical, psychological, etc.)
☐   6. To understand more about how language works (FL and native language)
☐   7. To develop intellectually (think logically and abstractly, understand underlying meanings, etc.)
☐   8. To express one's feelings more freely through a new medium (personality development, self-confidence, etc.)
☐   9. To facilitate travel abroad
☐ 10. To gain understanding of one's ethnic origin

☐ 11. To demonstrate willingness to meet other nations halfway
☐ 12. To combat chauvinism, parochialism, and ethnocentrism
☐ 13. To broaden one's educational experience through another mode of learning (another avenue of human knowledge)
☐ 14. To make this country bilingual and bicultural (or multilingual and multicultural)
☐ 15. To develop the feeling of belonging to an international community
☐ 16. To broaden opportunities for enjoyment of life (leisure, etc.)
☐ 17. To learn about other places, other times, other institutions
☐ 18. To see the world from a different perspective
☐ 19. To experience through language and language-related activities what it feels like to be a member of another linguistic/cultural group
☐ 20. To understand how communities are structured and operate
☐ 21. To understand how meanings are expressed and communicated
☐ 22. To learn the four skills for basic language proficiency
☐ 23. To satisfy an educational requirement
☐ 24. To be able to function in the second-language cultural milieu
☐ 25. Other (specify)

What kind of course should I design?

Read the following quotations from responses to the questionnaire. Consider the situation indicated by the attribution in parentheses. What approach would you take to course development to provide for the interests and needs expressed in each quotation?

1. [Students' objectives] tend to change as the make-up of the class does, but they seem to be the more practical reasons like: to get a job; to get a degree; to be able to use technical material in their jobs. (Ontario, adult classes, English)

2. Language learning is invaluable as a way to "get out of oneself," to become something (or someone) out of the ordinary, daily context of life. It affords a student the opportunity to communicate with persons having a completely different set of values and viewpoints. This "global" aspect of foreign language learning makes the role of the language teacher unique and akin to the role of the fine arts teacher, who attempts to get students out of their shells (theatre) and into communication with others. (New York State, college, French)

3. My students need to learn about the language and lifestyle of their forefathers. They need to learn that [the members of their community] are not a quaint and peculiar (and thus something to be ashamed of) people, but rather we are people who have a heritage of which we should be proud. If we understand our background, then we will understand ourselves better. (Pennsylvania, high school, German)

4. Our students do not want to *only* learn how to order meals in London, but how to understand the cultural, political, social, literary, and economic problems and issues of the Anglo-Saxon world. They do not want

to listen to tapes about tourists in New York; rather, they would prefer tapes in the target language from the Voice of America or the BBC dealing with issues of importance. Our students want content not frills. (Brazil, college, English)

5. The most important goal is that of learning to *understand* the foreign language: to understand it when it is spoken (in conversation; radio programs; songs; movies...), and written. This understanding, at more advanced levels, also requires an awareness of the social system, the values, the history, etc., of those who speak the language under study. Note: I put understanding above speaking (or writing) because communication is often possible if you understand another person's language – and then express yourself clearly and distinctly in English, or with signs, or with pidgin. (Massachusetts, college, French)

6. To learn a considerable amount of vocabulary and structures that enable the learners to understand lectures and take notes, to understand what they read in their specialization (engineering), to make notes and write reports on what they read or see in the laboratory/workshop. (Kuwait, junior college, Arabic, English, and French)

7a. I hope to expose students to other cultures and to impart the idea that different is not necessarily bad or "weird" as they are prone to believe. It is important also that foreign language learners particularly at the junior high level are exposed to the world outside Idaho. (Idaho, junior high school, French and Spanish)

7b. Breaking down the provincialism which so often typifies the young American student, neatly tucked away in the suburban ghetto. (Washington, high school, French)

8. Language is *communication*. Our goals should be (but aren't always!) intercultural understanding, increased awareness of other peoples and cultures and, hence, a better understanding of our own. Young people all over the world are eager to communicate with one another. (Massachusetts, college, French)

9. I write from Britain, now part of the multilingual European Community. It is clear that the educated citizen must henceforth be a multilingual citizen. The rapid spread of English facilitates communication, but unless the English-speaker reciprocates by showing *some* FL ability, he increasingly suffers a psychological put-down. On the side, FL can be fun, can be a useful tool, can be helpful to personal development, can illuminate understanding of the native language. But fundamentally FL is essential because we must enable future citizens to function in a multilingual world. (United Kingdom, adult classes and undergraduate, English and French)

10. Above all, students should learn to express themselves *creatively*, both orally and in writing. Whether he knows it or not, each person has the ability to be creative, and this ability can positively be brought to the fore with relatively minor effort, and the right amount of (and variation in) class and homework assignments. (New York State, high school, French, Spanish, English as a second language)

11. Des objectifs dont les apprenants eux-mêmes soient *conscients* parce que leur définition aura fait l'objet d'une négociation continue avec eux. Des

objectifs révisables si besoin est au cours du processus d'apprentissage. (France, adults and immigrants, French)

12. [This] is a career-oriented school. Students want to learn a foreign language – especially Spanish – because they believe it will be useful to them in their careers. Many students in advanced language courses are already using Spanish in their Co-op and after-school jobs. They benefit immensely from conversation courses stressing medical and business vocabulary. Students in basic language courses feel that knowledge of a foreign language will help them obtain jobs. In a nutshell, their goal is to *communicate* with the *Community*. (Massachusetts, college, Spanish)

13. I see a mission for foreign languages as one of the best curricular "eye openers" to be found at the university level. At a time when students are capable of understanding the global gestalt, are studying the intricate balances of nature and mankind in courses ranging from Geology through History through Literature and beyond, are firming up their philosophies of life, the FL class can – and should – center attention on the role of the human being in an interdependent collection of land/sea masses. Language is the vehicle that carries us down the multi-laned routes connecting people, all of whom are in motion. Language study can make the collisions on these byways meaningful rather than disastrous. (Florida, college, Spanish)

14. It is important for the foreign-language learner (in Denmark, everybody) to be able to use their second languages as an instrument of their emancipation. . . To be a good Dane you must learn foreign languages. This statement. . . implies that communicative competence is the focus. (Denmark, high school and college, German)

15. Students' goals are social in nature, as opposed to being intellectual or academic. Students want to know people who speak Spanish as other humans who live in a different culture and communicate in a different language. 3rd year students in a questionnaire administered at the end of the 1978 school year indicate their reasons for studying Spanish are to travel to foreign countries, to talk to people who speak Spanish, to be able to read magazines and newspapers, and to learn more about people who speak Spanish. All of the above reasons indicate their desire to know Spanish speakers as people. (Ohio, high school, Spanish)

16. To learn how to understand lengthy, highly technical articles written in English and intended for native readers, i.e., to learn the conventions for making grammatical cohesion, discoursal functions (hypotheses, classifications, etc.), and author's attitude. To learn how to read quickly in order to cover lengthy bibliographies. (Israel, college, English)

17. Since I have detected an opposite trend in the current talk of "communicative skills" I must state that I am strongly against setting up "Englishness" as a goal for English teaching. A Swede will always remain a Swede and whether he can mutter the right words at the bar of a London pub is of little importance. What does matter, however, is whether he is able to express his – inevitably Swedish – views and has such a knowledge of the interlocutor's – English, American, African or other – national background that he is prepared for an exchange based on good-will and understanding. (Sweden, junior college, English and French)

18. To add to motivation to learn by giving students an *application* to which they can put their skills to work on a practical basis: a course at the 11 or 12 grade level offered in a foreign language, for example U.S. History offered in Spanish for students having completed three years of Spanish previously. (Utah, secondary and adult, French and Spanish)

19. Social and intellectual relativism and cosmopolitanism; evolution of a personal style through confrontation with other national styles and idioms; the sheer visceral fun of linguistic playfulness. (Massachusetts, college, French)

20. The objectives are not very clear at the Secondary school level. Yet they do become clear as soon as one leaves school or accedes to the university. Hence the shift nowadays towards *E.S.P.* [English for Specific Purposes]: (1) English for secretaries: final year of Technical School; (2) English for Science students: final year of Lycée; (3) Special English for students of the Facultés des Sciences et Techniques, de Gestion, de Médecine; and (4) English for hotel people. The goals are becoming clearer here, as the secondary school *responsables* now have accepted to consider the needs of the prospective clerks, technologists, and graduate and undergraduate students. All the skills have to be developed but ultimately the main skill should be *the reading skill*. The other goal is to belong to an international community whose language is obviously English. French is still as important as Arabic, Tunisia's mother tongue. (Tunisia, Ministry of Education, English)

21. Insisto en que, a los grupos indígenas de México les es *indispensable hablar* el español porque las culturas indígenas de México son culturas ágrafas y el empeño porque escriban sus lenguas es una utopía; sin embargo, si no hablan español no podrán ser escolarizados porque todos los textos son en español y, además no podrán superarse económica ni socialmente. (Mexico, Indian education, Spanish)

22. To gain the ability to extract information in the foreign language and then apply this information in the native language. (Mexico, undergraduate, English)

23. For the non-major, I believe that the most important goals are humanistic – gaining insights into another culture and language, becoming aware of how languages work, increasing in tolerance for other ways of speaking and behaving – rather than practical. I feel, however, that the students themselves tend to focus on more concrete, practical and short-term goals. In my classes, I try to reach them through *their* goals – travel, careers, etc. – in order to keep them interested and enthusiastic enough so that I can lead them, or at least a few of them, to the humanistic goals which I think are an essential part of a liberal education. (South Carolina, university, French)

24. In this area specifically, many of our students see a need to understand what their Mexican-American friends are saying, and to communicate with them. (Arizona, high school and college, Spanish)

25. The world has become so small at this end of the 20th century and international exchanges so important and so vital that any human being who can only speak his mother tongue can be considered as a kind of cripple. The study of at least one other language as a way of increasing the

individual's power of communication ought to be an indispensable part of every secondary school curriculum. From a cultural point of view, one can hardly imagine a present form of culture within the narrow boundaries of one language, whatever its prestige and its international status. Monolingualism is a serious handicap indeed. (France, Ministry of Education, English)

Let's discuss

1   Is it possible to specify precisely what competencies language learners should be able to demonstrate at different levels? What kinds of competencies would you list for your own students? To what degree of specificity? What effect do you think these kinds of goals would have on teaching? On student learning? Would it be an advantage or a disadvantage for specifications like these to be applied to large groups of students (school districts, statewide, nationally)?

2   Conduct a survey in your area of the needs of local businesses and industries for personnel with knowledge of a foreign language. What kinds of competencies did they need and in which languages?

3   What provisions could you make in your language course to meet the special needs of blind and deaf students? How would you adapt your testing program?

4   What kinds of language needs do working adults in your area have? How are these being met at present? Draw up a proposal for providing more satisfactorily for these needs.

5   Develop some humanistic or affective activities for the language class. Try them out with the other members of your group. How did they feel while engaging in these activities? (For ideas, see Moskowitz, 1978.)

6   How would you design a course to develop intercultural understanding (*or* sensitivity to interpersonal relations)? Need such a course have a language component? How would you evaluate the effectiveness of the course?

7   How would you design a course with a language component to increase global awareness on the part of your students? With which other departments in the school would you need to cooperate? For what kinds of expertise? How would you go about obtaining enthusiastic cooperation from these departments?

8   If you had one extraordinarily gifted student in your language class, how would you go about meeting this student's special needs without upsetting the other students?

9 How would you set about developing a humanities through language course for your advanced students? What kinds of activities would bring out the full value of the materials?
10 Which of the Focused Approaches in this chapter seem best to reflect the objectives of your students? Your own objectives in learning another language? Can you combine objectives from these groupings to form an approach that would meet your students' needs more fully than any of these? What would you call it?

Selected bibliography

A short reading list for the harried:

Educational goals in the coming years

Randolph, E. S. 1978. "Maximizing Human Potential." *Educational Leadership* 35: 601–8.
Rubin, Louis, ed. 1978. *Educational Reform for a Changing Society: Anticipating Tomorrow's Schools*. Boston: Allyn & Bacon.
———, ed. 1975. *The Future of Education: Perspectives on Tomorrow's Schooling*. Boston: Allyn & Bacon.

Accountability, competency testing, basics

Born, Warren C., ed. 1975. *Goals Clarification: Curriculum, Teaching, Evaluation*. Middlebury, Vt.: NEC.
Steiner, Florence. 1975. *Performing with Objectives*. Rowley, Mass.: Newbury House.
Trim, John L. M. 1980. *Developing a Unit/Credit Scheme of Adult Language Learning*. Oxford: Pergamon Press, for the Council of Europe.
Trim, J. L. M., Richterich, René, van Ek, Jan A., and Wilkins, David A. 1980. *Systems Development in Adult Language Learning: A Unit-Credit System for Modern Language Learning by Adults*. Oxford: Pergamon Press, for the Council of Europe.
Valette, Rebecca M., and Disick, Renee S. 1972. *Modern Language Performance Objectives and Individualization: A Handbook*. New York: Harcourt Brace Jovanovich.

Career education

Lavergneau, Rene L., et al. 1974. "Career Education," in *Toward Student-Centered Foreign Language Programs*, ed. Warren C. Born. Middlebury, Vt.: NEC.

Lester, Kenneth A., and Tamarkin, Toby. 1974. "Career Education," in *Responding to New Realities*. ACTFL Review of Foreign Language Education, vol. 5. Ed. Gilbert A. Jarvis. Skokie, Ill.: National Textbook Co.

Turner, Solveig M., ed. 1981. *Foreign Languages for the Professions: An Inter-Cultural Approach to Modern Communications*. Boston: Northeastern University.

Equality of educational opportunity and mainstreaming

Charnofsky, Stanley. 1971. *Educating the Powerless*. Belmont, Calif.: Wadsworth.

Hosenfeld, Carol. 1975. "The New Student Role: Individual Differences and Implications for Instruction," in *Perspective: A New Freedom*. ACTFL Review of Foreign Language Education, vol. 7. Ed. Gilbert A. Jarvis. Skokie, Ill.: National Textbook Co.

Paul, J. L., Turnbull, A., and Cruickshank, W. M. 1977. *Mainstreaming: A Practical Guide*. Syracuse, N.Y.: Syracuse University Press.

Tursi, Joseph A., ed. 1970. "Foreign Languages for All Students," in *Foreign Languages and the "New" Student*. Middlebury, Vt.: NEC.

Lifelong learning and community education

Coppedge, Floyd L. 1978. "Lifelong Learning," in *An Integrative Approach to Foreign Language Teaching: Choosing Among the Options*. ACTFL Foreign Language Education Series, vol. 8. Ed. Gilbert A. Jarvis. Skokie, Ill.: National Textbook Co.

Monsees, Anita. 1974. "Public Awareness: How Can Associations and Institutions Use Public Relations Skills?" and Dona B. Reeves, "Public Awareness: What Can the Individual Teacher Do?" in *The Challenge of Communication*. ACTFL Review of Foreign Language Education, vol. 6. Ed. Gilbert A. Jarvis. Skokie, Ill.: National Textbook Co.

Self-actualization, personality development, self-enhancement, humanistic education

Galyean, Beverly. 1976. "Humanistic Education: A Mosaic Just Begun," in *An Integrative Approach to Foreign Language Teaching: Choosing Among the Options*. ACTFL Foreign Language Education Series, vol. 8. Ed. Gilbert A. Jarvis. Skokie, Ill.: National Textbook Co.

Moskowitz, Gertrude. 1978. *Caring and Sharing in the Foreign Language Class: A Sourcebook on Humanistic Techniques*. Rowley, Mass.: Newbury House.

Interpersonal relations and communication

Miller, George A. 1973. "Nonverbal Communication," in *Communication, Language, and Meaning: Psychological Perspectives*, ed. G. A. Miller. New York: Basic Books.
Rivers, Wilga M. 1983. "The Natural and the Normal in Language Learning," in *Communicating Naturally in a Second Language: Theory and Practice in Language Teaching*. Cambridge: Cambridge University Press.
Wardhaugh, Ronald. 1976. *The Contexts of Language*. Rowley, Mass.: Newbury House.

Multicultural education, values clarification

Grittner, Frank M. 1970. "Pluralism in Foreign Language Education: A Reason for Being," and Genelle Morain, "Cultural Pluralism," in *Pluralism in Foreign Language Education*. Britannica Review of Foreign Language Education, vol. 3. Ed. Dale L. Lange. Chicago: Encyclopaedia Britannica.
Robinson, Gail L. Nemetz. 1981. "Cultural Goals and Hollow Language" and "Where to Find Culture-Filled Messages," in *Issues in Second Language and Cross-Cultural Education: The Forest Through the Trees*. Boston: Heinle and Heinle.

International or global perspective

Hayden, Rose L. 1977. "Relating Language to International Education: Some Do's and Don'ts," in *Profession 77*, pp. 38–43. New York: Modern Language Association.
Leestma, Robert. 1978. "Global Education." *American Education* (June): 6–13.
Scebold, C. Edward. 1979. "Foreign Language and International Education in the Twenty-first Century," and Lorraine A. Strasheim, "An Issue on the Horizon: The Role of Foreign Languages in Global Education." ACTFL Position Papers. *Foreign Language Annals* 12: 27–34.

Developing the full potential of the gifted

Lacy, G. n.d. *Developing Defensible Differentiated Programs for the Gifted*. Albany: New York State Education Department.
———. n.d. "The Social and Emotional Development of the Gifted/Talented." Albany: New York State Education Department.
Naiman, N., Fröhlich, M., Stern, H. H., and Todesco, A. 1978. *The Good Language Learner*. Research in Education Series, vol. 7. Toronto: Ontario Institute for Studies in Education.

Revived emphasis on the value of a liberal education and the role of the humanities

Delattre, Edwin J. 1978. "The Humanities Can Irrigate Deserts." *Foreign Language Annals* 11: 7–8.
Moravcsik, J., and Juilland, A. 1977. "The Place of Foreign Languages in a Curriculum for Liberal Education." *ADFL Bulletin* 8, 4: 10–12.

3 From skill acquisition to language control

Some years ago, in an attempt to be helpful, I offered to give some lessons in English to a young Italian immigrant to Australia, who happened to have wandered into my church and was making rather futile efforts to make himself understood with the few words he had acquired haphazardly. Very soon, however, he stopped coming for lessons, since it was obvious to him that I did not know how to teach a language. I was trying to make him say things like "I went to work yesterday; I'll go to work tomorrow." This, he was sure, was not the way to learn English. What he wanted to know, and as quickly as possible, was the names of all the things he could see around him.

Labels or syntactic functions?

This young immigrant's attitude reflects a very common misconception about language use: that it is essentially a naming process, that the first step in language acquisition must be the learning of labels for all the features of the environment, so as to be able to talk about them to others. Many parents have this idea of language and spend time trying to teach their infants the names of all kinds of objects. Recent studies of child language acquisition, however, show that, from their earliest efforts at speech, children use words not as mere labels but with the operant force of more fully developed utterances.[1] *They learn functions and use even single words to express these functions.*[2]

When a baby girl says "milk," she can mean a number of things. She may, for instance, be naming a certain familiar liquid. Because this desired reaction is rewarded by the obvious pleasure of her parents, she tends to repeat this label to retain their attention. She may repeat the word over and over, engaging merely in word play, enjoying the repetition of sounds and the approving attention she receives as she continues. On the other hand, she may say "Milk?" with a look of puzzlement, meaning "Where is my milk? Isn't it time I was

Revised version of an article originally published in *TESOL Quarterly* 3 (1969), 3–12. © 1969 by Teachers of English to Speakers of Other Languages. Reprinted by permission of the publisher.

fed?" and if she is further ignored she may utter a peremptory "Milk!" as a command to her mother to attend to her needs. "Milk" in a tone of anxiety may mean "Look! I've knocked over my milk. What will happen now?" Or it may be a solemn inquiry: "What about my dolly? Isn't she to get a drink too?"

For the child, then, a single word may have all the force of a sentence and carry a number of different meanings that go far beyond its apparent lexical content. Very soon the child expands the one-word utterance to two words, and an elementary syntax develops as the child expresses an increasing number of semantic relations with simple word combinations. Bloom observed that the juxtaposition of two words like "Mommy sock" could express the possessor-possessed relation ("that is Mommy's sock"), as well as the subject-object relation ("Mommy is putting on my sock"). Bloom also identified in her child's early speech notions such as locative (as in "sweater chair"), attributive or adjectival ("party hat"), verb-object ("kiss Mommy"), requests for recurrence ("more juice"), rejection and denial ("no truck"), and a "noticing" reaction ("Hi, spoon").[3]

From this stage on, *the child's language evolves through a series of syntaxes*, identifiable and analyzable at any particular stage of development. The restricted syntaxes of the early efforts gradually approximate more and more closely the speech system of parents and caretakers until the child is finally able to control all of its essential syntactic operations to express semantic intentions. At this stage there is no limit to the number and variety of messages a small child can convey to fellow speakers of the language. (From then on vocabulary increases throughout life.) *From the earliest attempts at communication, children need a grammar; mere labeling will not suffice.*

In our foreign-language classrooms we have gone beyond isolated words, mere "vocabulary teaching": We have realized that what students must possess is the ability to use syntactic structures into which they can incorporate these words to communicate their intentions. They can acquire the many new labels they will need as their interests develop. In class we can ensure that they are familiar with a basic vocabulary that can be used for many purposes. This they can use to practice the syntactic operations they will need, if the rich vocabulary they will acquire later is to express their meaning appropriately.

The skill-learning approach

In the linear sequence of language there are certain strictly formal relationships, within the clearly defined limits of closed sets (for

example, verb systems such as *I'm going, he's going, they're going*).
These, we have found, can be learned by attentive practice, so that no
student will be tempted to say *I's going* or *they's going*. Similarly, by
consistent practice we can teach the restricted word order our language normally requires to convey certain meanings: *I saw him*, not *I
him saw* or *Him saw I*. These observations have led some to talk of
foreign-language learning as the learning of a skill, the acquiring of a
set of habits that must be learned so that they can be performed
below the level of conscious awareness. When we are speaking, we
do not have time to stop to think about word order, morphological
inflections, or invariant syntactic combinations. We need to be so
familiar with these details that they fall into place as we speak,
without distracting our attention from the combinations of meanings
we are seeking to express.

This skill-learning approach developed from the common observation that, in many classrooms, despite earnest teaching and many
exercises on the part of the students, ability to use syntactic structures like these with ease did not become firmly established. Because
this approach is still much in evidence in classrooms and teaching
materials, it is of interest to reexamine its underpinnings and its place
in promoting language learning. Teachers who turned to psychological theory to see what it had to say about the effective building in of
habits found inspiration in the *habit formation by reinforcement, or
operant conditioning*, theory of behaviorists like Skinner (this theory
is still widely applied in many educational contexts as behavior mod-
ification).[4] A word or two about the applications to language learning
that developed from this theory is in order before we reexamine the
skill-learning approach in the light of present needs.

In relation to teaching techniques and the writing of materials for
foreign-language learning, Skinner's principles have been interpreted
in the following ways.[5] According to Skinner, a response must occur
before it can be rewarded and thus be reinforced. He does not interest himself in what causes the response to occur in the first place.
There is here an obvious application to language teaching: Naive
students cannot invent foreign-language responses, but these can be
elicited by a process of imitation, which is a first step in establishing a
repertoire of responses. The familiar techniques of mimicking and
memorization of dialogue material, associated with audiolingual teaching, were developed for elementary language classes to provide opportunities for just such imitation. At this early stage, some practice
in variation is given, but the chief emphasis is on accurate reproduc-
tion. Once responses are established, then the question of their use in
autonomous interaction must be confronted, as we shall see later.

In operant conditioning theory, *immediate reinforcement or re-*

ward increases the probability of a response recurring: The teacher in the language classroom supplies this reinforcement by confirmation of correct responses, as in a structural pattern drill sequence, where the student hears the correct response modeled at each step by the teacher or the tape. With repeated reinforcement, according to Skinner, responses become established as habits that are maintained in strength by further reinforcement at intervals. This intermittent reinforcement is experienced as students use learned utterances, or variations of them, to express meanings in communication and are understood, or provoke the type of response they anticipated. *By judicious giving and withholding of reinforcement*, it is maintained, responses can be shaped to approximate more and more closely a desired model. Language teachers are familiar with this process, which they have long employed for developing finer and finer discriminations in recognition and production of sounds.

Reinforcement after a few occurrences of a response will not, according to Skinner, ensure that the response will be retained by the student as a permanent feature of behavior. Unless there is further reinforcement of subsequent recurrences, the response-habit will suffer *extinction*, albeit with some periods of spontaneous recovery before it disappears. Consequently language material has to be reintroduced at regular intervals, so that the student has the reinforcing, and therefore consolidating, experience of using it correctly on a number of occasions, particularly at the stage when many features of the language are being encountered as novelties in rapid succession. At advanced stages, when a great number of features have been integrated into a response framework, the student is forced to draw continually on previous learning, and habitual responses, both acceptable and unacceptable, are thus maintained. Unfortunately, incorrect responses can also be reinforced as habitual responses and become fossilized if students are not aware of their errors and are satisfied with, and even proud of, their production.

As a repertoire of responses is acquired, Skinner maintains that *further responses develop by a process of generalization* in which features of novel situations are identified as similar to those already experienced, and established responses find new areas of application. This psychological process is paralleled in foreign-language learning by the process of analogy, as students are encouraged to extend the range of their responses by applying in nearly similar situations the operations they have learned. Analogy is basic to the series of responses in a substitution drill and in other types of exercises that require variation within a limited framework.

A rather naive faith in generalization is perhaps the weakest feature of Skinnerian conditioning as applied to foreign-language learning. Effective generalization (or production of new utterances by analogy) requires the recognition at an abstract level of a relationship between a new situation and one already familiar, and the combining of new elements in a way that is consistent with this abstract categorization. In a new language, where the student's competence (or internalized knowledge of the rules of the language) is partial, this recognition of similarity is sometimes guided in really novel situations by knowledge of parallel structures in the native language. In English we say "I brought it from New York" and "I hid it from John." Misled by surface similarities in the native language, the English-speaking student of French will generalize from "je l'ai rapporté *de* New York" to "je l'ai caché *de* Jean," instead of the grammatical "je l'ai caché *à* Jean." Since valid analogy from one language to another applies at a more abstract level of analysis, it is not always a reliable guide to the many diversities of surface features of particular languages.

Even analogizing from one situation in a new language to another in the same language can be misleading. With conditioning techniques, students will have been drilled in transforming utterances either lexically or syntactically, to a point of automatic response. Here again the *learners are guided by surface features*. In many cases the analogy may be valid; in others, surface features will hide real divergences in usage, and students will fall into error because their knowledge of the language is insufficient for them to recognize the limits within which they may safely analogize. (Here, we may think of Chomsky's classic examples: *John is eager to please* and *John is easy to please*, where surface structure runs parallel but the underlying meaning is different, so that we can speak of *John's eagerness to please* but not *John's easiness to please*.)

Despite these limitations, experience has shown that skill practice, systematically developed, does enable students to produce acceptable syntactic patterns on demand in the carefully circumscribed situation of the classroom or laboratory. Properly instructed, the student who is working with the pattern "he's coming" will, on hearing the cue "we," produce the response "we're coming," which belongs to the same set, and will continue to produce correct responses in even more complicated sequences. We seem to have developed some useful techniques for the skill acquisition part of language learning, at least at a formal level. This does not mean, however, that students after such practice can participate freely in conversation in the language, producing these acceptable structural patterns at will. Teachers may well ask: "Where have we been failing? Why are so many of our students after thorough drilling still unable to use the language for their own purposes, when spontaneous situations demand more than learned associations?"

Is language produced in a linear sequence?

Satisfaction with the learning of responses to cues, and even of rapid substitutions, presupposes that language use is the production of language elements in a linear sequence, one item generating the next in succession, according to the habit strength of the association. On hearing "Where are you...?" most people will complete the utterance with "going." Studies of word associations cast considerable doubt on the validity of this approach to the essential processes of language production.[6] Given a cue like "cow," most subjects will produce the response "calf" or "milk," yet sheer strength of linear association would surely require "cow is...." "Cow, calf" or "cow, milk" rarely appear in succession. These associations, like so many others, spring from relations of parent, product, subordinate/superordinate, and so on. Moreover, word associations are frequently paradigmatic (producing words from the same grammatical class) rather than syntagmatic (or linear), and are drawn from fields of associative structures.[7] To the cue "good," most people will respond "bad" rather than "boy," which would be a common linear or syntagmatic association. (It may be noted that children tend to produce syntagmatic associations more readily than adults. With adults, adverbs produce syntagmatic associations more frequently than other word classes, but even here some paradigmatic associations are produced.[8])

Perhaps, then, we cite things found together or words frequently occurring in the same utterances. To the stimulus "sword," many will respond with "letter opener," articles that are conceptually similar but rarely found together or mentioned in close association in speech. Subjects who respond to the cue "fields" with the word "green" are producing neither a paradigmatic nor a syntagmatic association, "green fields" being the association built in by language habits in English. *There is clearly an organization among associations that has little to do with linear sequence.* Frequency of linear association as the major emphasis in language learning inhibits rather than facilitates real communication. Children learning the native language hear many items in close association, but they do not reproduce these in automatic fashion. They select from among these items and then use the selected elements for their own purposes. A small child who says "Allgone milk" did not hear this utterance in that form. The child's mother probably said "The milk is all gone" or even "Milk all gone." The child, having formed a concept for which the expression "all gone" is useful, then uses this expression to communicate personal intentions in a variety of contexts despite the mother's continued repetition of "milk all gone."

Concept formation in language learning

In foreign-language learning, even in a simple structure drill, it is concept formation we should be seeking to bring about, not mere rote learning of items in a sequence. As Miller, Galanter, and Pribram have expressed it: "To memorize the infinite number of grammatical sentences is to by-pass the problem of grammar completely."[9] "*The fundamental puzzle...is our combinatorial productivity*," says Miller elsewhere.[10] Even the attempt to memorize a useful selection of sentences for everyday use, as in most dialogue learning, evades the real problem that few sentences, apart from certain fixed formulas and clichés, can be used in actual situations exactly as learned in the classroom. Just as in perception an association cannot be made with previous percepts before there is recognition of a pattern,[11] so in speech learned associations (sentences, structural patterns) cannot be useful until speakers recognize that their requirements for communication are of a type for which this learned association is appropriate. Then, in most cases, they will need to adapt the pattern by substituting semantic elements called for by the situation.

Creative aspect of normal language use

Chomsky has attacked the view that language is a "habit structure." In 1966, he stated that "ordinary linguistic behavior characteristically involves innovation, formation of new sentences and new patterns in accordance with rules of great abstractness and intricacy."[12] He has spoken continually of "the creative aspect of normal language use"[13] – the fact that new utterances are similar to those previously heard or produced "only in that they are determined, in their form and interpretation, by the same system of abstract underlying rules."[14] This phrase "creative aspect of normal language use" has led some teachers to think that what is needed for language learning is not structural drill, but rather opportunities for the student to "create" new utterances in a free and spontaneous situation, as is the practice in direct method classes where students use only the new language from the beginning and try to communicate in it at all costs. Without some knowledge of structure and its flexible potential, this can result in a glib inaccuracy (Frenglish or Spenglish or whatever you will). This carefree indifference to the syntactic demands of the language is certainly not what Chomsky was referring to. According to Chomsky, the speaker-listener must internalize a system of rules that can generate an infinite number of grammatical sentences, and the innovation and creation of which he was speaking refers to the *production of novel combinations that result from the application of these rules.* In this sense, our students can only "create" novel utterances when they have internalized the rules, the system of rules then "generating" (in the mathematical sense of this word) new combinations as they are required.

Talking about "rules" frightens some teachers. From past experience they know that overt learning of abstract grammatical rules has not been conspicuously successful in producing students capable of using a new language creatively, that is, students skilled in speaking (listening, reading, writing) without having to hesitate to consider what is structurally permissible. Chomsky himself uses the term "internalize" for the assimilation of language rules because, as he states quite clearly, *the speaker-listener is not generally aware of these rules,* "nor in fact is there any reason to suppose that the rules can be brought to consciousness."[15] Here, he is referring to the native speaker, but foreign-language learners must also reach the point where they are responding to a rule system, without being aware every moment of the rules to which their utterances are conforming. It is as well to remind ourselves at this point that Chomsky is not referring to the common "grammar rules" of traditional textbooks, but to rules of "great abstractness and intricacy," the effect of which we observe, while being unable to formulate them at the conscious level. The deep structure and the transformations, which we encounter in the literature of generative grammar, provide a theoretical model that does not necessarily represent the psychological processes of language production.

Strategy and tactics

Miller, Galanter, and Pribram have proposed a model of language production by which we select a higher-level Plan (or strategy) that sets in operation lower-level plans (or tactics), that is, completely detailed specifications of every operation.[16] In acts of communication, *speakers have a certain freedom of selection initially.* For the meanings they wish to express, they select a certain sentence type, a time sequence, and certain relationships and modifications within the sentence. Once this initial selection has been made, however, there are choices they are obliged to make at lower levels of structure because of the rule system of the particular language they are using (obligatory inflections, word order, function words, substitutes), all of which devolve directly from their original selection. It is at the level of strategy, or meaning to be expressed, that speakers exercise choice, that the novel or creative element enters in, this choice necessitating further choices of a more limited character (the tactics) that oblige them to use certain elements in fixed relationships. *Creative, innovative language use still takes place within the restricted framework of the language*, that is, a finite set of formal arrangements, to which utterances must conform if speakers are to be comprehended, and thus to communicate effectively.

We cannot, then, underestimate the importance of practice in the manipulation of language elements that occur in fixed relationships in clearly defined closed sets (systems in which there are a few variable elements, but to which new members are not added, for example, the set "this, that, these, those"). This practice may occur in structured drills or in more informal situational practice, but such practice is needed in some form. The student has to be able to make the necessary adjustments to pass from "I'*m* going" to "he'*s* staying home." At this level the foreign-language speaker has no freedom of choice. On the other hand, the speaker may wish to say "I'*d* rather go, but she'*ll* stay," in which case the operation is at the higher level of selection. Having once selected the time sequence and personal references, however, the speaker has no further freedom at the lower level of surface manifestations of tense and person. Unless students are well trained at this surface level of operation, they will not be able to communicate freely the many novel messages they have in mind in a fashion that is comprehensible and acceptable to a native speaker.

It is at the manipulative level that structural practice (substitutions and transformations or conversions) is useful. Very early in this century, Thorndike had already shown that direct practice leads to transfer of learning where identical elements are involved: You practice *A* and *B*, and you are able to use *A* and *B*. Chomsky maintains that, in normal language, "repetition of fixed phrases is a rarity."[17] This statement is misleading because the word "phrase" is undefined. At the level of the sentence, or even for substantial segments of sentences, this is undoubtedly a faithful observation of language performance. If the sentence is further subdivided, however, into coherent word groups such as *I'm going, before he comes, if I don't see him*, or *to school* as opposed to *to the station*, it becomes clear that numbers of segments reappear again and again in identical form, and it is segments like these – *the building blocks of the utterance* – that are practiced in drills with variation of semantic content.

On the other hand, Katona discovered that for problem solving an understanding of structural principles led to greater facility in solving new problems and also to longer retention. "We do not learn the examples," he said, "we learn *by* examples. The material of learning is not necessarily the object of learning: it may serve as a clue to a general principle or an integrated knowledge."[18] This is the gestalt concept of transposition: "The elements are changed, but the whole-qualities, the essence, the principle are preserved in recollection.... and we may apply them under changed circumstances."[19] It is at the level of selection, of conscious choice, that foreign-language *speakers must have a clear conception of the possibilities of variation within the structural system*; they must understand the principles that determine the sentence framework and the relationships of the parts within it. Only then will they be able to set in motion the various elements that will combine in the ways they have learned so thoroughly, in order to convey the exact meanings they have in mind. It is this aspect of foreign-language learning that has been so frequently neglected in classroom teaching.

Students will acquire a realization of the possibilities of application and combination of what they are learning, not by listening to lengthy abstract explanations (tempting as this activity may be for the teacher), but by using the structural patterns they are learning, in combination with what they have learned, for purposes of their own. It is not sufficient for them to use patterns to complete exercises or to answer as the teacher requires; they must practice selection, from the earliest stages of instruction, in an attempt to combine what they know and what they are learning *in the expression of messages they have personally chosen* and are interested in communicating to others. In this activity, under the teacher's guidance, they learn the extent of permissible extrapolation or analogy. No matter how simple the structure, it is important in the communication system for its possibilities of occurrence and combination, and it takes its place in the foreign-language system the student is building up as soon as it becomes a medium of communication, rather than a simple manipulative operation.

Practical applications

All this may seem far from the practical demands of the teaching situation. How, the teacher may ask, can I apply this in the classroom? The following suggestions will, I hope, lead my readers to work out their own applications in conformity with the theoretical position I have been discussing.

Dialogue learning is a common classroom activity for which useful techniques have long been outlined. Nevertheless, in using dialogue material, many teachers never pass beyond the stage of manipulation: The dialogue is thoroughly memorized; groups and individuals make the appropriate exchanges. The teacher now passes to the next part of the unit. In this type of lesson the essential ingredient of *role identification* is missing. As soon as students act out the dialogue, as soon as he *is* John and she *is* Mary, they are communicating, not merely repeating.[20] Even inhibited students will speak out if they are being someone else. This acting out of dialogues by various students is not a waste of time. Students will repeat the same material over and over purposefully and listen attentively to others repeating it, if different groups are reliving the roles. When students act out a re-combination of the dialogue (one learned from the textbook, or one they themselves have created using variations of well-known segments), they explore further possibilities of combination and application of each structure to express a variety of meanings. In this way they are preparing for the act of selection when later they may wish to express similar meanings. Acting out a dialogue makes even memorization a meaningful activity, instead of an artificial classroom technique, since even great actors must memorize their roles. Memorization is thus accepted as a normal activity of real life.

Structural pattern drilling, as teachers well know, may become a parrotlike activity. Even with variations, students familiar with the technique soon learn to make the necessary adjustments, without having to concentrate their attention to the point of personal in-volvement. When, however, the student asks a question or gives an answer related to someone or something that concerns him or her personally, even an item in a drill becomes a form of communication. *Intensive practice need not, and should not, be divorced from real situations.* The lexical content of the drills should be applicable to things the student experiences in and out of class, so that items are useful even apart from the practice in which they are embedded; they should provide meanings with which the student can identify. An alert teacher can easily develop a practice sequence that could feasi-bly apply to the situation of some or all of the students, with an element of humor or surprise to keep their interest. Visual cues for drills not only keep students alert, but also force them to think for themselves, instead of merely adapting what the teacher is voicing for them. In a carefully structured lesson, students can be stimulated to provide the elements of drills themselves: They can be provoked into making a series of statements or questions of the pattern desired, through what are apparently only comments on the teacher's ap-pearance or activities, or on their own or other students' intentions or interests. Many a structure drill can be converted into a repetitive but exciting game that demands concentration. In all of these ways, *participation in the drill can be innovative,* providing for practice in the repetition and variation of language segments, but with simultaneous practice in selection, as students express their own meanings and not those of a textbook writer. A tape recording of such a lesson may not sound very different from one made during a stereotyped pattern drill session, the responses of the students following a familiar sequence. The difference, however, is not physical, but psychological: The active participation of the students is personal. Practice in selection should not be considered a separate activity for advanced classes: It can and should be included in class work from the very first lessons.

To summarize then, the student cannot perform effectively at the higher level of selection (putting into operation higher-level choices) unless facility has been developed in the effortless production of interdependent lower-level elements. So learning by intensive practice and analogy variation, under the teacher's guidance, will be features of the early stages of learning a new language, but with immediate practice in selection (within the limits of the known). Students will be continually placing new elements in the context of the functioning system as they understand it at that stage, by interrelating the new with the old. For this, they will need to understand what they have been trying to do in their practice exercises. They will be kept continually aware of the relationships of what they are learning to what they know, so that they can fully realize the systematic function of each new element they have practiced, as they endeavor to use it in wider contexts for the expression of their own meaning.[21]

To develop skill in communication in the foreign language the student must have continual practice in communicating, not merely in performing well in exercises, no matter how carefully these may have been designed. The teacher's reward comes on the day when students use the new language without prompting, and without embarrassment, for communicating their own concerns. This is language control. When students have acquired confidence at this level, they will be able to progress on their own, experiencing freedom of expression beyond the confines of learned patterns.[22]

Let's discuss

1 The nub of Chomsky's approach to language learning is the internalizing of the rules of the language. How do you think rules can be internalized without conscious rule learning?
2 Some techniques of language teaching emphasize learning labels for objects, whereas others emphasize learning how to express

syntactic functions. Describe the types of activities you would observe in a class of the label-learning variety and those you would see in a class learning syntactic functions.

3 What kinds of activities promote creative use of language for the normal purposes of language? For further information, read "Talking off the Tops of Their Heads," chapter 3 of Rivers (1983), or "Autonomous Interaction," chapter 2 of the *Practical Guides.*

4 Have you had personal experience of the skill-learning approach? What was your reaction (or that of your students)? What advice would you give to a teacher using this approach?

5 Make lists for the language you teach of structures that could usefully be practiced through various types of drills and others that require clear understanding of their functioning before they can be used effectively. How would you practice each of these types in "real situations"?

4 If only I could remember it all! Facts and fiction about memory in language learning

At times, it seems that we do not need to remember things any more. We have computers to do it for us. We have all these information retrieval systems that store everything we need to know – if we could only remember what it was we needed to know. Our computers are insatiable and seem to have infinite memory banks. But they too have problems remembering many things, such as who has already paid what to whom. These problems with retrieval of relevant information and identification of correct relationships make our computers seem exasperatingly human. A memory bank of itself is not sufficient to simulate a "good memory." It is the way the computer moves through various procedures and routines that counts, that is, its *memory in action – sorting, selecting, and interrelating.*

Just "remembering it all" can actually be a curse rather than a blessing. Luria, the Soviet psychologist, tells the pathetic story of a man who could remember everything.[1] He was not a happy man. He had difficulties functioning efficiently from the intellectual point of view, because "remembering it all" made forgetting impossible. As a result, all kinds of material that might be quite irrelevant at the time remained vividly present in his mind, making it, in Bruner's words, "a kind of junk heap of impressions."[2]

On first acquaintance, Luria's subject "struck one as a disorganized and rather dull-witted person."[3] He became very confused, for instance, when details of a story came at him at a fairly rapid pace, because for him each word called up images that, as he put it, "collide with one another, and the result is chaos."[4] Because he remembered specific images for each word, he was never able to single out the key points in a passage. When he later gave performances as a mnemonist, for which he had to remember long lists of numbers that had been written on a blackboard, lists from previous performances, although already erased, would appear before his eyes as he studied the board.[5] It seems, then, we can be thankful that we cannot remember it all.

Revised version of an article originally published with coauthor Bernice S. Melvin, in M.K. Burt, H.C. Dulay, and M. Finocchiaro, eds., *Viewpoints on English as a Second Language.* In Honor of James E. Alatis (New York: Regents Publishing Co., 1977), pp. 162–71.

What is "memory"?

When we talk about having a good memory, a bad memory, or a memory like a sieve, we are talking as though memory were an object: some part of us of a certain size, shape, and state of health that can be precisely located and into which we can stuff things to be withdrawn as we require them. Neuropsychologists tried for years to locate "the memory." (Phrenologists thought they had found it.) Aphasics who are injured in various areas of the brain "forget" some things, but certainly not all. They forget the strangest things: one language, but not another; the ability to write but not to read; the ability to read letters but not numbers. With aphasics, some parts of the brain seem to pick up where other parts have left off, especially with young children.

We begin to understand this failure to locate a "memory" when we consider Miller's statement: "Many psychologists prefer to speak of memory as something a person does, rather than something he has."[6] Or as Jenkins puts it, "The mind remembers what the mind *does*, not what the world does."[7] The mind does not just register impressions (visual, auditory, tactile, or kinesthetic), storing perfect images of them somewhere so that they may be conjured up anew at will at a later period. Rather, the mind takes what it experiences (not everything, but what fits its perceived purposes) and then processes these experiences in many different ways, not only while it is preparing them for storage but also while they are being held in store. *We interpret what we experience and then store the interpretation.* It is this interpretation that is available to us for retrieval, not the original unprocessed experience. (Here we may think of the ways different eyewitnesses recall what they saw and the ways in which their individual accounts may vary at a retrial.)

The interesting questions for us, then, concern what the mind does with the material it encounters and how we may present new knowledge, particularly of a second language, in such a way that it will be stored and be retrievable in a usable form. Without becoming technical, we can draw some interesting implications from recent research into memory processes and see what these imply for foreign-language comprehension and production. For the purposes of this discussion, we will draw mainly from information-processing and conceptual memory research.[8]

Memorization

In foreign-language teaching, the main form in which "memory work" has entered the classroom has been as memorization, or as repetition with minimal formal variation, as a means of storing potentially useful material from the new language in the memory. Phrases and complete utterances have been memorized (taken from dialogues or derived from classroom activity). Vocabulary has been memorized, often in lists with native-language "equivalents" or with pictures (a procedure that parallels the paired-associate list learning of early memory experiments in the Ebbinghaus tradition). Rules have been memorized in the form of paradigm tables or as verbal instructions like "put the indirect object before the direct object." Another form of rule learning has been through practice with frames demonstrating rules, as in simple substitution drills where the frame is committed to memory, through its repeated use, as minimal, cued changes are made in slots (for example, he gave them the book; *her*: he gave her the book).

Each of these procedures reflects the associationist stimulus-response approach to learning, which holds that if a stimulus and a response occur frequently enough in association with each other in a reasonably satisfying (successful) activity, the bond between them will be strengthened, and the stimulus, when it appears again, will tend to call forth the response. The repetition of the operation is presumed to strengthen the memory trace. This says something about a view of learning, but very little about the operation of memory, which is clearly regarded as a passive register of impressions.

If the stimulus is simple enough and designed to elicit only one particular response, the results of such procedures will be as anticipated. Students given the practiced cue will produce the learned response. The native-language word or a picture of the object will evoke the vocabulary word in the new language. An instance of the frame accompanied by a cue will elicit the frame incorporating the cue. An instruction to recite the paradigm, or even the first item of the paradigm given as a cue, will call forth the paradigm. A situation cue (Joe Doe meets Jane in the supermarket) will precipitate recitation of the dialogue ("Good morning, Jane. How are you? Fine, thanks. I'm doing my shopping. . . "), since dialogues memorized verbatim purely for the sake of memorization are a form of list learning. As a consequence, *tests that reproduce the original material in the form in which it was learned will yield commendable results.*

There is some place for simple stimulus-response association of this type in early foreign-language learning, mainly for associating the sounds of the language with new writing systems or different spellings, or even for associating new sound combinations with simple, unambiguous, concrete meanings like cat, book, or pencil (in the same way that we can learn to call a cat a fif, if that is what our social group likes to call it). The *memorization procedures* described, however, *have very little to do with learning a new language for use in unpredictable contexts* and bear no relation to the active memory processes that enable language learners to express their intentions (meanings) in new language forms. What the mind is *doing* during language-learning activities will determine what is stored, in what form, and whether it is retrievable and usable in new contexts.

The complexity of language use

One thing is clear, from both psychological and linguistic research: Language is an exceedingly complicated phenomenon that cannot be reduced to simple stimuli and responses without distorting its true nature and function. Each language utterance, no matter how small or seemingly unitary ("Stop!" for instance) has several layers of complexity: phonological (sounds, intonation, stress, duration), syntactic (its role as a complete utterance in a discourse or as an element in a complete utterance), and semantic (its meaning). Even the latter is not as simple as it appears. In the appropriate context, not only linguistic but also social, "Stop!" can really mean "I want you to continue, but I know from my upbringing that I should make at least a token protest." These layers are complexly interrelated, as are the individual sounds and, in a longer utterance, the syllables, words, breath groups, and sentences. How we are able to understand and produce such complex responses, and infinite variations of them, in what are apparently widely differing physical contexts is in no way explicable in a simplistic stimulus-response framework.

Furthermore, the mind extracts abstract features for storage from each linguistic situation, no matter how apparently limited. It interrelates these in *complex networks* in such a way that they can be retrieved from the network with quite novel associations whenever a key or cue is perceived (that is, recognized by the individual as relevant to his or her immediate or long-term concerns). The word to note here is *perceived*. The same cue can elicit vastly different responses from the same individual at different moments and in different contexts. For instance, a hand held out may elicit a hand extended in response and "Good to see you," or a brusque "Get yourself a job!", a turning away movement, or "A dollar forty, fifty, seventy-five, two. Thank you. Have a good day."

Such is the complexity of the internal and external responses even to an apparently simple cue such as "Do you know Esther?" that any attempt to teach standard, prefabricated responses to such stimuli is like shadowboxing: It is useful for practicing stance and possible movements, or even as a warming-up exercise, but only marginally related to the real business of anticipating and circumventing an opponent with these practiced movements.

Memory in language learning

Real language use is conceptual at base. People must have something to communicate. What they have to say, or what they comprehend, in normal circumstances is related in some way to the totality of their experience, which is a vast network of interrelated concepts composing their long-term memory, not just to their minimal acquaintance with the forms and units of a second language. What they are learning becomes intricately entwined with what they already know, and in this way it is stored in long-term memory (that is, it is remembered). This is why we often recall the oddest pieces of information at the oddest moments: Unobserved or unexpected cues dredge them up through the interconnections of the personal semantic networks we have built up.

Note that these networks are semantic or conceptual and therefore independent of the forms of any language. They are *networks of primitive meanings connected by relations*, not networks of words. Words of a specific language become linked with various interconnections of the networks when we find they evoke the meanings we intend for our listeners or help us to interpret what is said to us. Every listening or speaking experience modifies, expands, or strengthens these networks. The foreign-language learner has to connect new forms and new lexical items with known meanings and sometimes must register new meanings for which the first language has not yet established connections. Unfortunately, even for those word-related meanings that already exist in the student's semantic networks, derived for the most part from the first linguistic-cultural experience, only some exactly parallel meanings associated with seemingly equivalent words in the foreign language. And this can be a trap. The more meaningful connections that are established for the foreign language through *active use in authentic contexts*, both linguistic and cultural, the more readily will the necessary linguistic clothing become available to us as we need it for the expression of our personal intentions.[9]

Because it is experience, or use, that develops the necessary interconnections, it is experience in using the foreign language that permits the incorporation of foreign-language material in the long-term memory. For what we have learned to be usable in many contexts it must be *experienced in meaningful discourse* (through both hearing and speaking) *in all kinds of novel combinations.* The student has to become uninhibited in extrapolating from one known use to other possible uses in analogous situations (and situations can be analogous in many different ways, as perceived by the participant). Furthermore, it is the interrelationships of the conceptual networks that enable students to understand, in oral or graphic form, material that contains words new to them. These are the basis for projected expectancies and informed guessing. Inductive approaches to learning, such as the direct method, which require the student to hypothesize meanings, have always relied on this potentiality. From this point of view, stored experiences from use of a first language cannot be considered a burden or a negative influence on foreign-language learning; rather, they are a boon, facilitating in many ways the learning of a usable second, third, or fourth language.

"Meaningful" implies not only that all material used should have sequential significance beyond the phrase and the sentence, but also that its meaning, once the new-language code has been penetrated, should be accessible to the language learner. What is meaningful to the teacher is not necessarily meaningful to the student. "A trapezoid is a quadrilateral having two parallel sides" is meaningful and comprehensible to those who already possess this concept, or who have the constituent concepts in their stored experience, but is neither meaningful nor comprehensible to those for whom such knowledge is not available in their long-term memory. Foreign-language material must build on what students know, and what arouses their curiosity and interest at their age and in their circumstances, if it is to be effectively integrated into stored experience. The mind will not process what is perceived to be of little account by the individual concerned, and it is what the mind does that counts.

What about rules in this approach? *Rules are instructions to be tested in use.* They may be given explicitly or understood implicitly through seeing language in action. They serve as a support that ceases to be useful once the procedures they describe can be performed without conscious attention and monitoring. Rules seen as instructions for action will be presented in whatever form is most helpful to a particular group of students, and at the time when and for as long as they are clearly useful. They have no importance in themselves, but only insofar as they facilitate the establishment of essential structural routines that make the expression of nuances of meaning possible in the new language.

Vocabulary acquisition also takes on a new coloring in the theoretical approach we have just described. With every word comes a set of possible relationships, so that a word learned out of context is for the most part a useless bauble. Syntactic relations are relations among

Some have maintained that the reception of a message is determined by the operation in reverse of the same processes as those involved in its emission. For this view there is as yet little experimental evidence, and some that would seem to refute it.[3] Others consider that we perceive an oral message by covertly constructing a parallel message with which we compare it for fit. If this is so, speech perception must be considered a special case of speech production. Still others consider speech perception a distinctive process, in which the decoding rules draw on different factors from the encoding rules of speech production, with semantic cues playing a predominant role.[4]

Most linguists have concentrated on the system of rules that must be internalized if speech production is to be a theoretical possibility. Chomsky, for one, sees no difference between the knowledge of the language (the knowledge of the system of rules, or competence, of the individual) that must be posited for speaking and for hearing. In fact, he speaks of an idealized "speaker-hearer." (This position is challenged by the psycholinguist Bever.[5]) The model of the system of rules of which Chomsky is speaking is a description of competence, with no pretense at describing performance.[6] Psychologists, on the other hand, as distinct from linguists, must concern themselves with the behavioral reality, in performance, of the systems of rules elaborated by the linguists. Attractive as the latter may be as theoretical models, psychologists cannot accept, without experimental evidence, identity of process for the two facets of the communication act: speech perception and speech production. As applied linguists we are caught in the middle, and, for our practical purposes, we may be led sorely astray if we accept a theoretical model as a representation of psychological reality without looking for experimental validation.[7] Our language learners must also be language users, in the fullest sense of that term, both as comprehenders of messages and communicators of messages.

Processes of speech perception (listening)

Many writers have classified the comprehension of speech as decoding and left it at that. This term is deceptively simple for a process that involves first perceiving that there is a systematic message, rather than accidental noise, in a continuous stream of sound and then apprehending and identifying within this stream bounded elements (segments) the listener has never heard in exactly this form before, each segment having a distinctive structure and combining with other segments within a more extensive organized system. As listeners seek to interpret messages, this structuring within and among segments requires them to retain elements they have already apprehended, until relationships with succeeding elements have been established, and then to engage in a continuous readjustment of their interpretation of each developing structure in view of what has preceded and in anticipation of succeeding segments. Listeners are thus engaged in a continuous cognitive processing, in which factors of attention and memory are vitally involved.

Comprehending a message is not merely attending to a stream of sound and imposing on it some idiosyncratic structure of meaning: A highly complex structured system is involved that has an existence apart from this particular listener and speaker and which is known to varying degrees of complexity by both. Nor is comprehension the passive reception of an already structured message. Since the speaker and the listener in a communicative act are different persons whose competence in the language and knowledge store are never identical, and whose perception of the context of the utterance (psychological, as well as situational and linguistic) may be radically different, it is quite possible for the message perceived by the listener to be structured differently from that intended by the speaker. With a message in a language that is not the native language of one of the two participants, the discrepancy in competence and expectations may be considerable, and the probability that the message perceived will be identical to the message emitted will be correspondingly reduced. The message apprehended by the listener in the stream of sound will also be influenced by such personal factors as attention set, fatigue, and emotion. As a result, the message one person finally receives will not correspond precisely to the message another person would have perceived in the same communication sequence.

Listening comprehension is an area in which linguistic and psychological factors are inextricably interwoven, and as a phenomenon it can never be explained purely from the point of view of the psychologist or of the linguist. Insofar as it is a performance phenomenon, it can be investigated empirically as behavior (behavior involving two persons), but such investigation will be peripheral unless it takes into account what the linguist has to say about competence and the organization of the language system.

Perception as construction of a message

It must be remembered that the act of perception is not a purely passive one. It is an act of construction, rather than reception.[8] In continually varying sounds we recognize a phonemic system: combinations of sounds with certain complexes of distinctive features, which we have come to accept within a certain band of tolerance as sounds of the particular language to which we think we are listening. Should we anticipate that an utterance will be in a specific language, we will not perceive the same combinations of sounds as we would have perceived if we had been expecting another language, although the sound signal itself will not have changed. As we listen for a particular language, we will not be disconcerted by variations in sound sequences that represent the same morphemes, because we have internalized a system of morphophonemic rules that enables us to adjust our construction appropriately beneath the level of conscious attention and effort. In other words, we "hear" the variants as meaningful units that learning this language has taught us to expect.

Perception and retention

Beyond this phonological recognition, we perceive in a continuous sound signal units and groups of units that even advanced types of machines have difficulty in identifying consistently, except when utterances have been shaped to conform to certain restrictions of the program. These segments are perceived by the listener as belonging to groupings that possess a meaning at a deeper level of analysis, because of the categories to which we assign the whole, and often parts, of each segment and because of the interrelationships we perceive among these categories. This process of categorization extends to larger and larger internally structured segments, until the ultimate category of the discourse itself is reached. The groupings we perceive form a rhythmic pattern, which helps us retain what has been apprehended in earlier groupings long enough to interrelate it with later groupings, in such a way as to make the utterance meaningful. When we know a language well, these rhythmic groups seem to form a pattern of rise and fall of the voice in harmony with meaningful content, which may itself be a construction of the mind rather than an uncontestable acoustic fact, as certain experiments seem to indicate. Lieberman hypothesizes that it is meaningful content that suggests to us an appropriate learned intonation pattern in some cases, so that we perceive what we expected even when the speaker has deviated from what we had anticipated.[9]

Three stages of perceptual construction of a message

According to Neisser, we can detect in this process of perceptual construction three stages.[10] As I discuss these stages, I will show how

81

an application of this theory would affect the preparation of teaching materials for listening comprehension.[11]

The first stage, sometimes called *sensing*, is a stage of rapid impressions, only roughly identified and differentiated, and is relatively passive and receptive. At this stage, we impose some rudimentary segmentation on what we hear. We are dependent on echoic memory, which is very fleeting (it has been estimated to last for a few seconds only); actual items heard are not long retained unless they are interrelated in some meaningful way with other items. The rapid synthesis of impressions we form is a construction, resulting from our familiarity with the phonemic system, the morphophonemic rules, and the broad syntactic categories. As a result, much of what we have actually experienced aurally does not pass on to the second stage, because in our first rapid selection we have rejected as "noise" elements that did not fit in with our initial construction. These sensory items then pass from echoic memory and can have no further effect on our interpretation.

The second stage is one of *identification through segmentation and grouping*. We segment and group at various levels, as we apply the phonotactic, syntactic, and lexical collocational rules of the language to which we are attending. This identification is not the identification of an input identical with that of previous auditory experiences, because we may never have heard what we are now identifying in exactly the same form before. We identify configurations of attributes that distinguish categories and then wider categories of which the already identified categories are the attributes. In this way associations are aroused within the centrally stored information system. *This identification process is an active, detailed one that processes the signal it is receiving sequentially, interrelating the segments it has already identified and those it is identifying within the phrase structure of the utterance.* At this stage memory is still auditory; however, because the initial grouping was in a rhythmic form that was tentatively meaningful (insofar as the phrase structure had been apprehended up to that point), the auditory segments (or "chunks," in Miller's terminology[12]) are more easily retained. This increased power of retention enables us to suspend judgment where there is ambiguity of structure, holding perceived segments in our mind, ready to make the necessary adjustments as the form of the phrase structure becomes clear.

There is considerable discussion as to whether this process is one of analysis by synthesis.[13] It seems difficult to explain the conversion of auditory information, received from outside the nervous system, into cognitive meaning. According to the *analysis by synthesis hypothesis*, as we listen we construct a parallel message within our own cognitive system, according to the organized rules we have internalized, and compare it for match, or fit, with what we are perceiving aurally. This hypothesis seems to tally with our common experience of supplying words when others pause, or of believing we are following with comprehension another person's message, only to be suddenly disconcerted by the next element and forced to revise our projection of the form of the utterance. The hypothesis is in some ways attractive, but a satisfactory model of the process that could operate in real time has not yet been developed. Further, analysis by synthesis cannot explain common substitution errors. If the input on which our matching is based is an acoustic signal, then it should be impossible to "hear" words that have not been uttered, yet this is a common experience springing from our projection of the probable form of the utterance to which we are attending. It seems plausible, therefore, that we are engaged as we listen in some form of *anticipatory projection of the message, with adjustive correction* should the utterance not conform with our expectations. This projection is based on our familiarity with the phrase structure, morphology, and lexical collocations of the particular language to which we are listening, as well as the extralinguistic factors of situation and gesture. The less familiar we are with these elements the more difficult it is for us to comprehend and retain what we hear, because of our inability to anticipate appropriately. The development of an adequate model of comprehension must, however, await more substantial knowledge of the actual processes involved from the psychological point of view.

Whatever may be the precise nature of the identification process, we would not remember what we had perceived were it not for *the third stage*: rehearsal and recoding of the material, which must take place before what we have perceived enters into long-term storage. (Although this is called here a "third stage" it must be considered as taking place simultaneously with the ongoing interpretative process.) *Rehearsal* refers to the recirculation of material through our cognitive system, as we relate it to what follows and at times readapt what we have already interpreted in what we have already heard. Without rehearsal the auditory material in the memory would fade rapidly, and we would not be able to follow the line of thought in an utterance or series of utterances. It seems probable, however, that we do not store the material exactly as we first perceived it; rather, *we recode it* in a more easily retainable form. A number of experiments seem to support the hypothesis that long-term storage (after thirty seconds) is in deep structure form. In other words, the material perceived is detransformed and the basic semantic information retained (perhaps with transformational markers that enable the listener to recapture the original form if necessary).[14] This hypothesis is consistent with common experience. When asked about what we have heard, *we tend to give the gist* of it, usually in simple active affirmative declarative sentences (referred to by psycholinguists as SAADs). Such sentences are closest to base strings to which obligatory transformations only have been applied. Optional transformations (such processes as passivization, nominalization, and self-embedding) seem to be dispensed with for storage, although the semantic markers of such transformations as affect meaning (for example, question, negation) are retained in the base. A series of simple kernel-like utterances is more redundant than utterances with a number of transformations that combine information, and this redundancy aids memory. Recoding for retention must be performed immediately, and without conscious attention, or the listener misses part of the next grouping while rehearsing the recoding of the preceding segments. It is through recoding that the listener interpretatively clarifies relationships between what is being attended to and what has already been assimilated, and this establishing of meaningful associations is essential to storage and later recall.

At this point it is interesting to consider Fillmore's proposal that grammatical subject and object are surface features.[15] Real meaning, according to Fillmore, is in the deep structure: not only the semantic contribution of the lexicon, but also the semantic aspects of syntactic relations. It is of interest that in psychological experiments on recall, the logical subject (which Fillmore calls the agentive) as expressed in an agent *by*-phrase has proved to be a more effective prompt than a nonagent *by*-phrase.[16] This seems to indicate the psychological reality of Fillmore's agentive and to give added support to the notion that information is stored in deep structure form.

The three stages in speech perception that have been described form in practice one complex operation. It is reasonable, however, to presume that the efficiency of the whole process will be increased if listening comprehension materials for the early stages are so constructed that the student has specific practice in the various types of operations that must be performed almost automatically, in an integrated series, if speech is to be comprehended at a normal speed. Naturally, such early training must not be prolonged unduly, or students will not learn to perform swiftly the holistic operation that is the final goal.

Massed listening as an initial learning procedure

It has been suggested that students should begin the study of a foreign language by being plunged into a "bath" of foreign-language speech: that for some time they should listen only, until they begin to absorb the language through continual exposure. In the light of our analysis of the processes of speech perception, this massed listening approach does not appear to be sufficient of itself. If the segmentation we make in the initial stages is vital, and if ready comprehension depends to some extent on our ability to project an anticipated message, then massed listening in the very early stages, unaccompanied by some other linguistic activity, will familiarize the student to some extent with the general sound aura of the language, not the significant sound patterns (this, of course, has an initial usefulness); it will not help the student to segment the aural input according to the rules of the new language and may encourage an attempt at segmentation based on native-language rules. Where languages are very similar in word order and basic syntactic patterns, even having rather similar lexical items derived from the same roots (as with *Vater*, father; *table ronde*, round table), this again may have its uses, by encouraging students to put together meaning from semantic clues and to practice inference (both very important processes in listening). With very different languages, more problems arise and, without some guidance as to syntactic structure and the meanings of key words, students may become frustrated, discouraged, and too embarrassed to confess their failure to comprehend.

Initial listening should be accompanied by *visual cues to meaning* (pictures, objects, or actions), which focus attention and give direction to inference from semantic clues. Teachers should remember that, when the only response required is a nonverbal one (actions or pointing to items in a picture), it is sometimes difficult to judge how much of the interpretation is derived from actions of the teacher or the visual props and how much has been comprehended from the linguistic output itself. Some linguistic response will act as a corrective. This need not always be spoken. In the place of spoken responses, Postovsky and others have required written responses or demonstration of comprehension through reading, both of which require identification of segments just as much as do spoken responses.[17] Should all linguistic responses be excluded, care must be taken to check the students' comprehension from time to time by limiting the input to the purely verbal. Even with the visual help removed, students often remember expected responses to specific utterances. The teacher should probe further to see whether they have really comprehended individual segments of the utterance, as they will need to do later in decoding complex material. In the early stages, students should be building up a foreign-language competence that will enable them to segment and group meaningfully and carry in their memories significant segments while they anticipate evolving meaning. This ability becomes confirmed as knowledge of the language grows.

Techniques for segmenting (stage 1)

Merely to suggest that listening comprehension will improve as competence in the language is established is hardly a great step forward. We can do better than that.

The first stage of speech perception is one of rapid, fleeting impressions, crudely segmented before the echo of the stimulus has disappeared from the memory. The initial selection is vital and normally related to syntactic groupings. (Where the structure is complicated, the listener may resort to purely semantic decoding, which in its simplest form is based on the order of semantic elements and their probable relationships.[18])

We can help the student at this stage by ensuring the *prolongation of the auditory image*. In the early stages, students should be encouraged to repeat to themselves the segments they have apprehended, first as stretches of sound, then in an attempt at syntactic grouping. The very effort of repetition forces the student to segment the stream of sound in some fashion, the auditory image is retained longer, and the student has time to relate segments and to readjust the developing interpretation. Experiments have shown that speech can be speeded up within segments and still be comprehensible, so long as the pause between segments, which is essential for cognitive processing, is slightly lengthened, ensuring that the overall rate of presentation is not increased.[19] Students should be trained to *use the pauses for conscious processing*, until early segmentation has become automatic. Except where known lexical items form a sequence that makes inference feasible (*girl-sat-garden-tree*), early listening comprehension materials are most usefully kept within the limits of structural patterns being learned, so that rapid identification of syntactic groupings is possible. Once having made an incorrect segmentation, the listener has lost the sound image, and further adjustments must be made by conjecture and inference. (This is again an important process of which students must be made aware and for which they should be given plenty of preparation.) Training in *listening comprehension by parallel production* is more than mere imitation: It forces concentration on segmentation and provides guided practice in the production of well-formed segments, thus integrating with listening comprehension an operation that is basic to creative speech production as well.

Techniques for interrelating segments (stage 2)

At the next stage, students must identify more precisely and interrelate the segments they are holding in their short-term memory. Unless they are able to interrelate these meaningfully into larger groupings they will lose what they have so far retained. This is where students will gain from systematic training from the beginning in the *recognition of structural features*. If they are to reach an advanced stage of listening comprehension, where they can enjoy and later discuss all kinds of materials, they will need to be adept at rapid recognition of many indicators of structure. They must be able to categorize words and word groupings (in the practical sense of recognizing their function). They must be able to recognize rapidly sentence shape by identification of clues to question form, negation, coordination, or subordination. They must recognize clues that indicate condition, purpose, and temporal relationships. Such features are frequently signaled by initial words, which should be apprehended immediately so that the mind can concentrate on less clearly marked syntactic relationships. Listeners need to be able to recognize rapidly signals such as prepositions, articles, and auxiliaries, which help them discern constituents of phrase structure, and they must identify immediately, in order to discard them, prop words and hesitation expressions, which add nothing to meaning, but take up precious storage space (for example, *vous voyez, d'ailleurs, effectivement; kind of, you know, I think*). Students should have frequent practice in repeating as units, in meaningful contexts, word groups of high frequency that contrast with those of their own language and further practice in detecting these in listening materials. Exercises can be designed especially for practice in apprehending and matching orally certain types of structure (for example, left-branching, right-branching, or nested constructions). Progressively developed, these can be amusing exercises for laboratory practice. Once students have been trained to listen purposefully, and can identify readily the various clues to syntactic relationships that have been listed, mind and memory will be free to concentrate on the semantic content of the message, using what they know of reality to supply meaning when their knowledge of the foreign lexicon fails them.

Techniques for rehearsal and recoding (stage 3)

Next, there is recoding for retention. Here we may gain some ideas for teaching materials from the suggestion that information perceived aurally is detransformed for storage and is mostly recalled in simple active affirmative declarative sentences. We can aid the automatization of this process by giving students direct practice in such recoding. It is surface structure in the foreign language that is troublesome to the student, because it is here that languages are differentiated and contrast. Students need practice in detecting the main relationships (in Fillmore's terms, the agentive, objective, instrumental, locative, patient, and beneficiary, among others); they need training in abstracting these from the complications of the surface form, reducing the relationship extracted to a more basic form of expression. In other words, they need practice in giving the gist of what they hear in simple form. They can then store this, leaving the mind free to concentrate on incoming information. Exercises should be developed that force recognition of deep structure relationships like those of Fillmore by using as prompt words for recall those that correspond to the agent, instrument, or objective. The deep structure relationships constitute language universals, and in the recognition of these relationships students are able to draw on their cognitive abilities to penetrate beneath the level of surface structure complications. Students should also be given exercises in which they are presented first with the essence of what they are to hear in basic, kernel-like sentences, and then be required to listen to the same substance in more complicated form with numerous transformations.[20] Unless students have regular *opportunities to decode to a level of basic meaning and reconstitute interesting material* in the foreign language, they are likely to take what seems the easier path of converting what they hear into a simplified form in the native language, thus wasting much valuable time and energy in translation and retranslation, and never developing speed and ease in direct comprehension.

Applications to reading

One of the perennial problems in modern language teaching has been the *development of fluent direct reading.* Frequently students are trained to read fluently recombinations of foreign-language speech they have learned or even carefully graded readers kept within specified limits of known vocabulary and structure. Unfortunately, when these students are finally faced with less controlled or authentic materials (usually at the late elementary or early intermediate level), it becomes apparent that they have not developed a technique for extracting meaning directly from the foreign-language text. Many fall back on translation, grabbing at words here and there that they recognize and constructing a summary version. This may suffice for some purposes (identifying the general story line or seeking out sections of an informational text that will be useful for some particular project), but it is inadequate where precise information is sought, or if the assignment requires detailed study of a text. These students pay scant attention to the basic structuring of meaning in the text, those nuances that derive from the syntactic choices of the author. Consequently, they feel overwhelmed by quantity of pages and lose the train of thought.

It is important to keep in mind the three quite different goals student-readers may be pursuing: reading for precise information or for detailed analysis of a text; reading for enjoyment; and scanning as a time-saving method. Students must be trained in each of these ways of approaching the text. They need to be able to see how the author's syntactic choices structure precise meaning, while realizing that becoming bogged down in too much detail will prevent them from seeing the forest for the trees, and from developing into fluent, confident readers who read with unconcerned ease and enjoyment. Like native-language readers, they will need to be able to read rapidly (drawing essential meaning from the text without poring over every detail) until they find those sections that, for reasons of knowledge acquisition or pleasure in appreciation of good writing, they may wish to examine more carefully. The teacher is in something of a dilemma here: how to provide activities to develop both types of reading without hindering the students' development of a personal reading style. It is essential that each student learn early that fluent reading directly in the foreign language is the aim. This ability develops as one reads on, despite occasional mysteries: Fluent readers allow meaning to become clear as more and more is read, tolerating a certain vagueness at some points yet persisting.

At the early stages there is much students can learn that will eventually facilitate the process of reading for comprehension, helping them past that awkward stage, at which even many advanced students seem to be stalled, of reading meticulously word for word, or phrase by phrase, all the way through each text with the dictionary very close at hand. For students who have not acquired confidence in reading, a fifty-page assignment at the advanced level becomes an all-night chore, with the meaning of what one has already read fleeing the mind, as one moves stolidly on page after endless page, looking up words and piecing together meaning. We can improve the students' grasp of the reading process by drawing from two areas of psychological research: the cognitive approach we have been discussing, and Goodman's notion of reading as a "psycholinguistic guessing game." (The latter is discussed fully, with applications, in the next chapter, "Reading Fluently: Extracting Meaning for Pleasure and Profit.")

Processes of reading comprehension parallel processes for listening

To return to Neisser's three stages of perception, research into the act of reading for meaning has shown that the processes involved parallel those of listening comprehension. First, there is recognition in a fast, impressionistic way of segments that, for comprehension, must be identified as meaningful segments of phrase structure. Then there is the necessity to interrelate these according to basic relationships, holding one segment in the mind and suspending judgment, until other segments are identified and combined with it in a meaningful way. Finally, there is the same need for rapid recognition of categories, of sentence shapes, of markers, of constituents of phrase structure, and for penetrating beneath surface complications to basic relationships.

In view of this similarity of processes, *learning to read fluently could be considerably facilitated by combining it with a program for listening comprehension.* The effort at rapid segmentation (the identification of the essential relationships of the underlying phrase structure), the holding of chunks in the memory while awaiting confirmation of anticipations (that is, while waiting to see that the projected sentence is congruent with the actual sentence), the extracting of the gist (that is, the reduction to deep structure) – all these operations must be performed for both the aural and the graphic medium. When students are being trained in these specific operations for listening comprehension, they should be brought to realize their applicability to the graphic mode by being encouraged to read rapidly material based on the same content as that they have heard and, at other times, to listen to oral presentations based on content similar to what they have read. The reading should not be done aloud, however, as hearing oneself read and concentrating on how one is reading hinder rapid identification of the graphic text.[21]

Exercises similar to those outlined for listening comprehension can be developed for reading comprehension: reading the gist in simple active affirmative declarative sentences before reading a highly transformed version, practice in recounting in detransformed form what has been read, practice in detecting the deep structure relationships beneath the surface forms, rapid identification of cue words to structure and sentence shape. This is another area of concern, which must be set aside for another time.[22] All good teaching, however, is teaching for transfer (or, as in this case, transposition), and teaching of listening comprehension should be no exception.

Let's discuss

1 What factors in the process of listening act as impediments to our constructing a message that exactly parallels that intended by the speaker?
2 In what ways can we consider speech comprehension to be an "active, knowledge-guided process," as Slobin expresses it? Which types of listening comprehension exercises best fit in with this concept?
3 How can we provide in listening exercises for learning to recognize structural clues and structural groupings without inhibiting attention to the flow of meaning (that is, without encouraging students to hesitate unduly to check on precise details of the content)?
4 How would you design an intensive listening experience, for the first two weeks of an elementary course, based on principles elaborated in this chapter?
5 How does what you learned about memory in Chapter 4 supplement concepts in this chapter? How does this combination affect your views on the teaching of listening and reading?
6 How would you design a reading test of
   (a) ability to scan a text for specific information;
   (b) ability to detect subtleties of a writer's thought;
   (c) ability to use a text as a springboard for some other activity?
7 How would you go about designing a course to develop listening and reading comprehension as the main objectives? At the elementary level? At the advanced level?

6 Reading fluently: extracting meaning for pleasure and profit

Reading poses an acute problem the world over. Can we teach foreign-language reading? Do students learn it without teaching, drawing on their literacy in their native language? Or is there an interplay between teaching and learning in this area as in others? Is reading a late-developing skill that blossoms when students know the foreign language in oral form, or is it a useful preliminary to learning oral skills, familiarizing them with the language they are to learn? Some say all first- and second-language learning is really the same process drawing on innate abilities to acquire language. In this case, knowledge of the language in oral form should precede reading, as this is the order of native-language learning: Young children recognize what they already know orally in its graphic form, expanding their knowledge of the language from then on in part through reading. If learning the native language and learning a second or third language are different processes, at least for adolescent and adult learners,[1] then the approach taken to reading will depend on what the difference is and will exploit it. In this case, reading by already literate foreign-language learners may well go hand in hand with the development of early listening and speaking, consolidating and expanding what is being learned in the aural-oral mode and providing many opportunities for learning beyond what is actually being taught. In this chapter, we will first discuss the very live controversy about differences between first- and second-language learning, as well as the so-called critical period for acquiring a foreign language as one learned one's first language, and we will then examine research into reading processes to see what can be drawn from this area for improving foreign-language reading comprehension and developing confident fluency in reading.

Are first- and second-language learning the same process?

Recent findings clearly indicate differences between adult foreign-language learning and both first- and second-language learning by

Revised version of an article originally published as "Language Learning and Language Teaching – Any Relationship?" in W. C. Ritchie, ed., *Second Language Acquisition Research: Issues and Implications* (New York: Academic Press, 1978), pp. 201–213.

children.[2] The real problem, in discussion of these processes, is always this: *At what level of generality does one declare there to be a similarity or a difference?* We would expect to observe more similarities between the acquisition of a first or second language at age 2 and the acquisition of a foreign language at age 20 than between learning a language and learning to balance a book on one's head. In the following discussion, we will take into account both basic similarities of all language learning and specific differences that may derive from situation, age of acquisition and the cognitive development that this involves, and previous experience with language and language-related activities (in the first and other languages).

A critical period or Piagetian stages of development?

It has long been held that at about puberty one loses the ability to acquire a language in a "natural" (childlike) way, through much exposure to it, without actual formal instruction. This is the so-called *critical period.*[3] This view of Penfield and Lenneberg has been challenged by recent researchers, notably Snow and Hoefnagel-Höhle.[4] Rosansky and Krashen consider the observed differences in acquisition of a new language between small children and adolescents and adults to be related, not so much to neurological development (the notion of lack of plasticity of the brain tissue, put forward by Penfield and Lenneberg[5]), but to the stages of cognitive development described by Piaget.[6]

According to Inhelder and Piaget's studies, it is at about 11 or 12 years of age that the individual reaches *the stage of formal operations.*[7] At this age, students are able to use hypothetical reasoning. They begin to think in the abstract with propositions. They are able to isolate variables and deduce potential relationships. At first, they are satisfied with the search for a single constant factor in correspondences. They can perform the formal operation of implication, by which they assume that a determinate factor produces the observed consequences in all cases. By the age of 14 or 15, students are capable of hypothetico-deductive reasoning, performed as a mental operation divorced from actual material objects. They are able to isolate and combine variables that depend on a number of factors, performing all the sixteen binary operations of logical thought. They do not have to limit their considerations to one relationship at a time, but consider the possible effect of several variables, testing the effect of each by holding other factors constant. They feel the need to find the reason for the relations they observe and perform the operations of implication and equivalence, disjunction, and simple and reciprocal exclusion. They are ready, then, to think about and comprehend the many complexities of syntax.[8]

Because small children have not yet developed the ability to use these logical operations, they find an abstract approach to a new language (that is, explanations of rules and tables of paradigms) incomprehensible, irrelevant, and tiresome. Reading is also an abstract process and readiness for reading varies from child to child, some reading much later than others. On the other hand, older adolescent and adult learners feel the need for more explanation and, rightly or wrongly, they expect to find some logic in the functioning of the new language. To relate the Piagetian studies to reading, we may note that *many of these logical operations are essential for inferencing and holding meaning in the immediate memory* while interrelating new elements with previously selected material, as we will see in our later discussion. For this reason, many more repetitions and redundancies are worked into stories for young children, for whom inferencing is a problem. Because of the stage of cognitive development they have reached, we find them very "literal-minded" when we read to them.

Whether the changes Piaget identifies as young people pass beyond puberty are due to maturation or to educational factors in our society, as some have suggested, will not concern us here. These are our adolescent and adult students, whether native- or foreign-language learners. We must then take into consideration their mode of learning and the abilities they bring to the reading task, along with factors of interest and motivation that relate to the situation in which they find themselves.

Adolescent and adult language learning

Snow and Hoefnagel-Höhle's studies have shown that early adolescents (12- to 15-year-olds) actually learn a second language faster than very young children and propose as an explanation of the plateau in the language learning of adults, who begin rapidly and then slow down, the early satisfaction of their linguistic needs at work and in social situations, outside their intimate circle.[9] This research is illuminated by that of Schumann. In work with adolescents and adults, Schumann has demonstrated the importance of *psychological distance* as a factor in successful and unsuccessful second-language learning (that is, how much the adolescent or adult wishes, and is able emotionally and temperamentally, to interact with other-language speakers and take on characteristics of their culture). Of similar importance is *social distance* (the degree to which political, economic, and societal factors permit frequent contacts between the language learner and other-language speakers).[10]

Applying this to our main focus (reading), we may note that illiterate immigrants often see no need for reading in their new language, as reading matter and even forms to be filled in may be available in their native language and younger family members can help them. The material in newspapers and books often seems strange to them, even to the point of incomprehensibility, and certainly of little interest because of different cultural preoccupations. Tradition within the family and their normal way of life may also cause them to undervalue literacy as an essential goal. Even migrants literate in their native language may spend all their nonworking hours in pleasurable activities with speakers of their language and have available a liberal supply of newspapers and other reading material in their first language, which they find much more accessible in language and viewpoint. Thus, they also may be perfectly satisfied to use the services of a bilingual supervisor or a child go-between when it is essential for written instructions to be comprehended or transactions performed.

The specific problems of adolescents and adults

More and more researchers, then, are recognizing the distinct character of the language learning of adolescents and adults, both cognitively and psychologically. No longer is there that carefree attribution to pedagogical ineptitude of the very real problems posed by acquiring a language at a later age. When we have faced the fact that, for most adolescent and adult learners, a native-sounding accent and full nativelike competence in syntax and semantics in communication may never be achieved,[11] we may be willing to settle for less: the ability to convey messages comprehensibly and acceptably in the spoken language without inhibitions, and real fluency in extracting messages from both oral[12] and graphic material, the latter being recognized as of major importance to many. In these areas adolescents and adults can and do succeed very well.

We come, then, to our fundamental question: How can our teaching stimulate the language learning of the student who has reached the stage of formal operations, beyond the so-called critical period of natural language acquisition? In other words, *how can we draw effectively on the particular cognitive abilities our normal adolescent or adult student has developed with maturity?*

We have many approaches to the initial stages of learning the basic corpus of a language, which students must be able to use productively in all skill areas if they are to reach the stage of comprehensibility and comprehension. More and more demonstrations of "new" approaches to initial second-language learning fill the workshop areas of our national conferences. Too rarely do we see demonstrations of ways to attack the problems of intermediate and advanced learners, especially those who have valid reasons for preferring reading to speaking. Their problems, as every experienced teacher knows, are urgent and persistent. No wonder students at these levels drop out of our classes in discouragement when so little attention is paid to their acutely felt problems and to their legitimate personal goals in language learning.

Research in native-language use

For possible explanations of some of these problems of later language learning, especially in the areas of reading and listening, we can, I believe, look seriously at research into the teaching and learning of language and language-dependent activities in the native language, especially with subjects of a similar age and maturity, and see what kinds of problems they highlight for our foreign-language learner in the formal classroom. The native-language students who have been the subjects of this research do not possess a mature and rounded competence in their first language; in fact, many are impoverished in this regard. *They are still language learners.* The problems for the foreign-language learner are compounded, to be sure, by the need to acquire and use with flexibility another symbol system. Nevertheless, many of the skills and processes involved in language use are so poorly understood by foreign-language teachers in the first place that they are liable to identify as distinctively foreign-language learners' problems many that are essentially problems of language use wherever the knowledge of the language is incomplete. Consequently, teachers have little solid foundation on which to base their analyses and explanations of the difficulties they observe, or proposals for better teaching. The solutions they develop tend to be ad hoc, where they might be given firmer underpinnings if the observer possessed more knowledge of language-using processes.

Perception and production processes

According to much recent thinking, speech perception and speech production are different processes independently represented in behavior. If this is so, it has important implications for teaching reading (and listening). Perception, it seems, depends on semantic apprehension, moving from sense percept to idea, with recourse to syntactic knowledge where the meaning is not clear or an ambiguity, or misdirected interpretation, is detected. In a foreign-language situation, where the reader (or listener) does not have full control of the syntactic system, even the latter stratagem may be bypassed by resorting to processes of inference. The major planning unit in perception, according to Bever, is "something close to the 'deep structure sentoid,' "[13] the sense of which may be apprehended without close attention to syntactic detail. In speech *production*, on the other hand, the speaker is expressing an intention, or idea, through the operation of the syntactic system, which gives structure to the semantic intention of the message. Here the planning unit is "something close to the 'surface structure clause,' "[14] and the student needs to possess greater control over syntactic structure and morphological variation.

With this distinction between *independent, but interacting, systems of perception and production* in mind, the foreign-language teacher would expose the student to much authentic material for reading (and listening),[15] without worrying whether all the structures and vocabulary were familiar, while encouraging students, when expressing themselves in speech or writing, to keep as much as feasible within the framework of what they have been learning. This does not mean resorting only to learned phrases in production, but encouraging students to use their limited knowledge of the syntax to the fullest by paraphrasing, simplifying, avoiding, circumlocuting, and even extrapolating from rules they know in the new language when caught in a bind, so as to make the most of what they control without being forced to borrow surface structure realizations from their first-language system to meet their needs.

It is important for teachers to realize that the knowledge of the grammar required for reading (and listening) will be rather different from that required for speaking, a fact that should be kept in mind when designing specialized courses for reading or for conversational skill. The facts of grammar that need special emphasis for recognition as opposed to production have not been thoroughly researched in any foreign language. Teachers choosing textbooks and materials writers should be aware of the need to provide for *recognition and production grammars* and be ready to supplement or redesign materials that ignore this fundamental distinction.

Carroll's two-stream approach

This dual approach for comprehension and production parallels Carroll's two-stream proposal. Carroll points to the "two somewhat conflicting demands" that "arise from a consideration of language-learning processes" (and we may relate these comments to what was said earlier about the stage of cognitive development of the adolescent or adult language learner). Carroll suggests that "second-language learners appear to be helped by guidance and explanations with respect to particular aspects of instructional content. Some learners, at least, seem to need to have the instructional content develop 'logically' so that new learnings can build on prior learnings....However, normal speech contains an unpredictably large variety of content (vocabulary, grammatical constructions), and selection and sequencing of instructional content may never capture this full richness and variety." He proposes, then, that "a program of instruction should contain two parallel streams, one devoted to exposing the learner to materials containing a relatively uncontrolled variety of linguistic elements (for example, vocabulary and grammatical constructions) and the other devoted to a rather carefully developed sequence of instructional content. The two streams would presumably have interactive effects, in the sense that the second stream would give the learner the specific guidance that would help him in his efforts to master the materials of the first stream."[16]

Undoubtedly, the first stream of materials containing "a relatively uncontrolled variety of linguistic elements" is best provided by *authentic reading and listening materials* (the value of which has been emphasized in so much recent writing on language teaching), their use being paralleled, as Carroll suggests, by carefully sequenced and developed instructional materials for intensive study. (For production, the relatively uncontrolled element is provided by early and frequent attempts at creative expression in speech and writing, paralleling more carefully structured learning experiences with practice materials.)

Bever's psychogrammar

Bever postulates the existence of a "psychogrammar,"[17] whose function is to equilibrate the capacities of the two distinct systems of speech perception and speech production during their development, thus providing the interactive element, so that what has been acquired by the perception system may play into the production system, to some extent, and vice versa. According to Bever, this psychogrammar ceases to be useful once a native competence has been acquired in the two areas. It does not necessarily wither away, however, but remains, as it were, dormant. Its usefulness can presumably be revived at the late adolescent or adult stage, so that much of what is learned through the perceptual system by reading and listening to authentic materials can be sorted out and can provide an experiential basis for learning how to express the equivalent semantic intentions through the production system. The psychogrammar, having served as a mediator between the autonomous perception and production systems of the first language, can furnish useful inductions about the functioning of the new language, by identifying universal features of language and highlighting differences between the old and the new grammars at a basic conceptual level. (It is well to remember that new learning always draws on previous learning stored in the cognitive system.) In this way, the psychogrammar can serve as an *inductive filter*, which will help older language learners establish mentally a schematic overview of structural relations. This overview will make more comprehensible to them the place that new linguistic facts, which are being presented in the structured program, will occupy within that system. The goal of the language learner is to reach the stage in the new language where the systems of speech perception and production operate independently of the psychogrammar, as in native-language use, except at points of difficulty when we reflect on what was said in order to unravel its complexities, or when we deliberate on how best to express a complicated idea. Bever's theory of the psychogrammar supports the view that *much of language behavior must become automatic* in the sense that many of its operations are carried out below the level of conscious awareness.[18] Such a supremely confident operation can be developed at the adolescent and adult level only through a clear understanding of interrelationships within the language system.

Research into the reading process

With the needs of our older language learners still in mind, we can profit from looking rather more carefully than in the past at recent research into the reading process. In foreign-language teaching, we have been prone to lean far more heavily than is warranted on the fact that our adolescent and adult students already "know how to read." Unless there is a new script to be learned, we pay scant attention to how our students read, frequently putting reading material into their hands and sending them off to "read" it for the next day. Just what they do with it does not seem to concern us, so long as, on their return, they can tell us something about the content. We are particularly interested usually in the factual details. If our consciences smite us and we feel we should be "doing something about reading," we stand them up and make them read aloud, preferably from previously unseen texts, to demonstrate "how well they read." Then to cap our ineptitude we ask them questions on what they have just been reading aloud. Each of these common procedures could hardly be better designed to thwart the student who really wishes to learn to read the foreign language effectively, in the sense of drawing coherent meaning from the text.

For the older foreign-language learner, in a formal setting, who is already literate in one language (that is, the majority of such learners, in most countries today), decoding letters and words is not the major problem in reading. Even the need to learn to decipher a new alphabet is not of itself a prolonged disability.[19] Students may learn to associate a new sound system with an old graphic symbol system without too much difficulty, yet still find the extraction of meaning to be a problem. The more the foreign-language reader becomes bogged down in individual words the harder the task becomes. Goodman calls fluent reading *a psycholinguistic guessing game* that requires "skill in selecting the fewest, most productive cues necessary to produce guesses which are right the first time."[20] Robeck and Wilson call this performance "that of a reader with basic recognition skills confronted by material that is beyond his independent reading level."[21] What a vivid picture we have here of the average foreign-language reader – a picture that makes Goodman's approach seem all the more appropriate for our students.

Three radical insights

Here the "three radical insights," which Frank Smith highlights in his discussion of the thinking and research of linguists and cognitive psychologists with regard to reading, are worth serious consideration. Just stating these three insights, without examining further the research on which they are based, will give pause to the conventional teacher addicted to such procedures as those I have described.

> 1. *Only a small part of the information necessary for reading comprehension comes from the printed page.*
> 2. *Comprehension must precede the identification of individual words.*
> 3. *Reading is not decoding to spoken language.*[22]

What are the implications for foreign-language teachers of these insights? In what ways do they suggest changes in our procedures to ensure the nurturing of the efficient reading that is surely a priority in most foreign-language programs? Should we not share these insights with our students, so that they may adapt or completely change their approach to reading in order to comprehend content more effectively? In considering these implications, we will be thinking of both learner and teacher.

What is known beyond the printed page

First, only a small part of the information necessary for reading comprehension comes from the printed page, according to a number of reading researchers. We may find this insight rather startling when we first encounter it, since it certainly runs counter to conventional ideas on reading. Taking it seriously can have a most salutary effect on our practice.

Readers have expectations about the content of what they are about to read and its development, which are further stimulated as they continue to read by what they have already understood. *The function of the symbols on the printed page is to reduce the uncertainty of the reader*, as information (or meaning) is derived from the script. For this reason, an efficient reader needs only schematic indications of the actual visual forms. Here we can think of children's reading games where only portions of letters are given, or where the usual presentation of letters is distorted in some way.

This insight also explains why we often "read" from the page synonyms of the words before us, even when these equivalents have quite different visual shapes from what is actually printed: "friend" for "buddy," for instance. *We are reading "meanings," not specific words.* (We also report "hearing" such alternatives.) In an interesting series of bilingual experiments on reading, Kolers demonstrated this natural tendency of the reader to perceive words directly in terms of their meanings. French-English bilinguals, when asked to read aloud texts that mixed segments of the two languages, would read out some groups of words that were in the first language in the text as their translation equivalents in the second language, and vice versa. For instance, "des gouttes de verglas stuck to his manteau" was read out as "drops of ice se collaient to his cloak." Kolers comments that "the subjects were treating words in terms of their meanings rather than in terms of their appearance on the page."[23]

Further, it now surprises us less that *two readers can draw quite different content from the same script* (or "hear" different messages from the same signal), even when the input has been carefully composed. This is a normal and common experience in native-language reading, yet we often expect a perfect rendering of the details of the script, and the one "right" answer or interpretation of the content, when they are reading in another language. Here again we should reflect and observe. Redundancies built into language act as a backup when expectations are not realized, and comprehension falters. These redundancies act as a corrective for redirecting expectations.[24] They are even more of an aid to the foreign-language reader, for whom the extraction of meaning is a laborious and inexpert procedure. In preparing reading (and listening) materials for second- or foreign-language learners, then, we must be careful not to reduce the amount of redundancy below that of authentic materials.

It appears that inefficiency in reading is related to the amount of knowledge a person has, not only of language forms, but also of the conceptual and informational area in which the passage has been written. The less readers know, the more visual information they require. (This again is paralleled for listening. As Olson has observed: "If the listener doesn't 'know' what you are talking about you have limited linguistic resources to make yourself known."[25])

This brings us to the question of *"literal" meaning*. The first thing inexperienced foreign-language readers seem to demand is, "But what does it really mean?" as they rush to a bilingual dictionary to find "the meaning" of isolated words. We must change this state of mind. We have to encourage foreign-language readers to tolerate vagueness, so that they will be open to the unfolding meaning, as segment is added to segment and first impressions are corrected by later information. Miller and Johnson-Laird are emphatic on this point:

> Perhaps we should say that there is no such thing as the literal meaning of a sentence, only the literal meaning that a given listener [or reader] places on a given utterance of it. Or perhaps we should say that the literal meaning of a sentence (divorced from any particular context) consists of procedures that can be called in many different orders, even omitted in certain cases, by higher-order programs responsible for verifying statements, answering questions, obeying commands, storing information in episodic memory.
> The moral for the mental lexicon is clear. If the meaning of a word were a fixed set of procedures or structured set of semantic markers, it would be impossible to handle structures of a given sentence with sufficient flexibility.[26]

The acceptance of the *flexible, changing nature of meaning in context* is essential to the development of efficient reading techniques. The willingness to withhold judgment, to resist a tendency to closure, to fill in the gaps by inference – these require a certain courage on the part of the anxious reader. It is important, then, to have much reading for pleasure, for reading's sake, which is not tested at all: reading to develop confidence in reading.[27]

The adult reader and conceptual content

It may be argued that here we are talking about comprehension of the author's intention in a text, rather than "reading," yet this is what reading for adolescent and adult students implies. Carroll has made clear how difficult it is "to distinguish 'pure' comprehension of language texts from processes of inference, deduction, and problem solving that often accompany the reception of language."[28]

Our students are impatient to comprehend the content and import of what they are reading, as they do in their own language, and the new language should be merely a barrier they must learn to hurdle with confidence, not a fence to climb laboriously. Chall says that "to read at the highest level of maturity means thinking and reasoning, and to have an advanced command of language, concept, and experience."[29] Our adolescent and adult students are at an age when *they feel the need to think and reason about what they read*, and they possess "an advanced command...of concept and experience." The only similarity between them and children learning to read the native language is their lack of command of an extensive vocabulary in the new language, and their ignorance of some areas of syntax. However, their wider knowledge of concepts and their many life experiences enable them to bridge this gap with expectations based on the general theme and its development. Apart from further language work in the course that feeds back into reading, it is through much reading that the students' knowledge of vocabulary and syntax increases – for each student individually and independent of the teacher. This is the added bonus of encouraging much confident reading in areas of interest to the student.

With foreign-language reading, *some of the conceptual content is related to the values, institutions, and preoccupations of the cultural group*, or even of the subcultural group, from which the writer springs. Just as a passage about the process of nuclear fission can be incomprehensible to a person whose major interest in life is comparative economic systems, so can a passage in English be largely incomprehensible to an Arab who does not understand the American or British way of looking at life's experiences. In such cases knowledge of language forms is not enough for efficient reading. In summary, to quote Frank Smith once again, "there is a trade-off between visual and non-visual information in reading – the more that is already known 'behind the eyeball,' the less visual information is required to identify a letter, a word, or a meaning from the text."[30]

For this reason *reading specialized material in a technical area* in which the foreign-language learner is well versed is a recognition and identification problem, which is quite different, and requires quite different approaches to teaching, than the reading of foreign-language material by an elementary school child. Specialized reading material provides amplification of what well-informed students already know and confirms their expectations, even in areas of new and surprising details and conclusions, because these students are already familiar with a great deal of what is contained in the text. The same details would not appear surprising, nor the conclusion novel, to one who did not have this prior knowledge and whose expectations were much less precise as a result.

Comprehension is not a word-by-word process

As with all other areas of language use, then, one can "know" the forms of a language (the vocabulary and grammar) without being able to operate within it, because one does not have the necessary links within the conceptual networks to the new forms.[31] In this sense, comprehension must precede the identification of individual words.[32] As one pieces together the meaning, receiving confirmation of what one has inferred so that one may finally make judgments as to relationships, one is able to identify words in their essential roles in the evolving tapestry of discourse. (In English, it is clear that homographs, like *bear, lead,* and *bow,* cannot be identified, or in some cases even pronounced, until the passage in which they are embedded has been comprehended, and there are many ambiguous structures, yet we are able to read texts despite these problems.) If we ignore this process in our teaching, we will penalize students for many inevitable and natural confusions and mislead them as to what reading is all about.

Relationship of reading to spoken language

Similarly, reading in its fullest sense is not decoding to speech, but precedes decoding to speech. For this reason, reading aloud from a passage can be a pro forma relating of rules of sound-symbol correspondence to graphic material, accompanied by the activation of appropriate articulators, without indicating a high degree of comprehension. This lack of real comprehension will be evident from misapplication of stress, juncture, and intonation rules in particular, since these indicate proper allocation of words to meaningful segments. If there is sufficient reason for requiring reading aloud as a demonstration of comprehension, the *comprehension must come first* through a preliminary silent reading before the oral reader can give it full expression. At this point, it is the silent activity that may rightfully be termed "reading." The oral activity is not of itself useful, except for a future newscaster or court reporter, and can have the effect of training students to look closely at individual words, or even syllables, rather than words in context where true meaning lies. In this way, it can inculcate reading habits that are ultimately detrimental to efficient extraction of meaning from graphic material.

Experimentation has shown that *concentrating on sound-symbol correspondences and hearing oneself read aloud actually hinder* students in extracting a message from a text, by preventing them from rehearsing adequately the elements of the evolving meaning as they proceed and from retaining what they have extracted long enough to relate it to later parts of the text. We must remember that the "meaning" at one point in a discourse may be radically modified by later information, even by something we read much later, so that holding elements in immediate memory until the full meaning has been extracted is an important element in reading for comprehension. Reading aloud in a foreign language may be useful at times as an exercise in pronunciation and in the identification of syntactic segments from surface structure indicators, but it must not be confused with reading for meaning. Reading for comprehension of a message and of the writer's intentions may complicate life for the foreign-language teacher, but it is the only valid goal.

Reading and purposeful activity

The discussion to this point highlights the importance in language instruction of building reading practice into a matrix of purposeful activity, so that the attention of the reader is on the extraction of information from the text, rather than on the reading process itself. This applies equally to listening activities. In one sense, we cannot teach reading or listening, or any other language skill; all we can learn from research is how to assist its development more efficiently and provide for the student many opportunities to perfect its use. Sticht makes a distinction the language teacher may well take to heart between "teaching reading" (or listening) and "*teaching learning (comprehending) by reading*" (or listening). Here the emphasis is not on decoding and orthography, but on "teaching meanings of words, concepts, reasoning with the information gained by reading."[33] Similarly, testing comprehension by reading can also be through purposeful activity. Comprehension of what has been read can be tested through the performance of some task, using information derived from reading, or by completion of some project that requires the reading of material from a number of sources.

Carroll has pointed out the difficulties of testing "reading comprehension" as opposed to "learning by reading" (or "listening comprehension" as opposed to "learning by listening"). In a lengthy analysis, he shows how difficult it is to separate the extraction of meaning from a text (that is, language comprehension) from processes of inference and memory in any meaningful or useful way.[34] If reading and listening are developed as purposeful activities, these processes need not be separated out, because they are part of the macro-process of "learning by reading" (or listening). We must continually remind ourselves that reading (and listening) comprehension draws on *situational and contextual factors* as well as what is conveyed by particular words and phrases. Without an assessment of what is not in fact expressed, what is merely hinted at, the matrix of language in which a particular group of words is embedded, who the writer (or speaker) is, and the circumstances of the emission of the message, the meaning of a particular group of words may be completely misinterpreted. Bever distinguishes three "different kinds of knowledge that are components of every concept indicated by language": *semantic meaning, cultural ideas* (of which *linguistic ideas* are an important subset) and *personal ideas.*[35] Clearly, then, inferential processes must inevitably be part of any real act of comprehension.

In the early stages of foreign-language reading (or listening), it may be useful to pinpoint, through quizzing or testing, the student's ability to draw specific information from particular linguistic items or structures. This type of testing must, however, wither away, as soon as its limited usefulness has been exhausted, to be replaced by *testing the results of reading* (or listening). This approach has implications for standardized testing programs, as well as for local situations, and is demonstrably more useful and interesting.

I shall not pretend that I have considered all the specific problems of reading in a new language.[36] If I have set a few ideas coursing through your minds, that is all I can hope for in this complicated and little-researched area. Let us recognize the validity of the slogan "the right to read in any language" and do our part to encourage reading, and more reading, as a satisfying and useful activity, which will remain with our students and which they will be able to perfect without our help long after they have ceased to be "official" language learners.

Let's discuss

1 What characteristics of Piaget's stage of formal operations have specific application to reading by adolescents or adults? What does this suggest to you about ways to approach the teaching of reading in a foreign language?
2 What kinds of reading materials for the language you teach would you consider appropriate for the two streams suggested by Carroll? (Make lists of specific texts for future use.)
3 How would you design a course to teach science or engineering students to read material in their field in a foreign language? How

would this course differ from the regular foreign-language beginning course? What techniques would you employ? How would you test the students' ability to comprehend specialized texts?

4 What kinds of information is it necessary for readers to possess before they can comprehend the material in a newspaper from a country where the language they are learning is spoken?

5 List as many purposeful activities as you can that incorporate reading as an essential component. Which of these could realistically be used for developing reading comprehension?

7 Motivating through classroom techniques

How often we hear teachers complaining about their students: "What can I do? They just lack motivation." This, of course, is impossible. Every living organism to survive must have some motivation. Frymier has defined motivation as "*that which* gives direction and intensity to behavior."[1] This definition emphasizes the fact that little is known about motivation, which, in psychological terms, is a construct inferred from the way an organism behaves. By the direction and intensity of the behavior we infer something about the inner state of the organism, and in order to be able to discuss and investigate this "something" we call it "motivation." Studying this "something" in more detail, we realize it is a complex of factors, many of which are intensely personal. Further detailed study of factors in motivation reveals more of their nature, but does not enlighten us a great deal on their operation in combination and interaction within the complex.

The complaint "They just have no motivation to learn to speak the language" may seem a more accurate description of the behavior of some students, but even this statement reflects a lack of realization on the part of the teacher of the *complex, individual factors in motivation*. Certain experiments have been performed where teachers had the opportunity, by way of an intercom system, to instruct fictitious students for whom they were provided with names and a short description. Later they were shown the supposed work of these students. The experiments revealed that the teachers' conviction about the intensity of motivation of particular students reflected the image they had created for themselves of these students rather than any existing psychological state.[2] The students referred to in the second complaint may not lack motivation to learn to speak the new language at all, but they may not regard the kinds of activities the teacher insists on as "speaking the language," or as leading to natural speaking of the language at any foreseeable time. Very often teachers impose useful practice activities on students without explaining their role in eventually developing speaking skill, and without in any way making them communicative.[3] For "lack of time," they also bypass

Revised version of an article originally published in *Speaking in Many Tongues*, 1st ed. (Rowley, Mass.: Newbury House, 1972).

the essential next step, communication practice, and rush on to more exercises in order to complete the unit in a prearranged interval. Students must perceive what they are doing as leading to speaking the language, if their motivation is to carry them through what are often tedious and uninteresting preliminary steps.

Furthermore, in the case of a second language, where students can interact out of class with native speakers, they may have found a variant of the language (which seems to the teacher to be substandard or even "incorrect") to be quite sufficient for their communicative purposes in the community in which they live. This may also be the only variety of the language they hear from those with whom they wish to identify, for example, parents or neighborhood associates. Sometimes a kind of pidgin (simplified functional language) seems to meet their needs for communication quite adequately.[4] As far as they are concerned, all indispensable communication beyond this may take place in their home language, be it English, Spanish, Chinese, or Navajo. The real problem for the teacher may be: "*My students have no motivation to learn what I teach in my language class.*"

So the question, "How can I motivate my students?" is not well formulated, nor is the question, "How can I motivate my students to learn?" Our students may not appear to be learning what we are earnestly trying to teach them, but every organism, nevertheless, is continually learning. As Holt tries to show in *How Children Fail*, our students may be learning in our classrooms to protect themselves from embarrassment, from humiliation, and from other emotional concomitants of failure; they may be learning to give us "the right answer and the right chatter."[5] According to Postman and Weingartner, "*a classroom is an environment* and . . . the way it is organized carries the burden of what people will learn from it."[6] Consequently, some of our students may be learning from our classrooms that the new language is used for rather meaningless, mechanical activities, or even as a vehicle for a teacher's monologues. In either case, it is not surprising if they find it clearly unrelated to their own concerns and interests.

Two views of motivation

There are two main strands of psychological thought on the question of motivation: the hedonistic strand, which includes the various theories of reinforcement or reward, and the ego-involvement strand, in which the individual's self-image and level of aspiration play the determining role.[7]

The hedonistic approach goes back as far as the ancient Greeks, of course. In modern psychological study it reappeared in Thorndike's Law of Effect, first proposed in 1898. It is discernible in the explanations of behavior of many psychologists, notably those that emphasize reinforcement or reward, as well as in the pleasure principle of Freud. According to the hedonistic approach, the individual organism in its relations with the environment is continually seeking to maintain a state of equilibrium, or balance of tension, which it finds pleasurable. Excess of motivation disrupts this balance and increases tension, which the organism actively seeks to reduce by purposeful, goal-directed behavior. Just as an excess of motivation is painful to the organism, so is frustration in its goal-seeking efforts, which prevents the organism from regaining its state of equilibrium. In this view, motivation can be looked upon as *a continual process of individual adjustment to the environment.* The individual actively seeks experiences that are pleasurable and avoids those that are painful. This parsimonious view of motivation would seem to provide a straightforward guideline for the classroom teacher. Unfortunately, because of the complexity of the inner state of each organism, what is pleasurable for one is not necessarily pleasurable for another, and the teacher must keep these differences in mind, seeking to understand individual motivations and adjust conditions accordingly.

Basically, this view would indicate that the teacher should capitalize on the motivated state of each learner *by keeping the work within the capacity of individual students* so that they experience success, which is tension-reducing and rewarding. This is the theory behind the programmed learning approach. In a well-designed programmed text, attainable goals, clearly discernible in carefully elaborated steps, act as incentives and, as each is completed, students are given immediate confirmation of the correctness or incorrectness of their responses. This continual feedback provides reinforcement of what has been learned, so that each student is motivated to continue to reproduce responses that have been rewarded and to put forth effort in the hope of experiencing further reinforcing success. (Most modern textbooks have adopted some aspects of this approach, sometimes within the text itself and, in other cases, in workbooks or language laboratory manuals.)

Ideally, potential success for each student can be realized only in an individualized program where students are proceeding at their own pace. Unfortunately, completely individualized work, as currently developed with programmed assignments or computer-assisted instruction, appears to conflict with the concept of language as primarily a vehicle of communication in which at least two persons, by their interactions, influence and modify each other's production. We must wait for further technological development of audio components and more imaginative programming before this disability can be overcome. The sophisticated materials that are becoming available are still beyond the financial resources of most schools. Furthermore, *individual differences cannot be reduced merely to differences in pace.* Some students crave more personal supervision and help than it is usually possible to offer in individualized programs; others are not happy with the inevitably reading-oriented approach of most programmed assignments. Still others look for the stimulation of working groups engaged in mutually supportive tasks.

In typical classrooms teachers do the best they can in distributing reinforcement within the class group, or within smaller groups for particular activities, hoping in this way to shape behavior progressively in the direction they desire. The result is a classroom largely teacher dominated, as the teacher seeks to manipulate the environment to provide the most favorable conditions for inducing correct language behavior on the part of as many students as possible.

Ego involvement is the second distinctive view of motivation, which is reflected in much modern writing on educational problems. According to this theory, individuals are continually seeking that which enhances the self as they perceive it; that is, *they are striving to achieve what they perceive as their potential.* Students are motivated at first in a general, nonspecific way in any situation: In other words, they are ready to take from any situation what there is in it for them. This initial motivation energizes and directs behavior, causing the student to attend to and focus on what is new in the environment. This attention is facilitative of learning, but must be caught and maintained. It is at this stage that the teacher uses interest-arousing techniques to involve the student. Students are more readily involved if the teacher builds on areas of concern to them at their particular stage of development, thus making the new learning meaningful and increasing its incentive value.

Many psychologists believe that the human organism possesses certain autonomous impulses such as curiosity, the desire to know and understand, the desire to play and explore, and the impulse to manipulate features of the environment. These provide raw material with which the teacher can work to interest the student in the learning process. Through success in language activities, and through the satisfaction of recognized and recognizable achievement, the student comes to take an interest in the subject for its own sake (that is, *an intrinsic interest in learning to know and use the new language*), and a self-sustaining cognitive drive then develops.[8] The development of such an interest in learning the language for its own sake is, of course, the final aim of the teacher, and the best assurance that the student will continue to learn and to seek opportunities to use the new language after the classroom has ceased to provide encouragement for this activity.

In the ego-enhancement view, a student's reaction to a stimulus is not predictable from the external conditions as the teacher sees them, but rather is *determined by the student's individual perception of reality.* The student may perceive a particular situation as a threat and withdraw from it or react unpredictably to counteract it. This is likely to happen quite frequently in an authoritarian classroom. Unfortunately, many language-teaching classrooms are authoritarian. Because the teacher knows the language well and the student does not, the teacher is always right and continually correcting the student. In such situations, many students are forced to adopt strategies to protect their self-image, even to the extent of preferring in some cases to be wrong in the first place, because at least in this way they know where they stand and the outcome is less painful. Some students may set themselves unrealistic goals they cannot possibly attain, because certain failure that they can blame on someone else is less damaging for them than unanticipated failure where they expected to succeed. The teacher who understands this personal character of motivation can help individual students to set themselves attainable goals, no matter what their degree of aptitude, thus building up their self-confidence and increasing their motivation.

Integrative or instrumental?

A great deal of research has gone into the question of whether integrative or instrumental motivation is the most facilitative of language learning.[9] *Integrative motivation,* as defined by Gardner and Lambert, implies a desire to identify with native speakers of a language in certain ways, even to the extent of being willing to adopt distinctive characteristics of their linguistic and nonlinguistic behavior. *Instrumental motivation* is manifested by those who wish to acquire the language as a tool for practical purposes. Gardner found, with speakers of English in French-speaking Canada, that an integrative motivation and positive attitudes toward speakers of the language correlated highly with achievement in learning a language for communication.[10] That many instrumentally oriented persons also learn very well a language for which they feel an identifiable need is very evident in developing and emerging countries, where motivation is high to learn as tools the languages of former colonial powers with whom the learners have no desire whatever to identify to the extent of taking on characteristics of their behavior. This fact was borne out in a study oɪ Marathi speakers in India, whose instrumental motivation scores correlated significantly with their English proficiency scores.[11] Gardner and his colleagues have since modified the definition of integrative motivation to *"a high level of drive on the part of the individual to acquire the language of a valued second-language community in order to facilitate communication with that group."*[12] This new definition blurs the previous distinction between integrative and instrumental motivation, in that the Marathi speakers may well have "valued" the English-speaking community because of what could be learned from communication with them without in any way wishing to identify with them. To make the situation more confusing, Gardner, Smythe, and Brunet found, in a 1977 investigation of intensive French study, that the students' motivation to learn the language increased at the same time as their attitudes toward the speakers of the language deteriorated.[13]

Social and psychological distance

A more recent approach to the question will perhaps clarify this somewhat bewildering confusion. Schumann[14] has proposed, as more useful concepts to explain lack of communicative achievement in a second language, the notions of *social distance* (lack of opportunities to interact with speakers of the language[15]) and *psychological distance* (lack of desire for such interaction, which is an affective factor). Either of these can arrest language learning at a functional plateau where people can meet their immediate needs with a simplified form of the language, without manifesting any desire to advance further in language control. Without attempting to resolve a very complex issue,[16] we may note that both the Gardner and the Schumann hypotheses bring out the importance of *practicing the language in communication situations that the students perceive as worthy of attention and, in some way, satisfying.* Instrumentally motivated persons succeed as well as integratively motivated persons when they make or seize opportunities, as the latter do, to use the language for some form of real communication. This means overcoming feelings of psychological distance and surmounting social impediments, in order to use the language with native speakers and learn from two-way interactive comprehension what can and cannot (or should and should not) be said. (Where no native speakers are available, classmates and members of language clubs serve as surrogates.)

Many of our students begin their language course with a sense of psychological distance from the speakers of the language, even with

what they should do, they are learning to do exercises: They are learning to give "the right answer and the right chatter." *This psychological difference is crucial.* Students learn from the classroom (from the structuring of the learning activities) whether the language is for communication or not. They learn whether it is part of their reality or just some tedious, artificial chore that someone "up there" has ordained they must perform. Exercises, oral or written, should always be framed as communication exercises, with a credible sequence of ideas and with some relevance to the class group and the class situation (which are the child's reality during school years).[18] The teacher who lacks imagination must learn to involve that of the students. The student whose interests and concerns are considered respectable and worthwhile in the classroom develops an enhanced perception of self, which increases motivation to engage in purposive behavior within the class group.

What about the human impulses to play, to explore, to manipulate? These can certainly be harnessed to the language teacher's endeavor. Recently I saw a first-grade class in a bilingual elementary school practicing the full paradigm in Spanish of the verb "to go" – "I go, you go, he goes, we all go. . . ." A few minutes earlier they had been lying on mats for their rest period. What an opportunity was being missed! Children of this age love to imitate and mimic. They love make-believe and identify rapidly with roles, which they act out with great enthusiasm. They love movement and can hardly curb their desire to express themselves vocally. They love stories with much repetition and insist that each story be repeated exactly as before. Repetitive rhymes and songs are their delight. Instead of look-and-listen activities, or even listen-and-repeat activities, they become absorbed in *listen-do-repeat activities* where they concentrate on the active meaning of what they are saying.[19] Later they practice spontaneously at home, showing Mommy and Daddy how it is done, or proudly singing their new song to aunts and uncles. What an opportunity was being missed in that classroom by an elementary school teacher who, suddenly asked to teach Spanish, could think only of how she was taught long ago, instead of exploiting her knowledge of the characteristics and interests of the young child. (In her class too, I may add, many of the children already spoke Spanish as a mother tongue.)

It is not only very young children who learn through movement. Certain modern approaches have found *response to a foreign language through movement* a very motivational beginning technique (viz., Total Physical Response[20] and the Natural Approach[21]). The Direct Method has always begun with concrete material students can feel, touch, and manipulate.[22] The audiolingual approach[23] and the functional-notional approach[24] build out from situations with which students can identify, and through which they can learn material actively, by *acting out roles in probable situations* in which they might find themselves. Material learned in class should be such that students can try it out immediately with others in the neighborhood or even in the environs of the school, just as students of the Alliance Française School in Paris can go out with what they learn and shop for dinner in the Rue Mouffetard. The days when students would meekly follow the insipid activities of the Dawson family, or of the impossibly well-behaved Carlos, Julie, or Karl, are long past. Teachers must build on the interests and perceived reality of different types of students to channel their motivation, so that they will want to learn more of a language of such obviously realistic practicality.[25]

We must find out what our students are interested in. This is our subject matter. As language teachers we are the most fortunate of teachers: All subjects are ours. Whatever the students want to communicate about, whatever they want to read about, is our subject matter. The "informal classroom" is ours, if we are willing to experiment.[26] Do our students watch TV? This we can use by incorporating material they can watch into our classroom programs, or using videocassettes especially geared to our programs. *The essence of language teaching is providing conditions for language learning* – using the existing motivation to increase our students' knowledge of the new language. We are limited only by our own caution, by our own hesitancy to do whatever our imagination suggests to us to create situations in which students feel involved, individually or in groups – whichever is appropriate for the age-level of the students in the situation in which we meet them. We need not be tied to a curriculum created for another situation or another group. We must adapt, innovate, improvise, in order to meet our students where they are and channel their motivation.

As we design our program, it should be possible to *involve students in the selection of activities* according to their personal preferences. Should all students, even the inarticulate, be expected to want to develop primarily the speaking skill? Some children reared on television may feel more at ease if allowed to look and listen, with minimal oral participation, until they feel the urge to contribute: These children will learn far more if allowed to develop according to their own personality patterns than if they are forced to chatter too soon when they feel they have nothing to say. Teachers, too, should be aware of psychological research demonstrating that native-language development proceeds at a different rate for girls and boys, with the girls advancing more rapidly, and that the effect of this difference is cumulative.[27] At certain stages, then, one may expect girls to express themselves orally more readily than boys, and this again differentially affects their reaction to chattering in a foreign language. Some students may prefer to range beyond the rest of the class in reading, and for such children graded reading material for individual selection, covering a wide variety of topics, should be readily available.

Such individualization of choices requires *imaginative planning* by the classroom teacher, who should be willing and ready to go beyond a uniform diet for all comers as soon as children's individual styles of learning make themselves apparent. An experimental study by Politzer and Weiss shows that "better results were obtained by the pupils of those teachers who went beyond the procedures strictly prescribed by the curriculum, teachers who were concerned with supplementing the curriculum rather than merely implementing it." According to this report, efficiency of individual teachers increased with the amount of their *personal* stake and *personal* contribution to the instructional processes.[28] Can this be less so for the students themselves? We know that involvement in personally selected tasks is intrinsically motivating to normal students. This further source of motivation must not be neglected if we wish to channel the students' natural energies.

Ausubel has pointed out that "motivation is as much an effect as a cause of learning."[29] The relationship between the two, he says, is "typically reciprocal rather than unidirectional."[30] By this he means that, when we capitalize on the student's initial motivation, focus it, and direct it into satisfying ego-enhancing learning experiences, this satisfaction motivates the student to further learning along these lines. Nothing breeds success like success. As one meaningful learning task after another is mastered, the attractiveness of the tasks increases with the expectancy of further success, and students are motivated to practice, rehearse, and perform what they have already learned.[31] What more could we seek as language teachers? *Motivation increases as our students experience success in using what they have learned.*[32]

In all of this, who is the experimenter? It is not the expert, or the consultant, but rather the classroom teacher – the teacher who one day thinks: "I'll try reorganizing what I've been doing and see if some of these things really work." Progress in improvement of the conditions for learning comes not through funded projects here and there, but through the thousands, the millions of classrooms in operation every hour of the week. There has been much enthusiasm in recent years for educational improvement. We do well to remember Goodlad's observation in 1969, after a study of some 260 classrooms, that "most of the so-called educational reform movement has been blunted on the classroom door."[33] Has the situation changed? The responsibility lies with each of us. Think of this next time you go into your own classroom.

Let's discuss

1 Discuss the hedonistic and ego-involvement views of motivation as two facets of the same phenomenon.
2 From your own experience, discuss the reactions of students in an authoritarian classroom. What effect do these reactions have on attempts to develop communicative interaction?
3 In your particular teaching situation, what effects of social and psychological distance can you detect? What can you do to counteract these effects?
4 How can exercises and drills be personalized? Think up as many ways as possible for converting various types of exercises into activities that relate to the student's interests and objectives.
5 "We must find out what our students are interested in. This is our subject matter." How would acceptance of this view affect your choice of a textbook and your preparation of supplementary teaching materials in your present situation?

8 Teacher-student relations: coercion or cooperation?

In *Teachers and the Children of Poverty*, Robert Coles quotes a child from an urban slum who speaks of his school experience in the following terms: "Are you trying to figure out if school makes any difference to us, because if that's it, I can tell you, man, here in my heart, it don't, much. You learn a few tricks with the numbers, and how to speak like someone different, but you forget it pretty fast when you leave the building, and I figure everyone has to put in his time one place or the other until he gets free."[1] This child is not speaking of the foreign-language class specifically, but what he says may well express the attitudes of many of our early foreign-language dropouts and even of those who stay two or three years in the high school course. Harry Reinert, in an investigation of the attitudes of students toward foreign languages, found that "well over half of them indicated that college requirements – either for admission or graduation – influenced their original enrollment in foreign language classes" and that "both by word and deed these students showed that once they had completed these requirements, they intended to have nothing more to do with foreign language."[2] "Traditional requirements with their standards of credit hours and grades have unfortunately developed into a system of time-serving."[3] These words, written in 1944, might well have been written forty years later. It may be that the elimination of some foreign-language requirements has served foreign-language teachers well in that it has forced them to examine the relevance, in this late twentieth-century period, of their objectives as reflected in what actually goes on in their classrooms (as opposed to the aims set out in syllabuses and in the professional literature). Many have had to reconsider their views on whom they do and do not welcome in their classes and the types of learning experiences they provide for their students.

The existence of requirements has made it possible for many a teacher to present a stereotyped, unimaginative course to a conscripted

Revised version of an article originally published in *New Teachers for New Students* (Seattle and New York: Washington Foreign Language Program and ACTFL, 1970).

clientele. Not many students, we would hope, have had to suffer under such procedures as were employed in one advanced French class in a New York high school I visited. Most of the year had been spent "reading" one French novel; for this, the class was divided into two groups, each of which prepared alternate sections. The sections were then subjected to grammatical and lexical dissection. By this method, no student officially read the whole novel or even a consecutive half of it. Such nonsensical teaching would never be endured by successive groups of students, unless they were coerced into the class by some obligation extrinsic to foreign-language study itself.

Foreign language in general education

If foreign language is to maintain its position in the school curriculum unprotected by external requirements, we will need to convince students as well as administrators that it has *a fundamental and unique contribution to make to the educational experience*, a contribution the students can perceive as relevant to their real concerns. For years, protagonists of foreign languages have made extravagant claims about the remarkable vocational value of their subject. A foreign-language major, we have said, can become a diplomat, a foreign correspondent, an executive in an international business complex, or a private secretary to a business representative who travels from world capital to world capital. What we have not been willing to admit is that, *vocationally, ours is an auxiliary study*. A diplomat needs a solid background in history and political science. As an adolescent, the future diplomat does not know which languages eventual assignments will require. A foreign correspondent needs to be first and foremost a top-notch journalist. A company with international branches needs above all a person with engineering training, business experience, knowledge of computerized operations, or public relations expertise. The business representative who travels the world wants most of all as a helper someone who can handle correspondence and reports competently and keep unwelcome intruders on the other side of the door. The potential foreign-language student has a right to expect more from a study that is going to take a great deal of time and energy for a number of years than a half-developed skill, which may or may not prove useful at some hypothetical moment in the future. And the administrator needs more convincing reasons than the vocational ones usually advanced if the foreign-language program is to be justified.

Rationale for foreign-language study

The unique contribution of foreign-language study, which is truly educational in the sense that it expands our students' personal experience of their environment and truly humanistic in that it adds a new dimension to their thinking, is the opportunity it provides for *breaking through monolingual and monocultural bonds*, revealing to the students other ways of saying things and other values and attitudes than those to which their native language and culture have habituated them. Through this experience, they may develop new attitudes to ideas and people, which will reduce their bondage to the familiar and the local and increase their sympathy for persons of other cultures and languages. The present generation of students in our schools is internationalist and interculturalist in its aspirations; it is also brutally direct in demanding the rationale of what we are doing and what we are asking the members of that generation to do. This basic contribution foreign language can make to their development is one they would welcome, but they must see that what we do in our classrooms really achieves such a purpose or they will drop out as soon as they conveniently may. If "the first task of education. . .is to raise the level of awareness and response to *all* ideas, events, people and objects,"[4] then foreign language, taught with this end firmly in view, can still claim that it has a rightful place in the overall educational program of the school.

Demands on the teacher

Can our teachers meet the challenge of providing the genuinely mind-stretching experience of exploring other ways of thinking? Certainly teachers trained only in habit-formation techniques of skill training will find it difficult to deal with sensitive areas of attitudes and values, and teachers for whom cultural understanding means the description of picturesque costumes worn for religious festivals or the measurements of the Eiffel Tower will find it difficult to explain why students demonstrate in Berlin, in Paris, and in Tokyo. Teachers of the future will need to be well read, alert to current trends, receptive of ideas other than those of their own culture, and flexible enough to reexamine their own ideas at regular intervals, in order to keep in touch with each new generation in a rapidly changing world. Such teachers are not produced by a rigid teacher-training program where the "right" answers and the "right" techniques are imposed on those in training as they are shaped and molded. *Coercive training can only produce either a coercive teacher or a rebel* against all that this training held to be of value. Teachers today need a deep understanding of the bases of what they are trying to do, so that they can adapt familiar techniques intelligently and develop new ones, as circum- stances change and new demands are made upon them. Their association with those who train them must bring the realization that only a person of open mind, willing to consider and weigh many points of view, can develop such qualities in those who study with them.

For a number of years we have paid lip service to the cultural objective set out in the preceding discussion, but students and colleagues rarely see the evidence of any such enrichment in those who have spent a year or two in our classes. They sometimes accuse us of rationalizing the irrelevance of our subject. The approach of most foreign-language teachers is built on the belief that students must attain a high degree of language skill before they can really perceive and appreciate cultural differences reflected through language. Development of the ability to use the language is, of course, important; it is our primary task and must not be neglected. We must ask ourselves, however, *how we can bring some part of this mind-broadening experience of other cultures to each student*, at every level of study in the language. It seems evident that any degree of cultural understanding will require a depth of discussion and thought that lower-level students cannot cope with in the foreign language. Insistence on the exclusive use of the foreign language in the classroom, and the more recent emphasis in some circles on discouraging questions from students in order to maintain this artificial atmosphere, have meant the reduction of classroom "discussion" of cultural matters to trite questions and answers on the content of what is seen, heard, or read. The probing questions the students would really like to ask are thus suppressed, and their misconceptions remain unidentified. Acting out roles is one way for language students to get a feel for cultural differences, attitudes, and their expression. Without some frank discussion, however, a great deal of what is implicit in the behavior and relationship of others remains a mystery, and the study of another culture tends to take the form of a simplistic introduction to such overt features as greetings, festivals, monuments, or eating habits, viewed out of context and interpreted by the students according to their own culturally determined values and attitudes. The interest of the students in another culture must be fostered from the beginning with research projects using any and all materials available, whether in the foreign language or not, with the encouragement of vigorous discussion of similarities and differences and their importance in the life patterns of the people. Such projects need not take away valuable time from the language-learning activities that should rightfully occupy the time the teacher has with the students. Projects may be given as out-of-class assignments, with class time used only for discussion of the findings.

A study of two widely used Level 4 (fourth year high school) texts shows that, even at this stage, the questions on reading passages are still limited to mere recall or identification of specific details of content and are so structured that the one right answer must emerge. With this type of question, it is easy for the teacher to imagine that the whole class is alert and participating intelligently, whereas they are merely giving the teacher an obvious and trivial response that does not require reflection – a thing they learn to do with equal ease in the foreign or the native language. Such questions are stultifying to intelligent students who, out of class, revel in discussion of controversial issues with their fellows. Even at the advanced stage, some discussion must be permitted in the native language if the student does not yet have the fluency to handle complex ideas. Lively discussions are motivational and encourage the student to pursue more diligently the difficult goal of full control of the foreign language. In this period of open and uninhibited expression of ideas, students are no longer willing to endure passively one-way "communication" in which the teacher has all the advantages. The day of "the silent generation," to which many teachers themselves belonged, has passed. Today's teachers must be trained to handle discussion, to welcome expression of student opinion, to be willing to admit when they do not know the answer, and to cooperate with students in finding out the things they most want to know about the foreign people and the ways they think and react.

An experience for all types of students

Having established a truly educative purpose in foreign-language study other than mere skill training, the foreign-language teacher will have to answer the question: "Is this experience of value to all students?" *It is the task of the educator to consider the needs of all youth: the gifted, the average, the less able, the handicapped, and the disadvantaged.* For too long foreign-language teachers have sought a privileged role in the school: Only an elite of bright, alert, well-motivated students was acceptable in their classes; all others were, in their view, "incapable of learning a foreign language." Sometimes the mathematics teacher, the science teacher, the history teacher, and the art teacher have felt the same way about their students and would have

124

preferred a select group. Yet students of all levels of ability and diverse backgrounds still come to be taught.

Many foreign-language teachers in the past found themselves unable to teach any but the more intelligent and more highly motivated students because they had turned foreign language into an abstract study of grammatical forms and relationships, followed by the close analysis of modes of expression divorced from the stream of common life (for example, classical tragedy or nineteenth-century poetry), which with their academic approach they were unable to relate, as they may well be related, to the preoccupations and concerns of the present day. In a reversal of trends, some have moved away from a traditional presentation of this kind to one involving drills and repetitive practice of inert phrases, material that students have felt to be of little concern to them at a stage when the body of educative experience presented in other subjects emphasizes productive and creative thinking. Despite an initial advantage, then, foreign-language teachers have also frequently lost the gifted students, who see foreign-language study as sterile and unrewarding intellectually.

We may ask, with these students, why in most schools they must be forced to accept a uniform foreign-language diet established by tradition, or by the uncontested prestige of college professors unacquainted with, and often uninterested in, the interests and capacities of high school students. After elementary general-purpose textbooks have been completed, who has decided that all foreign-language students, no matter what their abilities or interests, must study a series of literary "masterpieces," often of a bygone era and in a form of the language no longer in use? How frequently are such senior students allowed to participate in the decision on what they will do with the time and energies they are prepared to devote to foreign-language study? Some may be interested in contemporary social problems, some in history, some in scientific development, some in the arts or the everyday experiences of a foreign people, and some in the modern novel or contemporary theater. Some schools do make provision at this stage for personal choice and decision, providing resource materials for individual and group research projects in which students read, listen to, and discuss all kinds of material in the foreign language. Such progressive programs are, however, all too few. If the final high school years provide only "more of the same," it should not surprise the foreign-language teacher to find even the most linguistically apt students reluctant to continue beyond the minimum requirement.

Even at earlier stages it is possible to allow students some autonomy in the selection of activities according to their personal predilections, if at least some part of the program is individualized. Should we expect all students, even the inarticulate, to want to develop their speaking skills primarily? Some in this television generation, if allowed to choose, may prefer to look and listen. Other students may prefer to range beyond the rest of the class in reading (graded readers that cover a wide variety of topics are available in the more commonly taught languages from quite elementary levels). Such individualization of choices requires imaginative planning by a classroom teacher who is willing to go beyond a steady, uniform, universal diet for at least part of the time. Furthermore, involvement in personally selected tasks is intrinsically motivating to normal students whose natural enjoyment of cognitive exploration has not been completely stifled by the formalism of an educational system that overemphasizes such extrinsic rewards as grades and promotions.[5] More teachers will need to launch out into *new instructional approaches*, and teachers coming into the profession will need to be made aware of new possibilities in providing the proper environment for learning, if foreign languages are to keep the interest and allegiance of a voluntary clientele.

To move down the scale of ability, not infrequently a student who has not been noticeably successful with academic study becomes fascinated with a foreign language. For this student, the language has provided a new beginning at a stage when an accumulation of undigested facts or principles from earlier years has engendered a feeling of hopelessness in certain other subject areas. Everyone begins the foreign language at the same time, and such students feel they have as much chance as their neighbors to assimilate it. *These students are often more successful with some aspects of foreign-language study than others.* Sometimes less gifted students will find that they can understand anything they hear in the foreign language, but are unable to use it actively with any fluency. The testing and grading practices of many teachers severely penalize students like these. Consequently, despite their high degree of motivation and undoubted skill in one area, they may find themselves advised not to continue with the language. The teacher may not realize that many people are very popular who merely listen appreciatively, murmuring from time to time such supportive utterances as "Yes," "Of course not," or "You're absolutely right." Individualizing the program to some extent will enable such students or students who can read with ease but have inhibitions in speaking, or students who can converse fluently but are poor readers, to continue to study the language with special emphasis in those areas in which they feel most at home.

Finally, what have foreign-language teachers to offer *handicapped and disadvantaged students*? Some will say, "I cannot teach a foreign language to the deaf or the blind, or to students who can't write!" This is an overhasty judgment. Deaf students can read and can learn to lip-read another language as well as their own. An individualized approach to student assignments can provide more learning materials in the graphic mode for such students, and face-to-face oral work as a substitute for laboratory practice.[6] Similarly, since blind students are accustomed to depending on their ear and auditory memory, they are frequently more at home with an aural-oral type of presentation than their sighted classmates. Handicapped students who cannot write can often read, listen, and speak; those who cannot speak can listen and read and, in many cases, can use a typewriter. A flexible approach to the material to be learned, the way it may be learned, and the areas for which grades will be assigned can solve many of these seemingly intractable problems.

Yet others will say: "I can't teach the disadvantaged. They are unable to learn a second language. Why, some of them can't even read or write their own language with any degree of success!" Again, if learning another language does have some genuine educational value it must surely have something to offer those whose backgrounds have limited their horizons. *It will not, however, be successful in the hands of a teacher who doubts the success of the enterprise even before it begins.* Studies of students of a low socioeconomic status have shown that they already suffer from a feeling of insufficiency and readily accept the implications of defeat that the unconvinced teacher finds hard to conceal in relations with them. The teacher expects them to fail, and they do fail. If success is to be achieved in teaching foreign languages to disadvantaged students, teachers in training and experienced teachers alike will need to study the preoccupations, value systems, and characteristic approaches of these young people.[7] With an understanding of their preferred modes of learning and attention to their interests and concerns, the teacher can choose materials and design lessons that will utilize these to the full.

Students of some minority groups may prefer the concrete to the abstract and respond to material for which they see an immediate application. They will therefore enjoy learning foreign words and phrases they can employ immediately in the classroom or with speakers of the new language among the children in their neighborhood. Some may not be motivated by deferred rewards but expect some immediate satisfaction: To these, the promise that they will eventually be able to use the language fluently may mean little, whereas actual use of the language immediately, even in simple forms, in face-to-face interaction, is motivating. Still others learn through activity, through seeing, hearing, touching, manipulating, and role playing. The teacher with students of mixed backgrounds should use visual presentations (flash cards, drawings, films); things the students can hold, open, shut, or pass to each other; music and songs with tapes, guitars, and drums; action songs and action poems. The vocabulary used should be practical and should deal with objects and actions familiar to the students. The characters and incidents presented to children close to street life should never appear "prissy" or goody-goody. Students accustomed to the cut and thrust of inner-city life appreciate firm leadership. Often they are not anxious to work in small groups in which they will need to make group decisions. Because, in their neighborhood environment, they are accustomed to learning orally rather than through the written word (which may even present them with some difficulty in their native language), reading the foreign language may not appear to them to be of vital importance.

What languages should we teach?

Since certain disadvantaged students are motivated by concrete, clearly visible rewards, it seems appropriate that the foreign language to be taught to such students should be selected with an eye to languages spoken in their home neighborhood; in this way, *the practical, tangible value of the language* becomes obvious. Many schools are gearing language study for inner-city students who prefer it toward career-oriented studies, Spanish for law enforcement, Spanish for firefighters, or French for social workers (in which case the cultural background and dialect of the group with whom the social worker will be involved are given special attention).[8]

As teachers, we must keep in mind that black students today have a yearning for a clear and unambiguous identity and are seeking this identity more and more through exploration of their African heritage. There is, therefore, a case for teaching Swahili, or some other African language, in high schools where there are groups of black students who would prefer it. Teachers of Spanish, French, and German should be foreign-language teachers first, rather than desperate defenders of hard-won fiefdoms; *they should be advocates of more learning of any relevant foreign language*, not of more learning only of Spanish, French, or German. If we genuinely believe in the fundamental value of some study of a foreign language and culture for all students, then we should respond to the desire to learn a specific language among certain groups of our students. Swahili, Arabic, or Urdu will give students insights into how language operates just as surely as the more commonly taught languages and will give them even more illuminating insights into other ways of thinking and other sets of cultural values.

The immediate response of many teachers will be: "But we don't have teachers of Swahili readily available." The answer is that we must acquire them. Swahili is considered one of the less difficult languages to learn in intensive language schools, and it does not have a strange script. The logical approach would appear to be to provide intensive training courses in Swahili for practicing foreign-language teachers or intensive training in foreign-language teaching for available speakers of Swahili, so that the language may be introduced as a further offering in more language departments. Would not an important language of Africa or Asia also help some middle-class students to understand a completely different culture and the aspirations of newly emerging nations striving to advance into modern statehood? (Arabic is another lingua franca, and Chinese is spoken by a billion people in China and by many millions in other areas.) Young teachers in training are sometimes invited to undertake the learning of a completely different language as one of their education courses, in order to experience afresh the problems of language learning. Courses of this type could be used for giving them some basic knowledge of languages like Swahili, Arabic, Urdu, or Chinese. It seems better for trained language teachers to take up the cause of the less commonly taught languages than have it left in the hands of linguistically unsophisticated amateurs.

This same line of reasoning should apply in areas where there is a strong concentration of immigrant groups speaking a particular language, since students learning a language for educational rather than vocational reasons will be more motivated if the language they are learning can be used and heard in everyday life. This will provide a response to the needs of other young people who are feeling the urge to reexplore their ethnic heritage.

Finally, the success of foreign languages in the years to come must lie with teachers we are training at the present time. They will need to innovate, to experiment, and to initiate new programs. *We must train them to expect and to respect a new clientele.* With experience from their training days of participation in decision making and planning for change, they will be much more qualified than preceding generations to work with students in developing new approaches, new techniques, and a new place for foreign languages in the educative process.[9]

Let's discuss

1 Write your own statement of what you consider learning another language contributes to the educational process. Discuss it with

129

others and try to determine which aspects of your statement could be met just as well through learning in some other area. What is left that may be considered unique to language learning?[10]

2 What factors must be taken into account in deciding which languages should be taught in a particular situation? (Do not forget the practical factors.)

3 For what work situations is a foreign language useful? Conduct an investigation in your area to determine the language needs of business and industry. What changes in your program would be necessary to meet these needs?

4 How should we approach the teaching of another culture? What are the major pitfalls to be avoided? What advice would you give a textbook writer to improve materials in this area?

5 How would the language program in which you teach (or the one in which you learned your major language) need to be adapted to meet the needs of all kinds of students?

9 Understanding the learner in the language laboratory

In this latter part of the twentieth century, the learning of languages has become increasingly important on the international, and even national, scene. We are experiencing the tensions resulting from two opposing trends in modern society: the growing interdependence of nations and peoples, as life becomes more complex and the division of labor more indispensable, and the assertion of individual and affinity group identity, with its accompanying demands for self-determination, that the pressures of such impersonal interdependence create. It becomes more and more imperative for individuals and groups to understand each other, to be able to communicate with each other, and to respect what others cherish and value. Now, more than ever, we need effective language learning.

Language laboratories have, over the years, become language-*learning* laboratories (LLL) or learning centers. To ensure that they are closely integrated with the learning process, I shall use the model of the *effectiveness circle* of A: language learning, B: language teaching, and C: instructional personnel, with D: the LLL director at the center. (Sometimes a language coordinator works closely with the director and this makes the task less difficult.)

LLL personnel need to understand findings in language learning and trends in language teaching, in order to help instructors to use the language-learning laboratory to facilitate effective language learning by the students. Research in language learning provides insights into the students' task, so that we may find ways of helping them learn more efficiently. Trends in language teaching affect the classroom instruction students are experiencing and determine the expectations of students and instructors as to the outcome of the language learning. Course instructors need the help of knowledgeable and experienced LLL personnel to make the most efficient use of equip-

Revised version of an article originally published in *NALLD Journal: Technology and Mediated Instruction* 16, 2 (1981):5–13.

ment in ways that are the most pleasurable and advantageous to the students and the most in step with what is known about language learning.

Historical perspective

First of all, let us look back for a moment to the early days of the language laboratory, pre-LLL.

Innovative language teachers – the few pioneers – have always been quick to seize new opportunities to bring foreign-language students into contact with authentic speech. Parker tells us that a French conversational course was produced in England on an Edison cylinder as early as 1904, and that this device was soon being tried out with classes at Yale University and elsewhere.[1] The first fully fledged laboratory was installed at Middlebury College in Vermont in 1929. It had ten booths, each furnished with a phonograph, a disc cutter, and instruments for work in phonetics.[2] We must wait until 1945 for the installation of the prototype of the now well-known language laboratory. This twenty-booth facility was set up at Louisiana State University by Alfred Hayes. Twelve-inch vinylite discs, recorded at 78 rpm, were used, with magnetic headphones and crystal microphones.[3] In 1950, this installation, now expanded to 126 positions, was completely converted to magnetic tapes, twelve simultaneous lesson programs being available through a student selector switch.[4]

Technology and innovative enthusiasm had done their part. Now was the time to create the outer circle and relate the newly refined aids to language learning, language teaching, and course objectives.

Because the 1950s were the heyday of habit-formation-through-reinforcement theory in language learning, it was inevitable that the early language laboratory should be seen as *the perfect setting for stimulus-response (S ——►R) learning*. Technology and the materials developer provided the S, which would automatically bring out the R from the student. Consequently, laboratories all over the world were soon emitting a stream of stimuli, and campuses and schools were filled with the muttering of responses. Correct and relevant responses? – no matter. Responses were being heard; they were often recorded, less often checked, and least often rerecorded after further individual instruction. Nevertheless, S ——►R and LL (language laboratory) seemed the perfect partners on the road to linguistic mastery.

For whom? This question was rarely answered. The machine and the instructor knew best. Since little account was taken of the person producing the responses, students began to yawn and then to tiptoe out, leaving the machines to converse happily with each other. If there was a sign-in/sign-out sheet to check attendance, complaisant friends would look after that. In any case, one could always slip back for a moment, if necessary, after a cup of coffee and a chat.

Paralleling the period of development of the language laboratory was a rising tide in psychology of *interest in what came between the S and the R, namely, the O – the organism*: the thinking, feeling, reacting person. In language laboratory terms, this meant the students sitting there in the booths. What did the students want? What was going on in their minds? *What were they actually doing in the booths*, when they were there? Questions of motivation, perception and cognition, attention, and attention focus came to the fore in psychology and began to interest instructors and language laboratory personnel as well.

By the 1960s, this current of psychological change (which had long been developing through research in functionalist and dynamic psychology) came to full flood in *the paradigm switch to cognitive psychology*. Language laboratory directors, who had always been closer to the students than materials developers, were quick to identify with this new mood, as evidenced by their selected change of name to language-*learning* laboratory directors – learning by the student being the central element linking the presentation of the language by the instructor and the laboratory practice. Thus the change of emphasis from S ⟶ R to S ⟶ O ⟶ R was reflected in the change from LL to LLL.

The new emphasis on O, and the central L, climaxed a period when it had become evident to all concerned with the laboratory that bored, frustrated, and irritated students were bred by tedious, long-drawn-out, mechanical drilling of structural patterns, especially, as so often happened, when these were in a form identical with those the student had already practiced in class and was studying in the textbook. So what's new? wondered the students. Inevitably the news soon spread through school, college, and university that the language laboratory had failed. Funds became harder to get. Why should expensive equipment be replaced if instructors and students were no longer using it, or were using it only reluctantly? *If communication was now the goal, how did one communicate with a machine*, even a talking machine? Communication is interaction, a give-and-take or a cut-and-thrust; it is something dyadic, for which at least two active, interrelating, reacting persons are essential. It became time to rethink the uses of the language-learning laboratory, its role in the language-learning process, and the kinds of materials that could best supplement the active, student-centered approach to language learning that was permeating the classroom. Ways were needed to motivate stu-

133

dents to use the laboratory in the first place and to hold their attention once they were there.

Let us look at some of the findings about language learning that clashed with the prevailing approach of listen and repeat with minimal changes, which had determined the form of so many early language laboratory materials.

Language learning

Although no definitive model of language learning has yet emerged, it seems clear that *any learning is an active process*. Language learners are not passive receptacles who receive and pour out correctly phrased utterances in some automatic fashion. The minds of the students are actively processing all kinds of impressions: filtering out some they do not consider worthy of attention; readily accepting others that seem important to them; creating messages from what they hear, by a process of matching with possible messages according to their knowledge of the world, the speaker, and the situation; verifying these as the input continues, and switching and changing as they find they are on the wrong track; making errors, correcting these (most often without help), and learning from this experience.

Learners in the language laboratory have their own approaches to learning (strategies or cognitive styles, if you will).[5] No longer should we insist that *all* students learn through the ear initially, being permitted to see the graphic version only after they have successfully mastered the oral form. We now know that *some need a visual support* for their learning. We also know that students think and reason before they respond (if material is meaningful, as it should be) and that better learning results if they are allowed time for this. Demand for quick-fire response to develop automatic performance is no longer tenable. Consequently, *we must allow learners to control the rate of presentation as much as possible*, with access to mechanisms that permit them to back up and go through an item as many times as necessary before moving on. In fact, many will prefer to take the material away, to work on it in their own time in the way that suits them best. We also realize that some students need to spend more time going over and over the same material than others, who would do better to spend the extra time on other language activities that interest them. Some can concentrate on demanding work for longer periods than others, and, consequently, we must pay much more attention to differences in attention span and memory span when designing learning materials.

Some students, we find, enjoy memorizing and profit from it; others prefer to work everything out step by step in order to understand exactly what they are doing before they utter a word. Some resist direction of their thinking and effort; others look for structure and teacher guidance. Some prefer to work alone, and, for these, take-home cassettes are the answer. For all, effective language learning is more readily achieved through language exercises that make sense[6] and have some relevance to their interests.[7] They respond more readily to *activities that challenge them to apply what they know in new contexts*, rather than to a monotonous repetition of what they already know, or think they know.

We now recognize that students have different objectives in language learning, and that one diet for all will not meet these personally perceived goals; we also know that what the students perceive as unrelated to their goals may be cursorily performed, but will not register in any permanent form. Purposeful learning (language learning that results in the performance of some worthwhile acts) will retain attention and establish learned responses more readily than mere verbal participation. Finally, most psychologists agree that perception and production are quite different processes and may well involve quite different grammars. This should bring about a differentiation in the kinds of materials we present for aural comprehension and for production.

We have, then, learned many things about language learning that bring into question quite a few of the time-honored practices that have become identified with language laboratory work: the emphasis on oral production, practiced to a point of automatic response, without the support of a script, and with a very short interval allowed for a rapid response; concentration on details of grammar with a minimal vocabulary, with the expectation that this practice will carry over to listening comprehension; the structuring of the materials in minimal steps so that students will not make mistakes; the withholding of explanations until students have reached a certain level of smooth performance on drills and exercises; the lockstep presentation of language laboratory material with unvarying content, standardized pauses, and a relentless forward movement to the end of the tape. With the advance to a language-*learning* laboratory, *many of these practices must be rethought and materials redesigned. Whose responsibility will this be?*

Language teaching

Times change. Objectives of students and community change. Approaches to language teaching change to meet new objectives. Language-learning laboratory directors must be aware of these changes in class teaching so that they can help instructors and materials developers to use the resources of the laboratory to their full effect. Language-learning laboratory personnel should be able to advise their colleagues on *effective uses of media for new methodologies*. The laboratory director is the kingpin in days of change, not a mere factotum to carry out routine operations at the direction of others who may not realize the full potential of the laboratory, resource center, or language-learning center. Many changes in course approach and teaching techniques have been taking place, and the director needs to be aware of these.

1. The *order of skill acquisition* is by no means a fixed listening, speaking, reading, and writing sequence, with listening and speaking concerning the laboratory, and reading and writing kept for the classroom or for homework. The order advocated by Marcel in the nineteenth century was reading, listening, speaking, writing. Toward the end of the century, reading and writing, with translation, became the initially taught skills, with speaking introduced at a later date, and listening hardly at all. In the 1890s, Gouin proposed that one begin with speaking accompanied by physical activity to be supported later by writing. More recently, Asher has advocated listening with physical response for a long initial period, and Postovsky has proposed that students begin with listening and writing, with speaking deferred.[8] In Gattegno's Silent Way, there is very little listening, at least to the teacher or a tape; students begin by trying to create oral utterances after one initial hearing. In Curran's Counseling-Learning/Community Language Learning, students mostly hear each other, as they try to create utterances from prompts from their counselor. In Suggestopaedia, students listen, then read and translate, before they speak.[9] One can make a good case psychologically for listening and reading being learned together, particularly for a special-purpose course. There is a growing movement not to require students to speak until they are ready. Order of learning skills, then, will depend on objectives and the methodology developed to reach these objectives.

2. There has been a shift of emphasis from what in the past was largely a *structural syllabus* (the learning of grammatical structures in the early stages to prepare for fluent oral use of the language) to a *functional syllabus* based on functions of language (like imparting and finding out factual information; getting things done; socializing) and notions within those functions (such as identifying; suggesting a course of action; or taking leave).[10] For the moment, the functional emphasis has been largely an expansion of a narrowly conceived structural syllabus. There has also been a definite swing toward a more *experiential syllabus*, where students are brought in contact

with as much authentic language as possible. Students are encouraged to communicate freely with each other, from the early stages, in situations created within the classroom, in free interaction, or in contacts with native speakers outside the classroom, whether in clubs, local community activities, home exchange programs, or short-term study abroad experiences.[11] This has led to the use in the laboratory of *unedited, spontaneous interviews with people engaged in all kinds of activities and occupations, and the making of videocassettes of the students' own activities in class*, which are later viewed and discussed.

Such changes should mean a new look at the types of materials used in the language-learning laboratory. Authentic materials imply conversations among native speakers in actual situations of the culture, speeches by public personalities, and advertisements and soap operas from television programs in countries where the language is spoken – these are being incorporated more and more into laboratory assignments. As a result, there has been an expansion of use of the laboratory at the intermediate and advanced levels. Authentic interaction, with visible kinesics (body language), and gestures in a setting of the foreign culture become much more accessible through the use of video, and these help students to speak and act much more like native speakers of the language. Consequently, videotapes and videocassettes are being used more and more from the early stages, to facilitate the acquisition, retention, and normal use of language material by this visually and aurally oriented generation. Songs and popular music enjoyed by the youth of the target culture also help to convey the spirit of the people, so the collection of discs must be kept current. The audiovisual laboratory is *an indispensable aid in conveying a feeling for the culture*, which is an inseparable component of another language. Here materials developers and instructors will again need help and guidance from LLL personnel, if they are to prepare effective materials and exploit the potential of the media to the fullest.

No matter what the approach, the audiovisual LLL can make a vital contribution to its success. Students need to be oriented toward the type of learning the instructor is requiring in the course, and this calls for close cooperation between instructional staff and laboratory personnel.

The LLL director and the instructor

In many institutions, the LLL director has to be the expert on language learning and language teaching. Instructors have frequently been trained in literature or linguistics and take charge of language courses reluctantly, even resentfully. If these instructors have never had close association with laboratory work during their own language studies, they may completely neglect the potential of the laboratory, or use it as a kind of unwelcome necessity. They know it has been paid for and the administration expects it to be used. Native speakers often feel that they themselves provide sufficient authentic speech in their classrooms and that it is an affront to them for others to presume that taped or videotaped material can usefully supplement their work. Some instructors are too preoccupied with their research interests to spend time developing, or even selecting, appropriate laboratory materials and will expect the laboratory personnel to churn out, in equalized chunks, whatever commercial tapes come with the book, irrespective of their content or quality. A laboratory program out of step with, or unrelated to, the real concerns of the course leads to frustration, irritation, bewilderment, and absenteeism on the part of the students. If such reactions become apparent, the situation should be discreetly brought to the instructors' attention, with suggestions for another approach. If the relationship has been cultivated, such proposals will be more readily accepted. Perhaps there are materials available in the laboratory about which a new instructor is ignorant, materials that have proven their worth on other occasions. Perhaps the commercial tapes are too long, the pauses too short, or the practice segments too protracted, with no variety of activity to refresh the students. These things are easily remedied, and most instructors will welcome help in meeting student objections, which are surely reaching their ears.

An instructor, naive in the use of media, may benefit from a discussion of what media can do that cannot be accomplished by instructor and textbook alone. Some such list as the following will emerge, which includes facts well known to language-learning laboratory personnel, but well worth repeating to new instructors.

The laboratory, properly supplied with carefully designed materials, can provide:

— contact with authentic speech, which can be heard and reheard without embarrassment to the speaker or the listener, and as often as necessary for comprehension;
— contact with a variety of accents, voices, and dialectal variants;
— opportunity to work at one's own pace, for as long or as short a time as one needs;
— privacy to make mistakes without embarrassment, to practice and repractice problems of pronunciation and production of fluent utterances;

138

- opportunities for remedial study: makeup work; extra study in areas of one's own weaknesses, repracticed in one's own way according to one's perceived needs (this may include written exercises: dictées, dictocomps,[12] résumés, cloze tests);
- opportunities for supplementary contact with authentic material of value for individual projects, for the language course or for some other course; for listening to plays, commentaries, news broadcasts, literary readings, or music; for viewing films or television material from a country under study.

The LLL director and the instructor will work out others. The opportunities to help the student learn a language, and learn to use it well, are there. *It is for the LLL personnel to make sure that it is not neglected or underused because of ignorance, timidity, or indifference on the part of instructors.* If too many instructors are clearly unaware of the potential of the LLL, a workshop may be the most pressing need. There is nothing like actually manipulating equipment and working with materials oneself to arouse interest and enthusiasm for improving programs in the future. The student is best served when LLL personnel and instructional staff are working closely in harmony.

Computer-assisted instruction, microchips, satellite reception, videodiscs for take-home study – *many interesting possibilities are on the horizon.* New technologies change nothing without a corresponding development in courseware (the province of the instructor). As long ago as 1964, Hocking observed that "perhaps the most popular and persistent misunderstanding, vaguely felt rather than expressed, is a naïve faith in gadgetry–a feeling that push buttons and electronics can somehow solve all problems."[13] We now know from experience that the major problems lie elsewhere; namely, with the persons who use the laboratory: instructors, students, and, yes, language-learning laboratory personnel. It is for the latter to take the lead, to see their role as more than that of maintaining and installing equipment and ensuring the smooth running of laboratory sessions. They must also be leaders in applications of theory to practice to ensure that the second *L* (learning), having made its way into the name of the laboratory, does not slip away inadvertently, because it is perceived as superfluous.

Let's discuss

1 Design a one-day workshop for new instructors to help them incorporate language-learning laboratory work into their

courses. Make a careful list of all the aspects of language laboratory use, in relation to language learning and language teaching,
that you would wish to bring to their notice.

2 What explanations would you give to an instructor who thought
that a functional syllabus referred to an elementary-level course?
What kinds of practice materials would you propose developing to accompany a functional approach? (See also Chapter 2 of
this book.)

3 At what levels can "authentic materials" be used? What kinds of
activities in the laboratory would you propose to exploit authentic materials?

4 What kinds of activities and materials would you recommend to
accompany an advanced course of the "living language" variety
described in Chapter 11 of this book?

5 How would you use a native speaker assigned to work with you
for a year who was totally ignorant of the functioning and uses
of the language-learning laboratory?

10   Testing and student learning

At an international conference some years ago a distinguished European scholar, whose English was not strong, suddenly burst into the discussion of an experimental project with the words: "*Why these old tests?*" Although he was referring in this case to statistical tests of significance, the words have remained in my mind: Why these old tests! These words are still only too often applicable in practical instructional situations, despite the excellent books and articles of such friends of the profession as Carroll, Davies, Harris, Lado, Valette, and Oller.

And tests are becoming older. What was new in the sixties does not adequately assess achievement in the educational climate of today. In this period of rapid change in all educational enterprises, we are foolish not to engage in a little futurology: to analyze trends, predict probable future developments, adjust psychologically to what the future may bring, and plan to meet future needs.

Whether we like it or not, in any foreign- or second-language teaching we are swept by the winds of change in general education, in attitudes toward learning, and in community needs. But what has this to do with testing? you may ask. As Pilliner has stated so succinctly:

> It is axiomatic that [the] content [of tests] inevitably influences the teaching and learning which precede them.... Properly constructed, [the test] can foster and reinforce good teaching and sound learning and discourage their opposites. To achieve these ends, the test constructor must start with a clear conception of the aims and purposes of the area of learning to which his test is relevant.[1]

Reversing Pilliner's emphases, we may say that *aims and purposes, construction, and content of tests must be congruent with the aspirations and learning approaches of the day and age.* As test constructors, whether for large groups of students from a variety of instructional situations or merely for tomorrow's class, we must not allow ourselves to become so bogged down in the peculiar technical problems of test design that we cannot see the forest for the trees, thus exerting,

Revised version of an article originally published in M.C. O'Brien, ed., *Testing in Second Language Teaching: New Dimensions* (Dublin: ATESOL and University of Dublin Press, 1973), pp. 27–36.

perhaps involuntarily, a retarding influence on the evolution of foreign-language instruction. As Carroll has pointed out:

> The kinds of tests that are used to evaluate students can often have adverse effects on students' learning.... It is only natural for students to shape their learning efforts so as to be maximally successful on tests, and if the tests measure objectives that are in some ways different from those of the instruction, students will work towards those objectives and pay less attention to achieving other objectives.[2]

A student-centered approach to testing

Why do we test anyway? It is salutary sometimes to go back and ask ourselves a question of this type. Is it because it has always been done – because it seems to us of the same order of necessity as the rising and setting of the sun? Is testing an essential part of the learning process? Can we class it as a natural activity? Here we may think of the feedback loop that Miller, Galanter, and Pribram propose as a model of the molecular unit of human behavior. Miller and his colleagues call their model TOTE (Test – Operate – Test – Exit).[3] "In its weakest form," they state, "the TOTE asserts simply that the operations an organism performs are constantly guided by the outcomes of various tests."[4] *The organism's capability is tested against an existing pattern or criterion.* "Action is initiated by an 'incongruity' between the state of the organism and the state that is being tested for, and the action persists until the incongruity . . . is removed."[5] This criterion having been matched, the organism moves into the next phase of its activity and is challenged to a new effort by the criterion of that phase.

Here we recognize immediately the principle of the thermostat, and we can derive an interesting analogy from it for our students' learning. In this model, the test acts as a plan that controls operations. The test phase "involves the specification of whatever knowledge is necessary for the comparison that is to be made, and the operational phase represents what the organism does about it."[6] The test is, as it were, a source of information or a set of instructions that enables the learners to keep up their efforts until they have matched the criterion, testing and retesting to see how close they are coming to the desired performance. Each time they fall short they make a further effort to reach the criterion; each time they achieve their aim they move on to the next phase of activity. In this way *the test is an integral part of the learning process*: a natural step in any advance.

How different this is from the old concept of the test as a hurdle to be surmounted, a hurdle that becomes a discouraging barrier to too many language learners. Here, instead, matching against the criterion becomes a challenge and a guide to further effort. What a gain it would be if we could convey this attitude toward the test to our students, if they no longer feared the test as a threat to their ego, but saw it as an indicator – a helpful, even indispensable, sign on the way. In this paradigm, a test is no longer a special activity, set apart from all others and loaded with unique significance. If we think about it, we can recognize here the distinction between the norm-referenced test, where one student's performance is compared with that of other students or matched against some artificial, external standard, and the criterion-referenced test, where the student knows exactly what knowledge must be demonstrated, and either demonstrates it and moves on, or cannot demonstrate it and goes back to see how the performance can be improved. This is a revolution in the concept of testing. *Students are now responsible for their own learning.* When they feel ready to match the criterion, they test. Note that *they* test: It is not we who test them. If necessary, they later retest. When satisfied that they have matched the criterion, they move on. Idealistic? Perhaps, but it is in keeping with the changing climate in student-teacher relations, in which the students and their needs are central, and in which all students have a right to the opportunity to learn as much as they are able and as much as they are willing to devote effort to learning. Once the test ceases to be a separate activity (its importance enhanced by ritual), but becomes interwoven with learning itself, it may well lose the appearance of what we conceive of as a conventional test.

The test as a selection process

Once this change is accepted, what happens to our "standards"? How do we select those with the level of attainment necessary for specific tasks? This is another question and not an educational one. The educational question must be phrased quite differently. How do we provide the opportunity for all students to attain the highest degree of mastery of a foreign language consistent with their language aptitude, their willingness to devote time and energy, their perseverance, and their interest in the various aspects of language skill and the potential uses of language? A test that is a sorting process for some purpose other than the educational one should properly be assigned to some agency outside the institution in which the student is studying. It becomes an admissions or selection procedure, testing for the competencies required for particular jobs, or positions of responsibility, or for future study in another environment. Such tests are not related in any specific way to the learning experience of each candidate. They indicate what some particular agency, employer, or institution is looking for. One agency may need only persons who can read instructions in Japanese accompanying imported stereo equipment, or alternatively experiments in nuclear physics published in English; another may wish to accept only those able to comprehend and make résumés of broadcasts from some foreign source; yet another may be seeking persons able to escort monolingual Russian visitors around town. An educational institution may be seeking students who can read and write the language well. Those wanting specific jobs, or certain forms of higher study, will undertake the necessary preparation before presenting for the test; others will not be judged on their inability to perform the same tasks. *The form of the test will again be a set of instructions for the candidates*; the appointment or admission sought will be an incentive; students will attempt to make their performance in the language congruent with the set of instructions and thus exit into the specialized realm they seek to enter. Standards of proficiency external to the educational process must be defined clearly in terms of what successful candidates may be expected to be able to do, and not in terms of so many structures or so many lexical items correctly identified, or so many phonemes accurately produced.[7]

The Interagency Language Roundtable (ILR) ratings (described in Chapter 2) set an external standard that students must attain in order to be appointed to certain positions in government service. The ACTFL proficiency levels (set out in the Appendix to this book) act as a guide to students as to the level they have attained in using the language. They are criteria against which students can test and retest until they are able to perform the various tasks outlined in the language-specific guidelines to the level of language control specified.[8] Should students wish to compare their level of achievement with that of the world of work or apply for a specific position that requires a certain level of language competency, they can match their ACTFL level with the corresponding numerical rating of the ILR scale. For most, this will not be necessary. The ACTFL proficiency guidelines will be ineffective if used as a checklist for preparation for a test or examination instead of a yardstick for estimating individual progress.

Tests related to the objectives of the students

In the case of certification standards, the source of the set of instructions is clear. At the general level of language control, the source is not so clear by any means. In the past the test was set by the teacher, guided by the syllabus and ultimately by the officials of the system; or it was set by the teacher "alone," guided usually by the textbook he or she had selected (and, therefore, indirectly by certain contemporary "trends," currents, or emphases of the profession, strained through the prejudices and preconceptions of the textbook writer). If the test is to be in reality a set of instructions against which students may test their developing skills and knowledge, then it must have some clear relationship to their aims and purposes. For this, there must be input from the students. There are no "aims of foreign-language instruction." *There are only aims of particular students learning a specific foreign language at a particular time and place.* This is the age in which the course must be tailored to the person, not the image.[9] At this point the expertise of the instructor comes into play – for assessing special needs, in consultation with the student, then writing the sets of instructions or tests in relation to these needs. In practical terms, this may mean a recipe from the student that the teacher transforms into a suitable test, as in some individualized and diversified programs.

We may at this point look closely at two directions in which stress on the student as learner has led us and see what implications these emphases have for testing. Apart from a few general suggestions, I shall have to leave it to our testing experts to decide what we can do about it. My intention here is to describe the situation for which modern tests need to be provided if they are to promote the language learning of individuals, rather than act as irritating roadblocks that waste time without being particularly useful.

Certain trends are clearly with us, and we must face their implications squarely. First, each student is an individual with distinct preferences as to modality, pace of learning, and course content. Second, each student is an individual with a personality to express.

The student as individual

A great deal has been said and written about "individualization of instruction"; yet the more one encounters the concept the more confused one becomes as to just what it means in actual practice. To some it is a new term for an old concept: self-paced instruction through the use of programmed texts – an activity that in practice draws extremely close to independent study. Independent study for all types of students? Is this providing for individual differences in learning styles and modality and content preferences, or merely for

largely superfluous, unless students request it for the pleasure of demonstrating their achievement. When students enjoy tests as a challenge and an opportunity for displaying what they know, we shall have reached the optimal form and timing of the test. If grades are necessary (and we may question whether, in many cases, they are), then the grades should be based on what the student has achieved as an individual; they should reflect personal effort and progress toward an individual goal.[13]

Once the one standard test becomes the goal of all students, we are back where we started. Because of the limitations of the job market or of college or university entrance, or because some other need for a highly selected group has arisen, it becomes depressingly inevitable that some of the most hardworking students will fail. This is built into the system. Is such artificial "failure" necessary or desirable? If not, let us change the system.

The student as an individual with a personality to express

Thus far, even our discussion of providing for the student as an individual has still been in the main teacher directed, with the teacher making decisions about what is best for the student. Of course, it has involved teachers taking students into their confidence, making sure they understand what they are going to do and why, just what they will be expected to demonstrate and how, and what criterion they must match before they move on. This is built into the concept of performance or behavioral objectives. In the words of a recent book:

> The teacher...decides in advance which features of the unit he intends to stress in his classes and what degree of proficiency he wants the students to develop with respect to those features.... It is up to the teacher to set the level of mastery, but his intention should always be that as many students as possible attain a high score.[14]

If students are full partners, however, they must also have the opportunity to tell the teacher what their expectations for the course are, what particular skills and course content interest them, when instruction is moving too fast or too slowly for them, and, at a particular moment, the specific aspects of their study on which they feel the need to test themselves.

In theory, performance or behavioral objectives seem a good idea: They enable both teacher and student to come to a clear understanding of the next step to be surmounted. *In practice, in foreign-language learning they can be very confining.* A foreign language cannot be

148

reduced for learning purposes to a multitude of small elements we accumulate like beads on a string (this phonological discrimination, that use of the past tense in indirect speech, ten words for parts of the body). Furthermore, who is to decide that in each case students must know items to such a degree of accuracy that they make only one spelling mistake in ten examples of their use, or fail to make some distinction in only two cases out of twelve?

For years now, leaders in our field have been pointing out that *use of a foreign language is more than the sum of its parts*, that there is macro-language use as opposed to micro-language learning. The micro-approach can stultify foreign-language learning even in its early stages. Naturally, if our students are to use a language, they need a basic knowledge of phonology, grammar, and lexicon, but these must be continually practiced through the production of meaningful messages. In other words, students as individual learners must have opportunities to express themselves through the language in terms of their own personality, using the language for the normal purposes of language: as part of an interaction of communication (both giving and receiving messages, in speech or writing).[15] If this interchange is a natural expression of personality, it cannot be predetermined with an established criterion level of mastery of the nine out of ten variety: The criteria in these cases are comprehension and comprehensibility, qualities that are very difficult to quantify.[16]

In all education (shall we say in all living), we experience *continual tension between our desire to organize (to bring order to phenomena, to quantify) and need for unfettered natural growth*, between the classical and the romantic impulses, between control and self-expression, between the approach of Robert Hutchins[17] and that of Ivan Illich.[18] As educators, we have to keep our balance between the two as the pendulum swings. Performance objectives seem to bring order, clarity, direction, and rational progression to foreign-language learning, yet, given preeminence, they stunt the fragile plant they are there to nurture, just as pruning and training that are too rigorous may produce an espalier, but not a freestanding tree in a natural garden.

Micro-language learning and macro-language use

Here I shall return to one of my favorite themes since 1964, namely, the fact that in language learning *we have to control language at two levels.*[19] There is basic core learning of the phonological, morphological, and syntactic operations of the language, and of the interrelationships of these systems with the semantic system. This is what I refer to as micro-language learning. Mastering it is hard work — essential, time-consuming, even tedious — and it is here that the performance objective approach, and its related modes of discrete-point testing, may be useful. It is the second level, or macro-level, where one uses the new language naturally for the expression of personal meaning, that we seem continually to neglect, yet it is absolutely indispensable if the study of a new language is not to be time-wasting busywork. This macro-language use is not the special bonus of a later advanced stage, which, to our regret, many of our students will never reach: It is the major purpose of foreign-language instruction and must be encouraged and fostered from the first elementary learnings. This level of language use cannot be confined by conventional performance objectives or fill-in-the-blank and multiple-choice tests, if it is to retain the spontaneity that is its hallmark. If we wish to encourage creativity and self-expression in the use of the second language, we cannot decide in advance what features our students will use and the degree of proficiency we want them to demonstrate in the use of those features.

How, then, can this spontaneous language use be tested? Valette says: "Until we know precisely what we intend to teach we cannot measure our success."[20] Perhaps with natural use of language we will never know *precisely* what we must teach, yet it seems clear that the natural use of language by our students that we can observe is more important than a clear-cut "measure" of our success. We cannot teach for creative language use, with functional comprehension and comprehensibility as the ultimate criteria, and then test for mere accuracy of detail as most conventional tests seem to do at present.

It is here that we need better tests than the standard interview for speaking and free composition for writing. Various possibilities have been suggested, involving our giving students real tasks to perform that require them to seek and convey information in the language (in speech or writing, as their needs require), and then evaluating them on the successful completion of the task. In concrete terms, this suggestion has endless possibilities for actualization at various levels of difficulty and can be adapted to specific uses of language that interest a particular student (conducting business affairs, enjoying a film or play, investigating a scientific problem).

At the most elementary stage, the test may entail approaching a monolingual or presumed monolingual speaker of the language, directly or by phone, to find out such information as name, age, address, telephone number, and occupation for entering on a file card. *At a higher level,* it may mean conducting some consumer research within a local community of speakers of the language; reading a recipe in the language and preparing a dish as directed; watching a

150

foreign-language film and preparing a résumé of it in the language for students at a lower level; or taking part in a group discussion of an issue of concern to the students, in which each student defends a particular position (the discussion would be recorded for later evaluation by the instructor). *At the highest level,* it may mean presenting oneself for a practice job interview; gathering information from native speakers for an article to be written (or alternatively from written sources in the language); monitoring news broadcasts in the foreign language and preparing a news bulletin for distribution to other students; or writing a film scenario or a one-act play for performance in a later course. It should be possible to think of many appropriate tasks that test macro-language use in similar purposeful ways.

More testing along these lines would *make the test a natural and enjoyable part of the learning.*[21] It would also provide a climax to a unit of study, which students could anticipate with pleasure as an opportunity to test themselves against a criterion of authentic communication. This type of testing requires imagination and ingenuity on the part of the examiner, and testing experts could perform a service for the profession by drafting and publishing a number of tests along these lines, with suggested adaptations to keep them varied. Security would not be a problem in these cases, because each actualization of the test would take a different turn as the situation was followed through by the student being tested. The result of the test would be rated either successful or unsuccessful (either the student was able to carry the task through to a satisfactory conclusion or was not), so that the "subjective" element in the judgment of the examiner would not be of any great significance. Clearly there would be variability in the amount and complexity of the communication taking place, but the student would have demonstrated ability to give and receive information, or to interact informally in an acceptable manner.[22]

Carroll tells us that

> from a practical point of view it may often suffice to construct tests that measure only integrated performance based on competence. For example, a general test of proficiency in a foreign language is often found to yield just as good validity when its items are complex, each drawing upon a wide sample of linguistic competences, as when each item has been contrived to tap competence in one and only one specific feature of the foreign language.... Apparently the extent to which a language test should attempt to measure specific aspects of competence depends upon its purpose – that is, the extent to which there is need for diagnosis of specific skills as opposed to a generalized, overall assessment of proficiency.[23]

If, as Pilliner says, *the form of the test gives direction to learning,* then it is essential that it be consonant with the aim of natural language use, if it is to be valid in the contemporary context. Validity is a much prized concept in testing, yet too many tests are still based on the objectives of a decade or two decades ago, lagging behind materials and classroom instruction. In this way they retard the evolution of a progressive view of language teaching, instead of clarifying goals for the less informed.

Accuracy or communication of meaning?

With all global or macro-testing, the perennial problem arises: How much accuracy in detail should we expect or require if effective communication is to be the goal? The answer to this question must realistically be relative. The person seeking a business contract cannot afford to misunderstand detail or to give assurances that can be misinterpreted. Scientists writing research papers must state exactly what they intend to state if the equipment is not to blow up when the experiment is replicated. These people need a degree of accuracy not usually essential for the tourist or the transient sojourner whose foreign-language needs are comparatively minor. Students in such fields would, by their training, realize the need for accurate expression in professional matters and presumably be motivated to work toward it. Business executives, more than scientific researchers, would understand the need for accuracy in intonational patterns and pitch levels, so that they would not sound angry or offhand, for instance, when they intended to be persuasive. On the other hand, many an emissary in a foreign country has found that *a certain degree of foreignness in speech patterns, far from being a handicap, elicited a greater tolerance on the part of local people* toward the inevitable early mistakes in adapting to the cultural patterns of their society.

More research is needed in all languages into those elements for which an absolute degree of accuracy is required if the communication is not to irritate a native speaker, and those which the native speaker will accept as amusing but pleasant indications that the stranger has really tried to learn the language, as a gesture of respect. We must remember that we can easily kill, or at least considerably dampen, the enthusiasm of a foreign-language learner by preferring accuracy of detail to sincere efforts to create spontaneous utterances or to write expressive prose. When it comes to micro-testing, we do well also to remember that the person capable of macro-performance can frequently cope with the details of the micro-test, but all those who can pass micro-tests are not necessarily able to perform acceptably at the macro-level. The fact that the micro-test is so much easier to administer is a danger to us as a profession. If we become addicted to fill-in-the-blank tests and multiple-choice items, we must not be surprised if our students think that this is what performance in a foreign language really is. Let us remember that *by our testing they shall know us, far better than we shall know them.*

Let's discuss

1 Why do we test anyway? Discuss this question frankly and in depth.
2 Of the discrete-point tests for micro-language learning that you have encountered, which seem to you to be the most valid for a communication-oriented class?
3 What activities in addition to those on pp. 150–1 can you suggest that could be converted into task-oriented tests for (a) elementary level, (b) intermediate level, and (c) advanced level?
4 How would you test students in (a) a language for business class, (b) a language for literary appreciation class, (c) a course in reading for science and engineering students, or (d) a course for airline service personnel?
5 How would you individualize an advanced language course with ten students with different objectives, without sacrificing the interactional nature of language learning?

11 From the pyramid to the commune: the evolution of the foreign-language department

The great monolith of the foreign-language department is splitting and cracking. Its foundation is disintegrating and falling away, or so it seems, and the effect is being felt right to the apex. *Our beautiful, aesthetically proportioned pyramid is threatened.* Of course, many of us haven't given too much thought to its lower structures for some time. We had our graduate students, our future professors with such fine minds (were there any others?). There were, of course, our majors or concentrators,[1] whom we regarded as potential graduate students, and then that lesser breed, the future high school teachers who helped us pay our way. Were there a few minors? Difficult to say, since they blended so well with our majors in class. Anyway, they obviously could not be serious or they would be majors. And that vast anonymous mass at the base in the "service" courses? Like the poor, they were always with us; for, after all, without the working poor how could a cultured class give its full attention to intellectual and aesthetic matters?

Paralleling this hierarchy of students, we had our own inner core. At the apex were the senior professors, the scholars, concerned only with the elite graduate student, preferably in thesis advising on a one-to-one basis: the established scholar engaged with the most brilliant of the incipient scholars. Next, came the aspiring younger faculty, the scholars of promise, interested only in the concentrators and, of these, preferably the few destined for graduate study. Somewhat lower were our less scholarly, practical colleagues teaching teachers how and what to teach, and at the base the graduate assistants doing their time, poor souls, with the required courses, as we've all had to do in our day. No wonder there are alarm and consternation at the threat to the base: We cherish our antique monument as it always was, because it memorializes in concrete form the glories of a past age.

Perhaps we need a new image for ourselves and for others. Instead of our well-proportioned pyramid, orderly and coherent, where each section fits into its place, supporting the whole in anonymity and

Revised version of an article originally published in the *ADFL Bulletin* 3, 3 (1972): 13–17.

impersonality, we need a real community: a community of scholars, of learners at every level (in keeping with the true meaning of the word "scholar"). I suggest that we renounce our historical monument and become a commune – *an untidy, nonhierarchical, interacting, interdependent, evolving commune.* And what shall we have in our commune? Plurality and diversification in unity, innovation and interaction in mutual tolerance and acceptance. In this way, if we are sincere in our conversion, we can provide for all types of students the truly humanistic experience our discipline offers. We must renounce the idea that foreign-language study is essentially laying a foundation for future study (although this may be true for a few) and concentrate on developing people, interesting people who have read and experienced beyond the limitations of their own language and culture, flexible people able to react with equanimity to new ideas and ideals and to see them in perspective because of their wider experience in another culture and another age. In this way, *what we have to offer can be of value to all who come to us,* no matter how short their stay and no matter what their future role.

Idealistic? Maybe. A little whimsicality will help us to take ourselves less seriously and to worry less, in this period of somewhat unpredictable change, which is affecting, whether we will or not, our institutional role and our clientele. The new image I propose is not as fanciful as it may seem, but its implications cannot be realized overnight. The establishment of our commune is not merely a question of breaking down caste and challenging authority structures. Of the latter there will always be some. Even in a commune natural leadership patterns evolve, as events and necessity sort out the decision makers from the followers. The significant change must be in our attitudes within the community: in the development of a new acceptance and appreciation of individuals, with their diversity of gifts and interests.

How does our commune differ from the pyramid?

First, the unitary structure of the pyramid disappears – that structure where each step is preliminary to the next, and each leads inevitably to the apex. Stop at one step and where are you? Nowhere in particular, merely somewhere on the way. Within the commune there is a plurality of tasks and achievements, each one a worthwhile accomplishment in itself. *People come and people go; some stay, some leave, some return.* Whenever they are within the commune, they are fully participating members: They belong, they count, they are respected, for every contribution of effort and interest helps to create and maintain the commune. Those who leave take away with them a complete experience, perhaps shorter and less intense than if they had stayed, but in any event not a partial experience that is merely anticipatory and unsatisfying in its incompleteness.

How does this affect our courses?

So much for our metaphors. Let us express them rather in terms of courses and student-teacher interaction to make them comprehensible and practical. We need courses at every level that provide for *a diversity of interests and time objectives*, courses that have satisfying content and are not merely preliminary to some future experience. In this sense a fair proportion of our courses can be designed as "terminal," that is, complete in themselves, so that students who have no intention of continuing[2] can take away with them a full and enriching experience, whereas those who go on to a higher level will find their later experiences facilitated and illuminated by what went before. The secret is in the approach we take when planning our courses. As we are forced more and more to compete for student interest in an open market, we will need to conceive and plan our courses imaginatively and realistically, with the interests of a diversity of students in mind. We can no longer afford to regard our lower-level courses, for instance, as "elementary" and "intermediate" (the very words enshrine a preparatory concept). Thinking of them as preliminary courses, we try to include in them all the grammar we think our future majors or concentrators should know, until our students gag with revulsion.[3] We often withhold until the fourth semester any material that is intellectually stimulating and then provide snippets from various centuries, surely worthy when seen in their literary context, but quite boring to the naive student with little background in literature.

Terminal courses differ from continuing courses

Does a terminal course, in the sense that it is complete in itself, necessarily have to be a "review of the grammar," ensuring that short-term students take away a thorough picture of the workings of the subjunctive and the intricacies of the pronominal system? Is this what they will quote with pleasure when looking back on their undergraduate days? Surely we can provide a choice for our students: a preparatory diet for those who intend to continue and are willing to prolong an arduous apprenticeship for the promise of future mastery

156

and, paralleling this, a stimulating and provocative offering for those who will in all probability leave us at the end of the semester. When are we going to do some serious research into the amount of grammar a person really needs to know actively in order to comprehend and the amount of concentrated learning required to be able to recognize the rest when it is encountered in a context of interesting material? Recent psychological research in reading and listening shows that there is a significant heuristic element at work in comprehension. Furthermore, functional communication can be carried on without active knowledge of many of the finer points of syntax. *Which structures are essential for this level of production?*[4] Should we not set some of our best graduate students to finding out which aspects of language structure must be thoroughly assimilated, and which can be avoided by paraphrase and circumlocution, or deduced in listening from our knowledge of setting and semantic associations (particularly in languages with a large commonality of outlook and cultural context)? Once we have substantial research evidence in this area, we may find we can reduce considerably the grammar content in language courses for our transients and use our time, and our students' time, for the type of confrontation with ideas and attitudes that we recognize as one of the major educational contributions we can make to undergraduate education.

Rethinking course content and approach

A language is a vehicle. What about content? Are all students at the lower levels interested in learning the language in order to read the *literature*? For those who are, and there are many, we bring the literature to them, carefully selected in theme and development to interest and stimulate them intellectually and aesthetically, while keeping our selection linguistically within their capacity of comprehension. We resist the temptation to impose upon them our latest critical theories. We teach them to love literature and to want to read more. Some, we must admit, however, are interested rather in *current affairs* and the preoccupations of their contemporaries in the other culture. For these we use the newspapers and magazines of the day, as well as television documentaries, radio commentaries, and authentic recorded interviews, as the major course content. The interpretation of such contemporary documents will certainly challenge our students' understanding of present-day life and institutions and their roots in earlier periods. We bring in native speakers with special knowledge of these areas to interact with them and provoke discussion. Yet other students are fascinated by the clash of *attitudes, values, and behavior patterns* between cultures. For these, we pro-

157

vide opportunities to see the other culture and their own through foreign eyes – often a startling experience. Is it *drama and film* they seek? These we can provide. Should they wish to learn only to communicate, *to comprehend and be comprehended*, it should not be such a struggle for us to eliminate from specialized communication courses the written exercises they will rarely need.[5] If they wish to read literature in the foreign language, but to discuss it only in their own, surely this too is a legitimate interest. If students want to learn the language for *career interests* in business, anthropology, or social service, can we not design useful short courses that provide material to meet these needs? For far too long we have allowed a commendable concern with fairness in grading across levels to preoccupy us, so that in order to ensure that all are rewarded alike we serve all an identical, often insipid and tasteless diet few enjoy. Variation in content, allowing for student choice in sections at the same level, is feasible and has proved to be of considerable motivational value.

For a plurality of student needs we must provide a plurality of content. But why not also *a plurality of approaches*? Once again, with the best of intentions we have often insisted that all be taught alike, despite the differences in their learning patterns and the equally important differences in the natural instructional styles of their instructors. Here again uniformity has led us to colorlessness and lack of spontaneity. A little less scrupulous identity of treatment may lead to some unevenness in the offering, but it can also liberate the natural talents of young instructors and the potential exuberance of the instructed. At this stage of vigorous rethinking of our programs, we do not need a voice *ex cathedra* to tell us the new pattern to which we must conform, thus establishing a new orthodoxy of the heterodox. We need the excitement of experimentation within our own institutions, a healthy enthusiasm for one's own brainchild, that child who flourishes despite the pessimism of those who do not recognize its hidden vitality. We need many flowers blooming, day lilies perhaps, but each in its day and hour bringing fragrance to the experience of some. Excellent teaching has always been uneven in its distribution, depending as it does on the presence or absence of gifted individuals who stand out in the memory of the instructed.

The long sequence of language study

I have talked at some length about the transients. Let us consider now *those who will stay in the commune* and draw from it a major part of their undergraduate experience. I cannot deal here with all aspects of the undergraduate program in the foreign-language department, although there is much one could say about each segment.[6]

Let me keep to one or two facets particularly close to my own interests and in serious need of development. Here I shall begin with the language program for majors (or concentrators), for minors, and for those language enthusiasts who, although specializing in other fields, wish to attain a solid level of language mastery equaling that of the concentrators. How can we improve their control of the language? It is not enough to say, ostrichlike, "Send them abroad for a year," thus saving ourselves the taxing effort of seeking solutions for some of the toughest problems with which we have to deal. The year or semester abroad, especially if it includes a home-stay program, undoubtedly helps, but not all can participate and in our commune the interests of all are our concern. Let us face the fact that the improvement of language skills at the so-called advanced level is one of the most difficult of tasks, and yet it is the area toward which the least research and inquiry have been directed.

Who teaches the language courses and how are they designed?

We must meet our students where they are. Students complain about the gap between their intermediate course (or their high school experience) and the advanced courses. How do we explain this gap? It is very real to instructors and students alike. Two folk explanations are prevalent: "Nobody taught them anything in their earlier courses" and "The students are a feckless lot; if they really cared they wouldn't keep on making the same mistakes." If the same situation persists from year to year with successive groups of students and we know that, in many institutions, the most energetic language teaching is going into the earlier courses, perhaps the time has come to look more critically at ourselves and our courses at the advanced level. Most of the instructors, being trained in literary scholarship, want to teach literature primarily, so they proclaim firmly that they are not there to teach the language. The students, they say, should know the language already. In their anxiety to protect themselves from such an unwelcome task, they conveniently forget the many years it took them to perfect their own knowledge of the language (and this also applies to the native speakers among them) and the pitifully short language programs still prevalent in this country.

Because extra language work is, however, clearly necessary, we set up some language courses and farm these out as *perennial chores to less influential or more accommodating members of the department*. It seems anyone can do it, so the task is sometimes undertaken by a young literary scholar who wants a semester with little preparation in order to write up that article from the recently completed thesis. Few materials are available at this level (publishers consider it too

159

small a market), so the same old book does the job. Since very few are really interested in the design of the courses, or know how to design courses for advanced language learning, the language is usually *chopped up into unnatural and unpalatable segments*: a unit of diction this semester (such terrible pronunciation!), a unit of syntax next semester, not forgetting a unit or two of composition (no one has taught them to write decently in the language, and they will need this skill for their literature papers). Finally, we allot four hours, or even eight hours, to intensive conversation (the hardest of all to teach, but fobbed off most frequently on untrained, and often completely inexperienced, native speakers who proceed to do all the talking for want of familiarity with techniques for eliciting speech). If this seems a lot of time to spend on nonwritten work (writing being considered the real thing at this level), the conversation course is combined with the composition course, despite the dichotomous difference in modality and the distinctive character of written as opposed to spoken language.

Have we ever stopped to consider seriously whether language can be learned effectively in this piecemeal fashion? To learn language well one has to enjoy learning it, so that one is eager to know how to express oneself more correctly or more elegantly. The many snippets of knowledge students need are assimilated into their functioning system only after conscious and alert attention is directed to them, and they have been organized by the mind into retrievable subsystems. *For this they need to be using the language continually for absorbing activities*; yet, at times, in language departments we seem to have a puritanical fear of students enjoying what is good for them.

How much grammar is indispensable?

A typical student comment from the course evaluation booklet of a well-known institution will arouse acquiescence from many unenthusiastic instructors shanghaied into language teaching: "No matter what the language, grammar reviews are all the same: distasteful but good for you, sort of the cod liver oil of language courses."[7] What we need to consider is this: Can syntax be learned efficiently apart from conversation, composition, diction, and of course, reading? Syntax taught in isolation is a linguistics rather than a language course, an important course to be sure but requiring a different content from that served up in the usual "syntax course." Sometimes the so-called syntax course takes the form of a rather simplistic course in translation, where students translate short, detached sentences containing specific "points of grammar." Sometimes the sentences are even phrased in a distorted form of the native language to make the syntactic or

160

idiomatic structure to be elicited more obvious. These courses are not conceived, however, as serious courses in translation, where students will study the nonmatching nature of surface structures and of syntactic representations of semantic substance. A genuine translation course would train the student to extract the thought content from stretches of English discourse and to reexpress this in the formal structures of another language. Here we would be teaching a specialized craft, which can become a passion. Such a course is a long way from these artificially constructed translation sentences, which violate language as a living, functioning entity.[8] *Living language involves simultaneously all of the aspects we are now teaching separately*, with perception receiving as much emphasis as production.

Living language courses

We need, then, a continuing series of imaginatively conceived classes, where living language is taught as a whole, where the seamless garment is despotted, stretched a little here, shrunk a little there, and worn places are invisibly mended, but where the fabric is preserved in its integrity. In such courses syntax is considered as it is needed, diction as it is needed, semantic structure and communicative or pragmatic competence as they are needed, but all within the context of purposeful activity, because only then does the language come alive. Instead of talking desperately about something or other for four, five, eight hours a week in a "conversation class," the group undertakes some project together and, in carrying it through, uses the language, improves its use of the language, and corrects its use of the language. Advanced language classes, living language classes – call them what you will – *it is the integrated activity that counts.*

A series of language courses of this type can be designed so that each will unobtrusively zero in on specific problem areas. Is it diction that is defective? The course may focus on reading plays and poetry aloud for pleasure, with class performances recorded on videocassettes for self-evaluation. Is written language the problem? Activities will be designed that require the writing of a large number of letters or reports that will have some destination, perhaps in the exchange of information with a group outside the university or one within; or an activity may be designed in the first part of the course that must be carried out in the second half, such as writing a scenario for a radio drama or a film based on an incident that took place in a country where the language is spoken. The class may take over the regular writing and editing of a daily or weekly departmental newspaper. Writing poems is another challenging and demanding task students enjoy.

161

If integrated language practice is sought, activity or "case packets" can be designed. These should lead the students into simulating problem-solving situations that require them to search out information in printed sources and from native speakers on campus, to discuss their findings together, and to write some form of report for final presentation. Well-organized case packets will require each person in the group to take a role in the final presentation in order to maintain a viewpoint. During such activities gaps in the knowledge of syntax will continually reveal themselves, but the students will be taught to seek out the facts themselves from reference material or from the instructor as they need them, or to teach each other rather than being subjected to the fourth (fifth, sixth?) formal exposition of the workings of the system of tenses.

Such an activity class may well be linked to literary or cultural subjects and serves as an opportunity for students to familiarize themselves with wider areas of interest, as they seek to discover how certain themes have been expressed at certain periods in literature, how certain ideas have been worked out in drama, or how certain aspects of life are experienced in another culture. *Interesting content is needed for a language class as well as any other.* Such a class will differ from an introductory literature course, however, in that the purpose of the course will be quite frankly the perfection of language in use.

If we make available a series of courses like these, of varied interest and emphasis, *we can provide for the discrepancy in student needs.* Four courses of this nature would not form a sequence to be taken by all in strict order: Some would need all; some only one; some would be interested only in the second and the fourth; others in the first or the third. Instructors could concentrate on improving and varying the offering of a course, with a particular emphasis on an area in which they themselves were most interested.

What do students want?

Here comes the crunch. Our students, we are told, "prefer" literature classes – they are "bored with language classes."

There are perhaps readily identifiable reasons why many students seem to prefer literature. Literature courses are at present taught by specialists who love their specialty; interesting, even exciting materials are readily available; professors spend much time preparing, finding supplementary materials, encouraging lively debate; students soon sense which are the "real" subjects that "count" in the department. Let us take the obverse, which applies in so many departments: Language classes quite frequently are not taught by specialists who love their specialty; interesting and exciting materials are not readily available, but must be sought or developed at the expense of much time and energy; professors teaching such courses as an imposed chore resent spending time seeking out or preparing personally materials that will not provide an idea for a future article and that will not be regarded as "scholarly production" when they are being considered for promotion or tenure; students soon sense that these courses are held in low esteem by fellow-students, professors, and their own instructor.

Yet students continue to seek out what language courses there are, and where a series such as that described has been instituted, classes are packed with enthusiastic students, who continually ask for more.[9]

The need for language-teaching specialists

Elsewhere the situation will continue as it is at present until foreign-language departments are willing to accept *the need for highly qualified, respected, imaginative, academically rewarded language specialists.* I am not speaking of linguists, philologists, or phoneticians, but language teachers who know how to design and write materials and who can integrate language use with intellectually stimulating, thought-provoking, exciting activity and content. To do this effectively, they will need to have an informed knowledge of many areas, but they will be devoted specialists nevertheless. We need specialists in contemporary language and language learning who are also informed about different approaches to teaching, who can teach in teams, who can use students to teach their peers, who can help students to learn without interposing themselves in the learning process. We need specialists who understand that testing is primarily a device to encourage learning; who do not consider group work a kind of cheating, or take-home examinations, or open-ended or open-book examinations, as "lowering standards"; who can see the virtue of free discussion of a student's paper in class, before the student rewrites it in a final version, and of students' retaking tests to improve their grades. There are many well-attested devices for improving the quality and quantity of learning that are suspect to the stalwarts of the pyramid, but that will seem humane and fruitful in the commune, where change is not feared but welcomed when it promotes the good of the greatest number. These language-teaching specialists should also be well informed about contemporary life, institutions, and values in societies where the language is spoken, and well acquainted with modern literature in its broadest sense (film, theater, folklore, and poetry, as

163

well as fiction and expository prose), so that they can select worth-while content for all types of students.

I have called for proper recognition of language-teaching special-ists, but it must now be clear that such a group could be subversive, *promoting a quiet revolution in our inner circles.*

So that we do not create a group of initiates at odds with the rest of the commune, and so that other areas may profit from a shared spirit of innovation and renewal, we need a seminar for study and discus-sion where all future professors can come to understand each other's preoccupations; where they will be shaken out of the ruts into which their own educational experience has settled them; where they will get to the roots of the educational problems facing the total com-mune and acquire the flexibility to solve these problems that comes from knowledge and understanding of their causes. In other words, we need enlightened training for our graduate students and teaching assistants, not in teaching techniques for tomorrow's class, but as preparation for a long career. We need imaginative professors who will accept graduate student instructors as co-workers, team mem-bers in the teaching of all kinds of courses, and who will give them the example of innovative and stimulating learning situations in prog-ress, while allowing them the freedom to create others, which may well differ in approach and content. This is a situation we can create in the free, unguarded, and unsuspicious atmosphere of the com-mune, as we could never expect to find it on our separate steps of the pyramid.

Redesigned undergraduate programs, teaching training within the academy, graduate preparation for a long career within the depart-ments? There are many other areas that need a fresh wind blowing into the corners and through the doors of offices and classrooms. Let us establish our commune and other areas, too, will gradually open themselves up for intensive discussion and cooperative action.

Let's discuss and work it out

1 What type of language course would interest an economics major, or concentrator, interested in working with an international agency whose task is to help Fourth World (least developed) na-tions improve their economies?

2 Describe in detail two language courses at the advanced level: one designed to improve the language control of majors, or concen-trators, and one proposed for nonmajors seeking primarily the

ability to interact orally, at a high level of discussion, with speakers of the language within their own culture.

3 For the language you teach, make a careful list of syntactic structures indispensable for all users of the language; a second list of those structures lack of knowledge of which does not impede comprehension and comprehensibility; and a third list of structures essential for good writing, which can be omitted in an exclusively oral course. Discuss your lists with those studying with you.

4 What problems did you experience in moving from the intermediate to the advanced level in your first foreign language? What problems do you still have? What do you do to overcome them? What implications does your own approach have for teaching?

5 Design a syntax course that encourages active use of the language in purposeful tasks. How would you deal with fossilized errors in your students' speech? In their written work?

12 The revolution now: revitalizing the university language departments

Declining enrollments, great success stories, no change – from different areas, reports vary. In some language departments,[1] enrollments have dropped drastically in the last decade, whereas in others there have been phenomenal increases.[2] In some parts of Canada, with its emphasis on developing bilingual institutions, French classes are full (but not everywhere or at all levels), while other languages are struggling. How should language departments plan for the future?

The Society for Research into Higher Education in the United Kingdom sees a malaise throughout higher education and attributes this to "loss of confidence by school leavers in the private benefits of higher education; loss of confidence by politicians in the social benefits;...and often, loss of confidence by academics in their own sense of purpose."[3] Perhaps a little attention to these three factors may throw light on some of the problems of those language departments with falling student enrollments and threatened budgetary restrictions.

Objectives must reflect changed conditions

All education is part of the life of a society. As such, it is continually subject to social pressures, political demands, and the perceptions of students and their parents as to the type of education and course content they feel is worthwhile at a particular time. Yet many language departments, more often through inertia than tenacious conviction, maintain today an approach and programs that reflect the pressures and perceptions of the 1880s, when foreign languages were trying to establish themselves as valid and respectable studies at university level. Literary criticism, philological research, study of linguistic structure, and translation were sufficient for their purposes in a different age with a different student body, who were living in a smaller, less interactive world. *Now departments must rethink their*

Revised version of an article originally published in the *Canadian Modern Language Review* 37 (1981): 447–61. Festschrift in Honour of H. H. (David) Stern. By permission of the editor, Anthony S. Mollica.

role, in changing institutions in a changing society, or suffer the fate of the irrelevant and passé. For many, this will require a vigorous and conscious effort to move in new directions, while conserving those parts of their traditional program that make a valuable contribution to liberal education.

The current situation could be most promising for the teaching of both language and literature, but its distinctive character must be realized and opportunities assessed. Departments need to review their objectives in the context of social and educational trends and the composition of the student body that these determine; they need to consider existing programs in the light of newly identified objectives and be willing to make the changes required to bring programs into congruence with these objectives. Nothing less will restore the confidence of public, students, and academics themselves.

Response to change

In *Future Shock*, Toffler describes four common responses to the need for change: outright denial, specialism, obsessive reversion to previously successful adaptive routines, and super-simplification.[4] These are not uncommonly observed in language departments. Awareness of their inhibiting effect is a first step toward change.

Deniers, according to Toffler, block out unwelcome reality. They are able to convince themselves "that things really are the same, and that all evidences of change are merely superficial."[5] They continue to give their 20-year-old lectures, from yellowed, dog-eared sheets, on the same texts that may have delighted, or at least kept the attention of, the parents of the present students. They still call their courses "Contemporary Literature," or "Recent Trends in Criticism," even though the most recent text to be considered may have a copyright date of 1942. They never doubt that teaching literature, and particularly what others have said about the text, is the supreme aim of the foreign-language department. They may, of course, concede a small place to philology (or even, with some reluctance, to theoretical linguistics), while recognizing that the number of students interested in these areas is not great. Should they notice that their own students are sparser, they attribute this to the philistine influence of television.

Specialists, on the other hand, do "not block out *all* novel ideas or information. Instead, [they] energetically...keep pace with change – but only in a specific narrow sector of life."[6] Deconstructive and neo-Freudian insights dimly illuminate their jargon-ridden interpretations. Who are their potential students? This they do not need to know, so long as they have a few devotees, with interests like theirs, whom they may enthuse for their own line of thought and research.

Reversionists stick to their "previously programmed decisions and habits with dogmatic desperation. The more change threatens from without, the more meticulously [they repeat] past modes of action, ...previously successful adaptive routines that are now irrelevant and inappropriate."[7] Reversionist language teachers, for instance, may have been, at the beginning of their careers, dedicated audiolingualists, in the forefront of the revolution of their youth. The answer they believed in then must be the answer now. It matters little to them that experience and research have brought into question earlier convictions. Their approach will succeed, they are sure, if the students will only work harder.

Super-simplifiers seek "a single neat equation that will explain all the complex novelties threatening to engulf [them]. Grasping erratically at this idea or that," they become "temporary true believers."[8] Super-simplifiers are certainly not deniers or reversionists. Their course is never the same for two years in succession. The latest approach to literary criticism, a new (if ephemeral) linguistic theory, this miracle remedy to the problems of language learning (sleep learning, self-hypnotism, learning Russian through chess), each in its turn, they convince themselves, is the only way. A new idea surfaces? Unabashed, they switch – never consolidating, rarely evaluating.

None of these reactions will revitalize the language departments. As Toffler points out, "unless the individual begins with a clear grasp of relevant reality, and unless he begins with cleanly defined values and priorities, his reliance on such techniques will only deepen his adaptive difficulties."[9] Foreign-language departments must look outward. They must anticipate the world in which they will exist in the next decade and consider the types of students who will be in the universities. Only then can they begin to rethink their programs, so that all students, no matter what their primary academic preoccupations, can profit from what language departments have to offer.

Today's world

As we study the world in which we live, we may observe both internationally and intranationally two divergent trends that are potential sources of tension and conflict: *worldwide interdependence coupled with the realization and assertion of identity*. As nations, and linguistic and ethnic groupings within nations, become increasingly aware that they must share and conserve the same natural resources, that they cannot exist without the products of each other's labor, and that they need each other's knowledge and expertise to meet the demands of contemporary living, they seem to rebel against the loss of identity such interdependence fosters, reasserting their independence as self-conscious entities. ("I am me. Respect me!") In our universities, we must prepare students for concord and productive living in a world where these two forces will determine the social and political environment in which they will live and work.

Essential to harmonious living in such a world will be the ability to comprehend others; not only the words they speak or write, but also their ways of thinking, their aspirations, and their spoken and unspoken demands. Ability to comprehend, and also to communicate clearly, will be essential to the conduct of mutually beneficial enterprises (in government, in business, in social amelioration), as well as to everyday life in the multilingual and multicultural societies that are coming into being throughout the world. Our students must learn to live with such diversity and to accept its self-conscious assertiveness. As a result of these changes, knowledge of more than one language and multicultural sensitivity have become urgent and essential elements of education.

Attention to linguistic needs and intercommunal understanding are already a priority in many parts of Europe, not only in traditional schooling for youth, but also in the education of adults.[10] Many developing nations have had to make provision for the learning of several languages by their children in order to survive. In the United States, the work of the President's Commission on Foreign Language and International Studies and of its successor, the National Council on Foreign Language and International Studies, is gradually awakening the American public to its ignorance of the world and its languages. Consequently, interest in other languages and cultures is slowly mounting.[11]

Who are the decision makers?

The direction that education will take grows out of national and community conviction. Much as they might like to, universities cannot stand apart from broader educational decisions. *The educational needs that should be met are not decided in a vacuum* by teachers or professors. They are determined by the deliberations of community leaders, as they respond to the needs of society. Their recommendations influence how parents and students appraise language-related career opportunities, as well as the value that communities place on developing the multilingual and multicultural potential of their young people. These community pressures impinge on the work of even unconcerned university teachers, through such mundane factors as the level of funding the community is willing to commit to their programs and the numbers of students registering for their courses.

Already two emphases of national significance are becoming evident: the desirability for a closer link between language learning and international studies, and the need for bilingual and multilingual personnel in national and international agencies and for business across national boundaries. A third direction, the fostering of intercommunal understanding within the national entity and in relations with newly arrived immigrant groups, has led to a search for ways of developing multicultural sensitivity. The renewed emphasis in public discussion on the recognition and cultivation of shared values within the community adds force to this third direction in that any attempt to understand another culture leads inevitably to a closer examination and a more informed awareness of one's own.

Communities worldwide are raising serious questions about the apparent failure of educators to teach secondary and undergraduate students to communicate their ideas and to understand those of others in speech and writing. An understanding of the process of communication and increased facility with it can result from the study of another language, if the instruction is directed toward such an outcome.

Finally, the relentless advance of technology and the impersonalizing effects of an increasingly mechanized society are reawakening many to the human need for reflection and the nurture of reflection that comes from humanistic studies. Here foreign languages have always had a role, bringing students into contact with provocative ideas, human experiences, and artistic production in print, in visual image, and in the live contact of theater. The human spirit requires more than efficient production and distribution, or rapid communication of the banal and trivial.

Language in the education of all students

The demands of the future will not be met by programs focusing exclusively on the needs of a small band of concentrators, or majors, who may wish to follow in the footsteps of their professors. Language departments must recognize their role in the education of all students and appreciate the possibilities this role opens to them. Future lawyers, anthropologists, social workers, legislators, administrators, journalists, or musicians can and will want to profit from new programs that take their needs and interests specifically into consideration.[12] But programs for nonconcentrators must be developed with as much attention to content, staffing, and presentation as the traditional literature and linguistics programs of the department.[13] *The interested students are there*, but they will not be willing to accept the scraps, casually left for them after a small elite has received the lion's share of the thought and attention of the department. The nonmajors, or nonconcentrators, who will constitute the bulk of the students in the future, rightfully demand respect for their needs and the best teaching that the most qualified teachers in the department can provide.

Here I am not talking about elementary- and intermediate-level required courses. These should receive careful attention and excellent teaching, as they already do in many institutions. The nonconcentrators who are the most neglected are at the optional, postrequirement level. Many educated men and women wish to be able to communicate freely in another language with some sophistication and to read about and discuss matters of import in that language. When courses are designed to provide what they need, there is no lack of applicants.

Moving even further from traditional patterns, universities worldwide are recognizing, or being forced to take into consideration, the instructional needs of nontraditional students and the continuing education of adults. In the past, many departments have preferred to ignore this area, maintaining that only full-time undergraduate or graduate students receive the intangible benefits a university education can provide. Many people are unable, for personal or financial reasons, to study in traditional programs. These students are now demanding, with reason, their full share of tertiary education. Everywhere, *extension or continuing education classes, open universities by television or correspondence, and centers for lifelong learning are expanding*; in these, language study is in high demand. Furthermore, all prognostications indicate that the greatest increase in students in the next decade will be in these areas. To seize this opportunity, departments will need to think imaginatively, so that they can provide new types of courses to meet the needs of a mature clientele that knows what it wants.

Five directions foreign-language departments should explore in the next decade

Foreign language and international studies

A union of foreign language and international studies is a useful direction, well supported by the 1979 report of the President's Commission on Foreign Language and International Studies.[14] Such a move would require *unusually close collaboration across departmental lines.* Since, in the past, departments in universities have clung jealously to their separate identities, one not trespassing upon the preserve of the other, such a change would need to be initiated by *contacts between concerned individuals.* The result might be team teaching. Current political and economic problems in specific areas would be discussed by experts in these fields, while language department instructors conducted discussion sections in the foreign language, using documentation and contemporary comment from newspapers, magazines, and reports. In the process, they would give attention to refining the linguistic skills of their students. (A similar approach is possible in other cross-disciplinary areas, such as foreign language and philosophy, history, sociology, anthropology, or fine arts.)

For this type of collaborative program to succeed, foreign-language instructors will need to have *a broader professional preparation,* so that they can discuss, with some depth of knowledge, areas other than literature and linguistics. For less commonly taught languages, area studies have long been a popular model, and some departments of Western European languages have, in recent years, attempted to broaden their offerings along similar lines. What is intended here is an even more radical reorientation than area studies, and this will demand an equally radical approach to the preparation of future instructors. Yet the large departments, from which come the majority of each year's crop of candidates, continue for the most part along conservative lines. Suitable instructors for more innovative programs are, as a result, in very short supply. Without a concerted effort on the part of the profession to allow for broader preparation for the academics of the future, such proposals will remain pipe dreams, rather than an option regularly available to students.

One of the most effective contributions of foreign language to international studies is organized *home-stay exchanges* with students in countries where the language is spoken, or *working internships.* These should be preceded by careful study of life, institutions, and economic and political policies and buttressed for each student by a clearly defined research project that involves reading newspapers and other documentation and discussing current issues with the young people of the country visited. These types of exchanges are generally more valuable and longlasting in their effect than the conventional study-abroad programs, where a group of students, ill-prepared linguistically, are instructed in another country by their own professors or by nationals brought in to ensure that they qualify for sufficient credits in their home institutions. Such students tend to cling together, venturing out in each other's company to observe the natives in markets, parks, or theaters, rather than interacting with them informally as they go about their daily business.

Language and intercommunity understanding

Harmonious living in the contemporary world implies tolerance, acceptance of difference, and willingness to cooperate with others whose ways of viewing and doing things is not ours. Assertion of identity by groups within a larger community can surprise and antagonize those with the conviction that their society is, or should be, homogeneous in beliefs, expectations, values, and lifestyles. Understanding other cultures, both within nations and between nations, is of paramount importance in this interdependent modern world.

Talking about other cultures is not enough. Students tend to retain from lectures and readings what confirms their prejudices and reinforces their stereotypes. What does not conform to their preexisting opinions frequently goes unnoticed, is easily forgotten, or is reinterpreted. To thoroughly understand another culture, students need to live, to some extent, in that culture, to experience it as one brought up in the culture experiences it, and to assimilate this new experience so that it enriches their thinking and their expression of self. Because so much of another culture is expressed in and through its language, foreign-language learners are in a better position to penetrate the culture in depth than those who view it only through accounts in their native language. Learners of another language are better able to relive experiences of the culture emotionally and intellectually, through first-hand contact with the popular, the aesthetic, and the intellectual output of its members, and through personal contact with those for whom this culture is their primary experience. As Robinson puts it: "Understanding involves emotional as well as conceptual processes. To understand emotionally implies empathy. Empathy, in turn, implies identification. Learning to identify means merging one's own experience with those of the target culture. Therefore, if we are successful in promoting identification with people from other cultures, each student's response will be unique in that it reflects a synthesis of past experience with the new cultural and linguistic experiences."[15]

Close experience of another culture is desirable, but not sufficient. It should lead to *comparative study of several cultures*, and, for this to take place, there should be frequent interaction among classes of students learning different languages. Round-table discussions should be held frequently to share material gleaned from newspapers and magazines, films, and songs, with students explaining the viewpoint of the peoples whose languages they are learning. Discussions should be held on how persons from different cultures would react to certain occurrences and the solutions they would propose to common problems. Representatives of the different cultures should be invited in person to express their views on fundamental life issues such as work, leisure, family, old age, sickness and death, community relations, justice, religion, politics, or societal structure. Food, drink, and manners may be attractive as starting points for students, but these must be viewed in relation to geographical and historical factors and the life of the individual within the community.

For languages like French, German, Spanish, and Portuguese, *this multicultural approach does not necessarily mean moving beyond the department.* Each of these languages is claimed as a primary language by more than one national entity. Just as English belongs as much to Alaska, Jamaica, or India as it does to the United Kingdom or Canada, French serves as a means of communication to a Haitian, a Tunisian, or a Tahitian, just as it does to a citizen of Montreal, Geneva, or Toulouse. Spanish and Portuguese are spoken by nationals of some forty countries in both hemispheres, with cultures as varied as Peru and the Philippines, Brazil and the Azores. German is claimed not only by Germans, Austrians, and Swiss, but also by many inhabitants of Pennsylvania and South Australia. Teachers of foreign languages must demonstrate much more awareness of the importance of the languages they teach as vehicles for communication and comprehension beyond their countries of origin and increase their knowledge of the many areas where these languages are indispensable for everyday communication. Extending cultural and linguistic discussion to areas other than the country of origin of the language being studied provides opportunities for interesting cross-cultural analysis, as students discover that even an alien language may be absorbed by a living culture and, while subtly changing, become a channel for other aspirations and values.

A cross-cultural study within a department is also important where there are a number of *variants within the majority culture*, the representatives of which speak different varieties of the language; these variants must be accorded due attention and respect. Where representatives of these cultural and linguistic variants are present in foreign-language classes, they can make a valuable contribution to the students' recognition and acceptance of the diversity of cultural attitudes and forms of action. (Should there be many such students their special needs may warrant the establishment of special classes where they can acquire professionally useful proficiency in the standard form of the language.) Communities in the local or neighboring areas who speak the language being learned, or any of its varieties, provide students with many opportunities for closer acquaintance and understanding of culturally different attitudes and the rationale for differing value systems. Students should participate in activities within the community, make friends with members of the community, and help the community in its relations with majority language speakers, agencies, and institutions. Often they can render a valuable service to such a community by assisting in the collection of historical material, folklore, and samples of speech of the different generations.

Any study of another culture forces a reconsideration and a deeper understanding of one's own. Familiarizing students with another culture should not be proselytizing. Students are not being asked to surrender or lose confidence in their own culturally related ways of thinking and valuing. Instead, they begin to bring these to a level of conscious awareness and examine them, as they may never have done before, in relation to those of others. The study of another culture thus becomes a liberating experience, in that students are encouraged to develop tolerance of other viewpoints and other forms of behavior, while understanding better those of their own society or cultural group. This is an essential experience if young people are not to feel rootless and adrift in a rapidly changing society and a more and more intrusive world.

Of itself, foreign-language study does not lead to appreciation of the values and viewpoints of people of other cultures, nor does talking about cultural differences. The cultural values of our students have not been consciously acquired and confrontation with other values can cause culture shock: Different ways and viewpoints may seem "wrong," or "unethical," or "impolite." This emotional reaction to people of other cultures may be exacerbated by textbook material that, often unintentionally, presents stereotypes and caricatures of persons from the other culture. Simplistic interpretations of the ways of thinking, the values, and the behavior of speakers of the language are frequently found in dialogues that students memorize and act out, and these, because they appear amusingly quaint and outdated, may be recalled much longer than the learned dissertations of the instructor. Other textbooks give such an unsullied picture of the other culture that students find it unbelievable, or the material is so chauvinistic that they feel their own culture is being downgraded.

Many of these unproductive reactions may be overcome, if the investigation of cultural similarities and differences is a cooperative effort. Instructors bring materials and students seek out materials, in the main from contemporary sources; both instructors and students raise questions; members of the other culture are involved in the discussions, wherever feasible. In this way both cultures are investigated, probed, and analyzed, the experience becoming one of self-discovery, as well as penetration of the values and viewpoints of others.

Speaking in many tongues

Unfortunately, few foreign-language departments, as yet, give future instructors sufficient *in-depth training for cross-cultural studies.* This must be remedied. Instructors also need guidance in identifying sources of useful materials and in devising interesting ways of using these materials effectively in class.[16] For some languages, professional journals are already available to keep teachers informed about aspects of the culture,[17] and much documentation can be obtained from agencies in countries where the language is spoken, or through cultural representatives. More culturally oriented materials should be made available on audio- and videocassettes and discs. Finally, nothing replaces personal contact for cross-cultural understanding. Teachers need it. Students need it. Teacher exchanges and student home-visits in the country of the target culture must be facilitated, until they are considered an integral part of any language-teaching or language-learning experience.[18]

Understanding the process of communication

We frequently talk about the importance of understanding how people communicate, how they encode meanings and convey messages, and of the dangerous lack of communication and frequent misinterpretations that mar personal, community, and international relations. Foreign-language teachers should be able to design courses that illuminate the process of communication. This important element of a liberal education need not be left to the linguistics department, which usually approaches language from an abstract point of view.

Teaching the grammar and lexicon of another language, particularly when the learning is by rote, does not ensure that students gain an understanding of *how meanings are expressed and how language functions in social situations.* Blanket application of the dogma that only the foreign language should be heard in the classroom eliminates de facto many opportunities, particularly at the early stages, to broaden students' understanding of the nature of language and the nature of communication. Consequently, we profess to be interested in doing what is in practice impossible until a considerable amount of language has been learned. Foreign-language teachers should broaden their vision and become involved in courses, or sections of courses, devoted to the phenomenon of language as such. Sometimes, this will mean collaboration with other departments, for example, English, Speech, Communications, Music, Psychology, Computer Science – those that deal with communication of messages through systems of symbols.

So many aspects of communication can be conveyed through the study of another language. Students learn how to listen to what is really being said and how to express meanings with carefully chosen

176

words. They become conscious of the sociolinguistic aspects of language use: the levels of language that are appropriate in different circumstances and in different relationships, the structures and vocabulary that encode familiar and formal exchanges, and the way language varieties enrich a national tongue. They become conscious of kinesics or body language, that is, the way we convey meaning and attitude through facial and body movements, gestures, and eye contact. These they can study through film and observe in contacts with native speakers.[19] They begin to understand, as they have not done in their native tongue, the importance of syntax and the elusive nature of semantics, as well as the differences in meaning conveyed by slight differences in sound, pitch, and rise and fall of the voice. They become conscious of the rules of conversational interchange, the ways meaning is negotiated, and how pauses, filled and unfilled, enable us to preempt or yield control of discussion.

Conversation classes at the advanced level are among the most neglected of courses. Although stimulating active communication in a language in which the students feel insecure is a most difficult task, this type of course is frequently assigned to an inexperienced and untrained native speaker, who either talks too much ("they need listening practice, don't they?"), or sits and listens to lengthy lectures prepared in advance by individual students, while the rest of the group think of other things. *Conversation should be part of a larger activity.* Students can converse only when they have something to say to each other and to the instructor.

For the many students who want to learn to communicate freely in the language, we need living language classes at the advanced level, offered at several levels of competence, where students become involved together in purposeful activity. They may read contemporary novels, watch films, read about subjects of current interest, engage in some project together, for example, preparing a play, making a film based on college life, or helping a nearby community that speaks the language. Conversation will flow, without embarrassment or inhibitions, when there is a controversial subject to discuss or an activity to organize. And students will come back for more. With exciting, imaginative teaching, we will find many students anxious to accept what we have to offer.[20] Through communicating, they will learn much about the process of communication.

Language for specific purposes or career preparation

An increasing number of foreign-language departments have been experimenting with the provision of language-related training that will be useful to students in their chosen careers. The earliest of these

177

efforts were the now familiar courses in reading for science and technology, or reading for humanities research. A few universities offer courses at a level of professional competence in interpreting and translating. Some community colleges have provided courses in Spanish for inner city police officers and firefighters. Serious efforts have been made in various places to provide courses in business methods or secretarial skills, often with case studies of business situations and even summer internships abroad. Much remains to be done in developing this area.[21]

Any course of language for specific purposes or for career preparation should be preceded by a solid basic course that introduces students to the four skills of listening, speaking, reading, and writing, with coverage of the major points of the grammar, the acquisition of a vocabulary for general use, and some knowledge of the culture. *After such a basic course, options may be offered that prepare students to use the language in specific work situations.* More and more materials are being published with the needs of specific careers in mind, but much more research is needed into realistic requirements for courses of this type.

Before adopting a career-oriented option, a foreign-language department should study the potential clientele within the university, identifying their career aspirations, in order to create options that provide for their specific needs. Since needs will inevitably vary from university to university, these types of courses are not necessarily transferable. Contact must be made with other departments, to ensure that the courses offered complement usefully what is available elsewhere in the university. The students will then acquire a coherent, rather than a hit-or-miss, preparation for work in a particular area.

Departments wishing to provide courses that are oriented toward specific careers will need to familiarize themselves with *the actual foreign-language needs of these careers* – business, law, the health professions, social work, international management, travel services, and so on. The differences are not only in vocabulary. Some careers require considerable aural-oral ability, but not writing; others require ability to read, but not to comprehend aurally. The best example of in-depth preparation for instituting an occupation-oriented approach is the research of the Group of Experts advising the Council of Europe on the institution of a unit-credit system for adult learners. In preparing for this program, researchers analyzed the linguistic needs of adults in forty-four occupational categories. The actual activities in which persons engaged in specific occupations would need to use a second language were studied, and estimates were made of the degree of proficiency they would require in specific skill areas.[22] If occupation-specific courses are to be taught with any degree of seriousness, professional organizations will need to carry out or commission job analysis studies of this type, as a guide to course developers, materials writers, and instructors.

Furthermore, instructors themselves should have, or will have to develop, some familiarity with the work situations in which the language is to be used. Realistic activities can then be proposed for *role playing and simulation games* to add authenticity to the material being learned. Finally, teachers should not use the bait of future jobs to encourage students to continue the study of foreign languages, unless they know that such jobs are available and that the expertise they are communicating will be recognized as an asset by the employers in these occupations.

Language as the key to humanistic studies

Historically, foreign-language study entered the universities, and later the schools, as a poor cousin not entitled to the respect accorded the study of the classics. After all, millions of uneducated people spoke modern languages. It was generally held that the only educational value they could possibly have was as a key to the works of great writers and philosophers, whose contributions to thought could not be fully appreciated by anyone who could not read the language in which they wrote. The resulting overemphasis on literary studies, particularly literary criticism, has tended to obscure *the genuinely educational value of intimate contact with the writers and thinkers of any language.*

As the world becomes more technologically oriented and control of life seems to pass out of the hands of the individual, it becomes increasingly urgent to educate thoughtful, intellectually disciplined citizens who can recognize when the quality of life is being eroded and who consider problems and issues from a viewpoint that transcends the present. Foreign-language study must reassert its role in developing educated individuals who can examine issues, discuss viewpoints, and enjoy the aesthetic stimulation of a good book, play, or poem.

There will always be a place for the foreign-language course that excites discussion and debate through bringing before students well-written literature and well-developed ideas. Advanced language courses should be developed in which students whose careers will be in technology, science, business, law, or medicine can think through ideas and relate personal experience to the wider experience of persons in other cultures as seen through their aesthetic products. Courses of this nature take literature in its broadest sense: A proverb, a children's rhyme, or a peasant's tale provides food for thought as rich as a classical play or a modern film. It is *the vividness of pursuing ideas*

179

in a lively context that makes the experience of lasting educational value. Discussing, imagining, acting out, and creating are the techniques for such classes. Students heavily loaded with technological, mathematical, and scientific studies appreciate the opportunity to grapple with perennial human issues in a free exchange of ideas. Preparation for a future career in literary research has its place in courses for specialists. Humane studies, on the other hand, are for all and must be accessible to all.

Where does the revolution begin?

The present requires that departments reexamine their foreign-language programs in relation to the types of educational needs their students are experiencing. *We cannot rely on the models of the past.* Some of the approaches discussed here may be appropriate in a particular situation, or even others not discussed; the final decision must be based on research. The department must study the student population (or populations, since no student body is homogeneous): their ages, their career orientations, their daily preoccupations, and the way in which study of another language can meet their felt needs or expressed desires.

A questionnaire assessing students' perceived needs is a beginning. This must be supplemented by teacher observation and attentive listening to students and community. Next, experimental courses will be proposed. Student response to these should be studied to see how they can be further developed or adapted. As demand increases, additional courses of a different orientation or degree of intensity will be added, so that students may discover opportunities within the language program to study what they would like in the way they would like, instead of being forced into one mold determined by the department's, or the individual instructor's, preconceptions of how language learning should take place. Only with thoughtful attention to flexible course development, and options that meet the needs and interests of many different students, will foreign-language departments be ready to meet present-day demands in ways that will restore their confidence in their educational purpose.

Who will teach these courses?

The future of foreign-language departments will be largely determined by the degree to which they are able to adapt their programs to changing demands and assume new roles within the university. In the years to come, departments will be required to take much more

180

seriously the teaching of undergraduates and the provision of programs that interest and attract students other than majors or concentrators. *Yet the teaching program of a department can be only as innovative and forward looking as the attitude of its faculty members will allow.* Some academics will be able to recycle themselves through study of new areas that interest them. The major responsibility for providing the kinds of courses a new approach requires will, however, inevitably fall on young instructors now preparing to enter the profession.

Some departments have excellent training programs for their graduate student assistants, or teaching fellows, which lead them to reflect on curricular innovation and adaptation.[23] Others provide little or no preparation for teaching and see no need for discussion of alternative programs. If we are to prosper in the future, we must rescue foreign-language departments from the inertia that results from shortsightedness or lack of interest in change. *The preparation of the faculty of the future must be taken much more seriously*, so that there will be available a supply of candidates well prepared, not only in the language, the literature, and the foreign culture, but also in designing and teaching interesting and intellectually challenging courses for all types of students. If there is no one already on the faculty with the imagination and expertise to prepare such candidates, someone must be brought in. The person who will develop the new program must be appointed at a sufficiently high rank to have the freedom and authority to redesign and experiment, so that future teachers may not only learn about what can be done but also be involved in its execution.

In 1971, I called for the recognition of "highly qualified, respected, imaginative, academically rewarded language specialists" in our foreign-language departments "who know how to design materials,...write materials, and...integrate language use with intellectually stimulating, thought-provoking, exciting activity"; in other words, specialists with informed knowledge of a number of areas, but particularly of contemporary language, culture, and language learning. "Such a group," I said, "could be subversive, promoting a quiet revolution in our inner circles."[24] A decade later, I say "the revolution is now." Foreign-language departments, if they are to survive and flourish, can wait no longer to reexamine their programs in the light of today's needs and the interests and aspirations of today's students.

Let's work it out

1 Study the course listings for your university. Which departments offer courses that seem to indicate the presence of faculty who

have interests in common with your language department? Design a course of study that would combine language with specific courses you have noted. How would you go about setting up an interdisciplinary program with the members of this other department?

2 Design a language course that requires students to go into a nearby community where the language is spoken to perform specific tasks or collect certain information. Be precise about what you would expect. What would you need to do before launching such a course?

3 You are asked to teach a communication-oriented course that prepares students for a home-stay exchange program. Your students will need to be familiar with pragmatic functions in the language you teach (that is, acceptable uses of language in social interaction). How would you incorporate this aspect of communication into the course?

4 How would you go about choosing the linguistic content for a course for social workers in the inner city? How would you evaluate the effectiveness of the course?

5 Discuss ways of presenting contemporary literature in the language you teach to students specializing in the sciences.

13 Conservation and innovation: foreign languages in two-year undergraduate institutions

In "Precaution," Robert Frost has said:

I never dared be radical when young
For fear it would make me conservative when old.[1]

At first reading I found this rather startling, but on reflection it linked in my mind with a statement of Günther Grass: "I think there are many realities, and all these realities can exist at the same time."[2] Radicals and conservatives converge in believing that they have *the* answer, that there is one right approach to a question, whereas foreign-language teachers, to be effective in different types of institutions, must accept the reality of *many* answers, to be selected according to the diversity of need and circumstance. I am not speaking here of conservatism or radicalism, but of the interplay in any evolving situation between conservation and innovation.

Conservation is not merely clinging blindly to the old and established because it is the known and secure. Conservation means recognizing that something has value and working actively for its survival. For anything to survive, it must be able to respond to new circumstance and new demands. Innovation, then, is essential to conservation, if what we believe to be of value is not to become a mere museum piece, retained for reasons of prestige although no longer serving a useful purpose in its changed setting.

What do we, as foreign-language teachers, wish to conserve? As educators, we wish to conserve for all liberally educated students the opportunity to get outside their own language, to get outside the thought molds of their native culture, to get outside their own value systems, if only momentarily, in order to see their own ways of thinking and expressing themselves, their own conceptions of the normal and the obvious, their own responses to situations, ideas, and people from a different perspective. This is something we feel to be worth conserving in the education of the individual, because it develops a flexibility of thinking, which is becoming more and more essential for all, as we are challenged daily by the continually evolving

Revised version of an article originally published in W.M. Rivers, L.H. Allen, et al., *Changing Patterns in Foreign Language Programs* (Rowley, Mass.: Newbury House, 1972), as "Conservation and Innovation."

ideas, values, and demands of a fast-changing society.[3] Broadening our perspective from individual to societal needs, and bringing its implications nearer home, we may through this effect on individuals contribute to the breaking down of that "provincialism and parochialism which threaten a nation which feels psychologically isolated from its neighbors,"[4] and which as a result may tend to turn in on itself, instead of facing boldly the challenge of new concepts and new relationships.

Conservation, then, refers to the values of foreign-language study, and innovation, to their realization in a new setting. Foreign-language teachers in two-year undergraduate institutions, such as junior and community colleges, are in the midst of this new opportunity.

A new look at the curriculum

If students of today with their yearning to roam, physically and spiritually, beyond national boundaries, and their questioning of traditional values, do not enjoy learning a foreign language, then (to parallel Shakespeare):

> The fault, dear [friends], is not in our [subject],
> But in ourselves that we are underlings.[5]

An unadulterated diet of frankly preliminary learning for persons who will never reach the consummatory stage is indigestible and unpalatable; yet this is what many of our students are served, and served exclusively. In two-year undergraduate institutions, the type of elementary course that is offered is often the one considered most suitable for students intending to transfer to a senior institution, whereas most students in these programs have no intention of transferring. Even when they do transfer, they rarely do so to become foreign-language majors or concentrators. (A survey conducted in Illinois in 1971 showed that of the 5,619 students in foreign-language programs in two-year institutions only 43, *or well below 1 percent*, could be considered foreign-language majors.[6]) We talk glibly about our objectives and our goals but, in the step-by-step program for foreign-language mastery that we offer, these goals are only dimly perceived by students as attainable, even after several arduous semesters of tedious grind. Student motivation, whose apparent lack we often deplore, is stimulated and channeled, not by the setting out of reasonable and relevant objectives that salve the instructor's conscience, but by *student perception of the attainment and attainability of these objectives.*[7]

184

It is here that two-year institutions can, and should, lead the way. A two-year college is not an elitist institution, drawing on the top 20 percent of the high school graduating class. It is not an established institution, sunk deep in ivy and centuries of habit. It is a new concept with a new clientele, and it should be pulsating with new life. As foreign-language teachers, we may consider that this new clientele needs the age-old experience of language learning as much as, and perhaps more than, the traditional undergraduate population. We will wish to conserve the essence of this experience in these new institutions. This does not mean that we have to, or can necessarily, conserve the forms, the institutionalized modes, of initiating students into this experience. Instructors in two-year institutions must innovate: They must *experiment in renewing the forms, while retaining the essence.* Content, organization of learning experiences, modality of learning, pace, and gauging of progress should all be reexamined in order to make accessible to all kinds of students the unique educational experience of encounter with another way of thought and expression.

Such innovation requires understanding, imagination, and courage:

— *understanding* (perceptiveness): to see what the student needs, not in a utilitarian sense, but in a human sense;
— *imagination*: thinking beyond the confines of past and present experience; assessing, in relation to the needs of the students, possibilities that have never been tried;
— *courage*: to know the students as they are, to recognize what must be provided for them, and to accept them as full partners in their own educational experience; courage to do what has not been done before and is not being done elsewhere; courage to accept the mistakes one has made and learn from them; courage to withstand the criticism of others who remain safely on well-trodden paths.

The two-year undergraduate institutions are, for the most part, young. Let them also be adventurous. Imagination and courage come more easily to the young.

Foreign-language teachers in two-year institutions often feel very isolated. It is essential that they come together and share freely, allowing imagination and insight to flow from one to the other, in order to develop new patterns and new attitudes appropriate to new situations. What matter if we are called dreamers! All great innovators have been dreamers. We need the courage to set down our convictions, to work them through realistically, and to return to our institutions ready to insist on our right to experiment rationally, with the equanimity to face criticism, indifference, and discouragement as we try to implement our ideas. Of course, we will make mistakes. Of course, some of our ideas will not work, but all progress comes through experimentation. Each failure provides as much information as an experience of success when we function as a sharing, mutually supportive community.

Practical suggestions

Here I would like to present several concepts of curriculum that are worth careful consideration in the context of two-year undergraduate situations: continuing and terminal courses; the hors d'oeuvre or two-stage approach; diversification of content; and variation in pacing.

Continuing and terminal courses

With a diverse student population we must consider carefully the following questions: Who is going where? and What does the student want and need?

Traditional foreign-language courses at college level have been *continuing courses,* in the sense that they have been designed with the mastery required of the future major or concentrator in mind. Setting the foundation with care, building on it methodically and soberly, instructors have moved steadily toward the objective of a complete and fully equipped edifice. At any stage on the way the edifice is incomplete, unfunctional, only minimally usable in makeshift fashion. If construction ceases at an early stage, the embryonic edifice deteriorates and finally crumbles to dust. So it is with a continuing course: Those who go on to the stage of mastery are well equipped, solidly grounded, able to function in the language; those who drop out after the foundations have been laid soon forget, finding no use for the small accumulation of knowledge and skill they acquired so laboriously.

There is, and always will be, a place for the continuing course for those who want and need it. We have many ideas for the design and operation of such courses. But for those other students who stay with us a short while, who come to see what we have to offer as our contribution to a liberal education, can we not do better for them?

Here the concept of *the terminal course* can help us. A terminal course sets a goal related to the interests and needs of the students in that course and achieves that goal, no matter how long or short the course may be. The goals vary. Some will take longer to achieve than others, but this is known to and accepted by the students who undertake the course. Are the students to remain with us only one semester? Then, instead of deploring this fact and force-feeding them the usual introductory diet, we design a course that will give them a complete experience during that semester. (Here, the hors d'oeuvre approach, discussed in the next section, can be helpful.) Are the students likely to remain for four semesters? Then we design a course in which they will have acquired something they can perceive as an achievement in those four semesters. Perhaps they will be able to understand films and broadcasts or take part in general conversation at an uncomplicated level. Maybe they will have acquired the ability to read magazines and newspapers, or articles in a specialized field, but can do no more orally than find their way from one place to another. At least they will not go away with only preliminary learning for more advanced courses they will never take.

The two-stage approach

Once the distinction between continuing and terminal courses is accepted, all our planning is affected. We can then consider the advantages of a terminal-type first-semester course (Stage One), before students commit themselves to the arduous task of achieving functional control of the language at Stage Two. This Stage One course will allow some to retire gracefully from the field with an important increase in knowledge and experience that will enable them to decide whether foreign-language study interests them. The same course will motivate others to continue with enthusiasm to Stage Two because new perspectives have opened up to them that they are anxious to explore. The Stage One course would be a complete entity in itself, so that all who passed through it would have gained something of educational and humanistic value, even if they never studied a foreign language again. The Stage Two course, on the other hand, would lay the foundations for further language study for students who realized what this would involve and were genuinely interested in such study.[8]

I shall call the terminal one-semester course the *Hors d'Oeuvre course*, knowing full well that this very title will cause some to dismiss it as a frivolity that cannot be taken seriously. Such an attitude springs from a rather widespread, often subconscious, feeling that really educative activities cannot possibly be, or at least ought not to be, enjoyable. This being an attitude we should combat, let us keep the term for the present. Dictionaries sometimes translate or explain the word *hors d'oeuvre* as "little appetizers," their function being to arouse our appetite for more substantial food.

One of our problems in the foreign-language field is the early dropout rate, which is uncomfortably high after one or two semesters in institutions where foreign-language study is purely elective. With the conventional program, what do these dropouts gain in an educational sense after one semester? With the two-stage approach, the hors d'oeuvre first-semester course would be designed to give each student insight into the nature of the subject, some practical experience of the language and the culture of the speakers of that language, and a feeling for the fundamental differences between languages. It would be *an interesting course in itself, exciting some to continue, illuminating all on the nature of the discipline*, and making a valuable, if small, contribution to the educational experience of each student. As an approach it is worth serious consideration.

Why should our foreign-language menu be stodgy and unattractive? Is there any serious reason why students should not thoroughly enjoy their introduction to a language, so that they anticipate their next course with genuine pleasure? We all know that motivation is necessary to carry students through the inevitably solid, and sometimes tedious, learning necessary for acquiring any lasting control of a language. If the hors d'oeuvre course arouses in some a real desire to learn the language more fully, it will have made an important contribution to the program. Furthermore, if those who go no further retain in later life favorable attitudes toward the whole language-learning enterprise, this in itself will yield dividends in a gradually improving community attitude toward the foreign-language program at the local two-year institution and elsewhere.

In detail, the Stage One course would have four facets:

First, an introduction to language itself through a specific foreign language: gearing our study to the way language operations express meanings and the many ways meanings may be encoded; the way our language expresses how we look at things and the way another language expresses another people's way of looking at things. This study would be frankly contrastive.

Second, an introduction to another people through their language: the way another people thinks, feels, values, and acts in contradistinction to our own preoccupations, attitudes, and reactions. This segment would be illustrated with much contemporary material, not only photos, magazines, and artifacts but also films, discs, and videotapes. There would be discussion of similarities and differences and ways of coping with new situations.

Third, an experience of being another people: communicating as they do, acting as they do, relating as they do. Here our students both learn and live the language. Language knowledge acquired is immediately acted out. Rules internalized become channels of communication. Practice in production is immediately incorporated into some form of interaction.

188

Fourth, an experience of communicating with another people: speaking with them where possible, writing to them, working and playing with them where a neighboring community makes this possible, sharing with them in joint projects.

Methodologically we would aim at student involvement in planning, in group research and interaction, in interdisciplinary exploration, and in human contacts in nearby communities or through correspondence.

Obviously the development of such a radically different approach will involve carefully planning and preparing materials, with perhaps pilot projects to work out the best way to proceed. The situation at the present time requires some intensive original thinking and here is a good place to begin.

Stage Two, beginning in the second semester, will be more akin to the language-learning situation to which we are accustomed. We would, however, now have a better-motivated and a better-prepared group, from the point of view of both linguistic awareness and cultural comprehension, a group that had chosen to study the language with the acknowledged purpose of seeking a higher degree of mastery. These students would have acquired favorable attitudes, which would enable them to enjoy the disciplined language study awaiting them.

Student choice

Beyond the two-stage introductory course, our objective should be a *diversified offering*. We are continually being told this is the age of pluralism. What people have wanted to see as a monolithic society has proved on closer examination to be a great diversity of cultures, subcultures, groups, subgroups, and individuals – all with their own goals, aspirations, and interests. The foreign-language programs of the present and the future must reflect this diversity.

In the foreign-language field we are very fortunate: Language is a vehicle of expression, not an end in itself. A multiplicity of possibilities therefore opens before us. Language that is being used purposefully will be learned. There are, then, a great number of possible contents and activities from which to choose. Suitable approaches and pace of learning can be as varied as the personalities and temperaments of our students. Language can be learned through conversation; through reading; through singing; through drama; through carrying out tasks; through listening to radio; through watching films or television; through writing or translation; by library research; by independent study; in group activities, social activities, or community action; with the help of computers, or through a home-stay period in the country where the language is spoken. A diversity of possible courses awaits the attention of those who, with imagination, energy, and confidence, are willing to experiment with new structures and new content. Where better to begin than in nontraditional undergraduate institutions like the junior and community colleges, where a spirit of innovation manifests itself in the very fact of their existence?

Let's discuss

1 Which aspects of the traditional undergraduate foreign-language program would you wish to conserve? Which aspects seem to you outdated? Why?
2 Why do students choose to study in two-year undergraduate institutions? Identify four different types of students and their motivation in this choice. What kind of foreign-language program would best suit the needs of each of these groups? Can these needs be reconciled in one course? If so, how? (You may wish to refer back to chapters 11 and 12.)
3 Design a syllabus for a hors d'oeuvre course in the language you teach. In which ways would you need to adapt it to make it useful also for an extension, continuing education, or evening class for adult working students?
4 Is it possible to design a terminal course so that students who wish to continue their study to a more advanced level will not be short-changed? (You may draw some ideas from Chapter 5 of Rivers (1983), "Individualized Instruction and Cooperative Learning: Some Theoretical Considerations.")

14 Students, teachers, and the future

"Teachers teach as they were taught," we are told. How are they being taught? Some schools of education have renounced the task of training teachers altogether, declaring that one cannot teach people to teach. "They either have it or they don't," they maintain. "In any case, they will muddle through to an eventual style of their own." In our society we also accept this approach for politicians, but not for doctors, engineers, or plumbers. Surely the education of future generations of citizens for a productive life in this very complex world is a professional activity that warrants a careful apprenticeship or period of preparation? *But what kind of preparation?* If we expect young teachers later to innovate, experiment, and initiate new programs appropriate to the situations in which they teach, then preparatory programs should be innovative and provide opportunities for identifying problems, studying possible solutions in the light of theoretical knowledge and the experience of others, and producing materials and devising techniques to implement these solutions. Because teachers tend to teach as they were taught, we must also attack the problem of the preconceptions and prejudices young teachers bring from their own experiences of language learning in high school or undergraduate studies. We must work for the apprehension of modern conceptions of the task, as well as the acquisition of modern techniques.

In the everyday hurly-burly of the school, it is easy to become time bound. Yet the future is pressing in on us. If the future is purchased by the present, as Samuel Johnson maintained,[1] our best preparation for it is to recognize the directions of change in our present situation, so that adjustment and adaptation become natural, nonthreatening processes. Knowing that change, sometimes continuous and imperceptible, at other times sudden and jolting, will be a way of life for us all in any educational enterprise, we must ensure that those joining our profession are prepared mentally and temperamentally to comprehend and accept new purposes while retaining the essence of our

Revised version of an article originally published in *Foreign Language Annals* 8 (1975), 22-32.

discipline. As a first step, let us look at certain changing relations and changing directions in the classroom teaching of foreign languages that have become evident in recent years.

Changing relations

Teacher-student relations are changing from the traditional teacher-directed situation to one of teacher-student interaction with shared decision-making. Foreign-language teachers, along with colleagues in other fields, must identify what each student needs and wants; as educators they must maintain a balance of these two if the student is to be motivated to learn. The emphasis must be on attention to individuals, sensitivity to their needs and interests, and closer rapport between teacher and students in a student-centered program and in cooperative teacher-student planning of learning experiences.

School and community are no longer separate entities, with the student moving out of one and into the other. The school must go out into the community, as part of the community, to learn from the community and serve community needs; conversely, the community impinges on the curriculum and activities of the school. Foreign-language teachers must know and use their community and design foreign-language programs that reflect the preoccupations and interests of the community. This becomes particularly important when there are in the area communities in which the languages being taught are spoken.

Foreign-language programs and other subject areas can no longer operate in the same institution in hermetic juxtaposition. For a meaningful educational experience all aspects of the curriculum must interrelate. Foreign-language teachers must consider what they can gain from and bring to an integrated curriculum. Sometimes their contribution may be in developing an auxiliary skill to widen the student's perspective in other areas. Certainly it will mean looking beyond their traditional preoccupation with belles-lettres to involvement with the ways of thinking and acting of people who speak the language, their history, their environment, their community structures, their influence beyond their own shores, and their ways of interacting politically, commercially, economically, and artistically with other peoples. Not all foreign-language teachers are prepared professionally or emotionally to move in this direction at present. Those being trained to become foreign-language teachers should receive special preparation in this area.

Changing directions

1. The educational emphasis is moving *from the mechanistic to the humanistic*. Foreign-language teaching is no longer seen as the inculcating of certain skills, but as part of the formative education of human beings, an experience that broadens the way individuals view life, the world, and the people they encounter. To survive in this changing atmosphere, foreign-language teaching must show that it has something to contribute to the quality of life. At present, foreign-language teachers talk about this need, but only a few have been able to develop programs that achieve this effect. More experimentation is needed with the kinds of learning materials and the types of learning environments that will make such an outcome possible and probable.

2. Foreign-language teaching is moving *from an elitist to a comprehensive view of its task*. As a profession we must consider much more seriously what the study of a foreign language can contribute to the education of all students, with their widely diverse abilities, interests, and modes of learning. We must give serious considerations to ways of presenting languages so that all kinds of students can learn them efficiently and pleasurably.

3. Interest in languages is now turning increasingly *from the languages of faraway places to languages at home* – the languages of local areas and minority concentrations, or nearby countries. This trend is demonstrated not only in bilingual programs but also in moves to preserve the ethnic heritage of immigrant groups. For instance, in the United States, there is much interest in variants of the standard languages, which are in use in countries sharing borders or which have special meaning for students because these are the areas from which their ancestors came to a new country. Here we think of the Spanish of the Americas, of Puerto Rico, and the Southwest of the United States; the French of Louisiana, Quebec, Haiti, and certain countries of Africa where French is still a lingua franca; the German of Austria, Switzerland, or Pennsylvania; the Portuguese of Brazil and the Atlantic islands; and the Italian dialects spoken by immigrant communities. Teachers must be prepared to readjust the perspective of their teaching accordingly, taking their students into local and neighboring communities, where this is feasible, and bringing representatives of these groups into the schools.

4. The profession is moving rapidly *from orthodoxy to heterodoxy*. With this in mind, teachers must be on their guard against any tendency to impose a monolithic approach, no matter how estimable, as the surefire solution to problems in all situations. In methodology

this means a clear preference for eclecticism: selecting the approach, the content and materials, the organizational pattern, the techniques, and the pacing to meet the needs of particular individuals in a specific situation. Teachers and students should be encouraged to think through the implications of each situation as it arises and to develop their programs to meet the perceived purposes of their encounter. In this way the exhilaration of the personal innovative project will be more widely generalized, and more students and teachers will profit from at least some exciting classes.

5. Innovation in language teaching is becoming a movement *from the base to the apex*. Teachers are less anxious to listen to "experts" and are becoming more willing to learn from other teachers. As a profession we should encourage classroom teachers to try out their own ideas and provide them with frequent opportunities to share their successful experiences with others.

The state of the field from the point of view of the classroom teacher

To the ordinary classroom teacher the field appears confusing, demanding, and threatening.

Confusing. The classroom teacher often feels like a pawn in a game played for professional advancement through leadership in "innovation" by "experts" with little or no experience of the realities of today's classrooms. Teachers feel pressured into new approaches (which, for the experienced teacher, are often cyclical), only to be left stranded, and vilified for their insufficiencies, when the tide turns. Teachers who were coaxed or coerced into audiolingual teaching were then told it was a failure, despite clear evidence of successful learning in many of their classes and the periodic revivals of "new" methods that look very much like it. These teachers also saw much evidence of successful learning in their pre-audiolingual classes and this is likely to continue, since success in the classroom emanates much more from empathy between teacher and students than from choice of methodology. Understandably, they are in no mood to respond to pressures to switch and change from year to year without strong justification. The shocks of accelerating changes in society, in the curriculum, and in student-teacher relations are exacerbated by constant demands for experimentation before the last, or next-to-last, recommendation has been consolidated or seriously evaluated. For long-term improvement, we need to encourage absorption of the best of what has been tried into the fabric of ongoing practice, rather than forcing on teachers continual reversals and new beginnings.

For any realistic evolution, *teachers themselves must be involved in determining new directions for the profession.* Instead of rapidly conceived and prematurely acclaimed "successes" in new approaches, we need carefully planned pilot experimentation in which local teachers and students are active participants at all stages, widespread inservice discussion and training, appropriate restructuring based on the experience of many, and considered longitudinal evaluation of effectiveness in specifically stated contexts, before recommending the adoption or discarding of any set of techniques or materials.

At the moment there appear to be in the profession a number of thrusts that are not necessarily convergent. As primary objectives we find emphasis on communicative and pragmatic competence; cross-cultural understanding; development of reading skill; integration of foreign languages in humanities and international studies programs; learning languages for career utility; and fostering listening comprehension through authentic materials (interviews, films, radio, TV, and plays). We hear strong advocacy of behavioral objectives and the systems approach; individualization of instruction; peer teaching and group work; the natural approach, the cognitive approach, the Silent Way, Suggestopaedia, Counseling-Learning; minicourses, intensive courses, and total immersion programs; home-stay exchanges; the long sequence and the terminal course; computer-assisted instruction; the use of videocassettes and videodiscs; and learning through community involvement – all laudable in themselves but as varied as a smorgasbord. Which path is the classroom teacher to follow?[2]

Demanding. As well as being expected to rethink their philosophies and reorient their techniques at intervals of five years or less, teachers are the recipients of a plethora of recommendations that require the development of new materials and the adaptation of old ones. To perform these tasks effectively, the teacher must have near-native fluency and accuracy, the technical training of a textbook writer or materials developer, excellent organizing ability, a superlative memory, a flair for drama, knowledge of the linguistic requirements of a number of occupations, and the temperament and capacity to provide answers and design activities for all kinds of levels, a variety of student abilities, and new approaches to presentation at the same time. Moreover, our teachers have no assurance that extra time will be provided for them to do all that is expected of them professionally, or that they will be given the opportunity to acquire the specialized training they will need to do it efficiently.

Threatening. The superior teacher can meet these demands, given sufficient physical stamina and resourcefulness, a cheerful disposition, teaching aides, and some money for acquiring supplementary materials and technological support. The average or less-skilled teacher finds all this impossible. The latter may try, with ineffectual results and much discouragement, or may prefer to take refuge in a closed-door, traditionally textbook-dominated classroom.

For many teachers, then, there is a *continuing need for inservice workshops, institutes, and training sessions* for the maintenance and development of language skills, and for practical experience in materials development and pedagogical techniques, to enable them to implement a variety of approaches and courses for the types of students in their groups. Such training sessions should be planned and taught by experienced and successful teachers, who can demonstrate what they are discussing and guide in the practice of techniques and the production of materials of immediate use in the participants' own classes. In other words, we need much more teacher-to-teacher exchange of ideas and experience.

Primacy in any planning should be given to the continuing development and consequent emotional serenity of the classroom teacher, who will remain the key figure in any lasting advance by the profession.

Future demands on the classroom teacher in view of changing relations and directions

An unpredictable future will require of our teachers first and foremost flexibility – the ability to work out many things for which they were never trained.

Flexibility in their attitude to the students and the curriculum. The teacher can no longer be the expert passing down to the disciple what he or she has learned. New knowledge is accumulating and multiplying too fast for this approach to continue. The teacher must cooperate with all types of students in optimizing their opportunities for learning and self-teaching in developing new content and appropriate activities for acquiring really usable language, and in meeting community needs and interdisciplinary demands.

Flexibility in working patterns. Teachers will be expected to break up the more easily controlled lecture-practice class hour to allow for a variety of groupings, scheduling patterns, and differentiated teaching approaches, according to specific objectives and student needs.

Flexibility in approach and methodology. Teachers will need to be able not only to select methods and techniques that suit the particular requirements of certain students in a given situation, but also to switch from techniques of one type to techniques of another as the situation changes. For this, they need a thorough grounding in methodology (how techniques relate to objectives) and in ways to apply in practice what they have learned so that they are freed from textbook domination. They must have knowledge that enables them to implement textbook recommendations and to supplement materials to make them more exciting, realistic, and current.

Flexibility in approach to student achievement. A plurality of student needs and objectives and diversification of content and activity will require a variety of ways of evaluating the appropriate level of achievement in specific cases and situations. Many teachers, traditionally trained and oriented, find a flexible viewpoint toward evaluation very difficult to achieve. Rigid demands imposed by some administrators make their position even more difficult. Teachers need help in providing the best they can for their students within the demands of the institution.

What steps can be taken to ensure development of a flexible, future-oriented profession?

Innovation at the undergraduate level

Development of an approach to teaching begins with the way we have been taught. Most future teachers spend a large part of their four years of undergraduate study, and perhaps a year or two of graduate study, in rigid, conventional, lecture-discussion classes for which they are examined in two- or three-hour regurgitation sessions at the end of the semester. At present, many instructors in elementary schools, high schools, and nontraditional undergraduate institutions are open to experimentation with content and presentation, but such innovation is still uncommon at the undergraduate level of foreign-language departments in senior institutions. It is here that the problem must be attacked – with proper training at some stage for those teaching undergraduates.[3]

Flexibility in undergraduate programs means willingness to broaden the curriculum to meet the needs of today and tomorrow, as well as a new approach to presentation, participation, and evaluation. The value of the undiluted lecture must be reassessed and opportunities provided for students to select topics, find out for themselves, take the lead, work in groups, and share in the development of their learning experience, bearing personal responsibility for their level of achievement. If such a radical change at the undergraduate and graduate level is to be achieved, the profession must be convinced of the

197

need for *thorough training of future teachers of undergraduates* not only in the advanced study and research of their chosen specialty and related interdisciplinary areas, but also in broader areas of general pedagogy (the not-so-simple practice of teaching) and second-language learning, ways of developing appreciation of and insight into another literature and culture, materials development, and the principles and techniques of evaluation.

Once the college classroom is open to innovation, diversification, variations of approach, new alliances, and the recognition of the validity of a variety of objectives, we may expect teacher trainees with a quite different outlook to begin appearing in teacher-training programs.

Careful selection of teachers

We may then begin to apply selection criteria to our teacher-training applicants that will screen out the rigid, authoritarian personality from the adaptable, outgoing, and community oriented. Not everyone who knows a foreign language well, or who has studied it conscientiously, is a suitable candidate for our foreign-language teaching corps. We need guidelines that will help us select the type of person our unpredictable and unconventional future demands.

Review of teacher-training programs

We must then reassess the adequacy of our present teacher-training programs. Some are excellent, and it is these exceptions that are reported in the journals and at professional meetings. We would do well, however, to face frankly some of the long-standing reasons why much foreign-language teacher training provides insufficient preparation for the real life of the schools.

Teacher training typically takes place in either the foreign-language department or in the college of education (more rarely in both, in which case it is often repetitious because of lack of coordination among the various courses). In neither case has the instructor necessarily received any specialized training for this task.

Teacher training has a low priority in faculty assignments in foreign-language departments and increasingly in colleges of education. Those who do train teachers often try to get out of it as soon as they can, or are caught in it for want of an acceptable "field of research."

In foreign-language departments, the teacher-training instructor often has not experienced high school (or elementary school) since leaving it as a student (apart, perhaps, from a six-week stint as a student teacher). Sometimes the instructor was educated in another country and has never experienced the local school either as student or teacher. Such instructors may or may not keep abreast of educational developments and needs in the schools; in any case, they may have more absorbing "intellectual" preoccupations (theoretical linguistics, the study of poetry, comparative literature), which provide the few vivid presentations of the semester. The rarer individual who has actually taught in the schools may be fighting to "rise above it" in the eyes of colleagues.

In colleges of education esteem for foreign-language teaching is often low. A part-time instructor is considered sufficient, or students are trained in classroom practice with students of other subjects for want of an expert in the area. Where qualified foreign-language instructors are available, they may or may not keep in touch with current trends in the schools, and they may or may not know the various languages their students are to teach and the problems peculiar to those languages.

As a profession *we must publicize the qualities and qualifications we expect of those who prepare teachers for the schools* of today and tomorrow. We must seek to recruit open-minded, perceptive persons who will grow as they teach, and we must take steps to see that the qualifications we expect are readily obtainable in responsible institutions and are respected by accrediting bodies. It is only in this way that we can build up the prestige of what is presently regarded, in the main, as a low-grade activity, and thus attract to it first-class, professionally trained personnel who will be willing to devote their undivided efforts to this field.

Keeping up with any field is difficult in a period of rapid change. For this reason trainers of teachers should have some close association with an ongoing teaching program, whether in a laboratory school, within a foreign-language department, or in association with a local school district. Their teacher-training work should not be a second string to a "more scholarly" pursuit. Until such an ideal situation obtains, sources of information are needed that will draw the attention of teacher trainers, as well as administrative personnel in school districts who are responsible for inservice training, to important trends, useful recent publications, reports of experimentation, and sources of assistance to teachers.[4]

As an interim measure, serious attention should be paid to providing further training for those teacher trainers who have been shanghaied into the task with insufficient background, as well as for others who have gradually slipped behind or come back into the work after years of absence from the field.

The nature of the training offered needs to be reexamined at regular intervals. One cannot emphasize too much the necessity for a

199

thorough command of the language the trainee is to teach and the culture of its people (in both senses of this word). Linguistic and psycholinguistic insights tied closely to the needs of the classroom teacher are also valuable and important. For the rest of the teacher's professional preparation, from a theoretical or a practical point of view, there is frankly too much that is essential for it to be covered in one short, rushed course. The all-too-brief methods course is often packed into the same semester as the student-teaching experience, so that students' ideas and perspective have no time to mature before they are hustled into the always nerve-racking first attempt at controlling a class and stimulating worthwhile activities at the same time. It is no wonder that, to many young trainees, actual problems of classroom management appear to be much more important than developing communication situations, so that much of what they learned in their methods course is perceived as irrelevant to the "real" task.

Hitherto, we have been too modest in our requirements. We should advocate a dual system of a general methods course, to establish interest and perspective in the semester preceding the student-teaching experience, and a specific-language methods course, which would be essentially practical and tied to the needs of the teacher in the classroom. The latter would be given during the practice-teaching semester. Why two such courses? It is obvious that our flexible teachers of the future need a thorough theoretical background if they are to adjust and adapt their teaching to varying needs and a changing clientele, but they also need a thorough practical training in the design and development of teaching and testing materials in the language they will be teaching for courses they may not yet have encountered or foreseen.

The general methods course, which can be given with future teachers of various languages in the same class, may be taught in the college of education, where the instructor is in close touch with colleagues in educational theory, curriculum, and the teaching of germane subjects, or in one of the language departments if a person of suitable interests and training is available. The specific-language methods course would normally be taught by a suitably trained instructor from the language department concerned, who is in a position to keep up with new developments in the study of the language itself, the contemporary culture and institutions, the literature, and the artistic manifestations of its people.

The general methods course prepares future professionals, giving them a wide overview of the ramifications and complications of the field: the various theories of language, of learning, and of the learning of language that must be taken into consideration in designing activities for students of various ages, aptitudes, motivations, and needs (present and future); the long-accepted procedures and the experimental; the recurrent, often cyclical attempts at solving apparently intractable problems; and the areas of controversy and their relationship to theoretical considerations and objectives.

The general methods course is the course for wide reading, for familiarizing oneself with the classics of the field and for following personal predilections, as one discovers the many sources of information and stimulation available to the practicing teacher. This course reveals to our future teachers the potential of their chosen field. It gives them the background of knowledge that frees them, at a later stage, to innovate and develop their courses to meet the needs of changing and evolving situations beyond what they could have anticipated in their early training.

For content in the general methods course, we can list at least the following: the place of foreign languages in the curriculum and in the general education of the student; their interaction with other areas of study; the intricate relationships between objectives and approaches or methods, and how these affect techniques; the theoretical background to language acquisition and use, and the development of the various skills necessary for communication in speech and writing; interpersonal relations in the foreign-language class, between teacher and student and among the students themselves; the psychology of groups, the sociolinguistic and emotional problems of communication; the rationale and organization of individualized programs, community-oriented programs, and programs for special-interest and career objectives; the theoretical assumptions and operation of various types of bilingual programs; when and how to design intensive courses and minicourses; patterns of scheduling and staffing; team teaching, peer teaching, group work, and independent research, with their implications for effective foreign-language learning; principles of evaluation and their effects on testing, both oral and written; aptitude and motivation; the role of media in foreign-language learning (films, tapes, video, microcomputers); where to find information to keep abreast of educational trends; the problems and changing objectives of different levels of institutional instruction; how to organize exchange programs, immersion weekends, camps, and festivals; and research and recent experimentation in foreign-language learning and teaching.

A general methods course can combine future elementary school, junior high school, and high school teachers, even instructors of undergraduate elementary and intermediate courses, thus ensuring that future foreign-language teachers in the various types of institutions will have some understanding of each other's aims, problems,

201

and working conditions and will be prepared to contribute to regional and local cooperative endeavors and articulation between the levels.

What of *the specific-language methods course*? It is in this course that the student practices techniques and day-to-day operations, designs activities and situations, studies materials and how to adapt and supplement them, refines evaluative procedures and instruments, and learns how to interest and motivate various types of students. Because the course is taught while the student is actually participating in some way in the life of a school community, students will now understand the importance of the meticulous work of materials evaluation, adaptation, and use, and the necessity for imagination and resourcefulness in creating learning situations and in stimulating genuine interaction.

The teacher trainer now has time to involve the students in actual construction of materials and design of exercises and activities they will use very soon. Since the class is language specific, students use the language they will teach and learn to cope with the major problems learners of this language encounter. Opportunity is provided for students to discuss and work with the appropriate components of various levels of instruction; for microteaching and videotaping the experience for discussion with the trainee; for planning and preparation of elementary, intermediate, and advanced courses, units, lessons, kits, individualized learning packets, culture capsules, games, and situational encounters; for practicing the organization and conduct of small-group learning; for detailed evaluation of textbooks, recorded materials, visuals, and tests; for learning to operate equipment and integrate it into the lesson; for seeking suitable authentic materials to supplement the standard fare; for discovering and recording sources of realia and contemporary information about the language, the speakers of the language, and the countries where it is spoken; and for discovering the relative usefulness of professional journals. Students try out what they have designed on each other, meanwhile profiting from the instructor's expertise in the language to correct faults in pronunciation and language use. In this course, the needs of teachers at various institutional levels will be different, and this fact can be exploited by providing students with the opportunity to experience individualization and personal planning in action, recombining the group for sharing where needs coincide.

It must be emphasized that neither of these courses should be designed merely to support future teachers through their first week or month of classroom teaching, although some of this preparation will be provided to instill confidence. Rather, they should lay the foundations for a lifetime of professional growth and involvement by providing students with both the theoretical understanding and the practical experience they need if they are to be able to adjust, and readjust, whenever new emphases and objectives require unanticipated responses from them. The inevitable trauma of the first day or the first week, however, can be faced and overcome only in an actual encounter with a class of students.

Preservice internship or student teaching practice

The reality of interaction with students in a group in an internship will give the future teacher the experience that creates confidence, rather than a simulation of this experience through peer teaching in a methods class or in a videotaping session where the students are obliging, well motivated, and already know what is expected of them. Microteaching during training is useful for the study of techniques, but its artificiality should be recognized and its place in the training program delineated. *A period of practice under guidance is essential* if what is being learned is to have reality for the trainee.

Regrettably, some institutions do not provide for an internship at all. Much has been and could be written about the inadequacies of what actually takes place in those that do. Many students have to work with teachers who are out of touch with present needs. Some teachers require students to do exactly as they do; others leave their student teachers to do as they please with no help or guidance, and sometimes without even a supportive presence in the classroom. Many student teachers never see an exciting lesson during their whole internship. The length of time in schools is frequently inadequate and often in one block, so that students have no opportunity to reflect on their experiences and then try again in another setting. For many students the experience is a bitter one, coming too late for them to change their career plans, whereas others have had a carefully organized experience of classroom visits and involvement with a teaching program, which gave them an early opportunity to decide whether or not their career choice was congenial to them.[5]

It is time for the profession as a whole to realize that, with all the demands that will be made on the teacher of the future, a preservice training period, no matter how well organized, will not be sufficient. Schools must be encouraged to provide *a mentor for each new teacher* during his or her first semester of autonomous teaching, that is, an experienced teacher with whom the new professional may discuss the design of courses, activities, and tests, as well as the inevitable day-to-day problems that result from lack of experience with student relations and classroom management. Such supervised initiation into the profession must be recognized as an essential element of a teacher's training and not a haphazard increment for those who are lucky. It is the first semester with full responsibility for the learning of one's students that is crucial for the development of professional skills and attitudes, rather than the short interlude of preservice experimentation.

How can the profession help the teacher trainer to improve the training program?

Easily obtainable films and videotapes of successful teaching of all types for all kinds of objectives are needed to strengthen the practical side of preservice and inservice training. Professional organizations should establish libraries of these materials for specific languages and make them readily available for rental or purchase.

Professional organizations should seek out and identify teacher-training programs that the users (students, classroom teachers, and department heads) recognize as successful. Their characteristics should be described and accounts of their operation circulated to stimulate the improvement of other programs.[6]

Inservice training

1. More teacher-to-teacher workshops should be organized at the local and regional levels to *reach teachers from the base*. National organizations can help by providing packaged workshops that energetic teachers can utilize as they please in their own districts. These should contain tapes of significant lectures, discussion materials based on simulated situations, films or videotapes of pilot programs of an innovative nature, or of extracurricular activities such as language camps, fairs, and projects for community involvement. Teachers should be encouraged to give their own demonstrations at local and regional workshops and initiate discussion of problems of immediate practical concern.

2. *Dissemination of teacher-prepared materials and ideas* for other teachers to use should be encouraged at the regional and district level, rather than the national level, so that teachers can interact in workshops and inservice conferences with the originators of the materials.

3. Opportunities for *interaction among instructors at different institutional levels* should be organized locally – not so that one group may "talk at" the other groups, but for exchange of information and combined action for the improvement of programs and for publicizing what is really being accomplished. Elementary school-teachers and instructors at two-year undergraduate institutions particularly need this help because of the lack of collegial support in their local setting.

4. We must *break down the parochialism of the French/German/Spanish/English as a second language teacher* without arousing feelings of insecurity about future jobs. Teachers of well-established languages must be kept informed of national and local needs for a variety of languages and be encouraged to involve themselves in efforts to broaden the range of language-learning opportunities by arousing local interest, training persons fluent in these languages in teaching techniques, and helping develop programs for teaching them. Where a need is clear but trained teachers are not available to meet it, practicing foreign-language teachers should be encouraged and enabled to take crash courses in the less-taught language for which there is a need, with a view to establishing a program from a base of experience rather than leaving the field to enthusiastic amateurs with no notion of how to teach a foreign language.

5. Local foreign-language teachers should be encouraged to *interest themselves actively in current movements and language-related activities* that go beyond their usual sphere: exploratory language courses, the bilingual and ethnic heritage movements, language and international studies, the opening of lines of communication with Third World countries, through language and the study of culture, language in multicultural societies, the open university and the development of continuing or lifelong education, and the possibilities provided in many communities by cable television, satellite reception, and home video recording.

Influencing the decision makers

What goes on in the classroom will continue to depend to a large degree on the types of materials readily available. Since these are, for the most part, produced commercially, the profession must *invite the editors of publishing houses to share in their discussions* and try to influence the orientation of new materials, rather than leaving such important considerations to the ad hoc decisions of editors and individual writers.

Teachers should be given more training in evaluating materials for specific purposes and the needs of particular groups of students. In journals directed to the needs of the classroom teacher, the traditional book review should be largely replaced by *user's reports*. Several such reports grouped together can help teachers to gauge the usefulness of the materials under discussion for their own situation.

In view of the tendency toward diversification of courses for a plurality of student needs and interests, the trend in published materials should be toward flexible groupings of interrelated (and sometimes alternative) materials from which teachers may select those that develop the particular skills or content they wish to emphasize.

The *public and the administrators* must be reached. These two interact, since administrators are sensitive to the priorities set by the community.

To improve the image of the profession we should do less public breast-beating. We can educate the public on the values of foreign-language study by *keeping the press, national and local, well supplied with succinct, well-reported accounts* (accompanied by photographs) of successful and innovative language teaching, that is, of interesting things actually taking place, not just vague statements on what the profession ought or hopes to do. Accounts of worthwhile programs elsewhere in language for careers, community involvement, home-stay exchange programs, or bilingual education, or the introduction of less commonly taught languages should be made available inexpensively for distribution to newspapers, school boards, parents' groups, administrators, or radio and television stations in local districts. Teachers should talk to neighborhood groups or write short items for local news media. Their task will be simplified if national associations make available informational kits, regularly updated, from which they can draw factual material. Some of this factual material should be in pamphlets for school administrators and counselors. Students should also be able to take home interesting facts and figures to their parents.[7]

To improve attitudes toward foreign-language learning in the wider community, we should *encourage and promote more learning of languages by adults* through programs planned to meet their needs in evening courses in their local area, in centers of lifelong learning, and in elementary and intermediate courses at senior institutions. This strategy will succeed only if adults have interesting and successful learning experiences, related to real uses of language in their personal or professional lives. From this point of view, improving the teaching of foreign languages for specific purposes in nontraditional two-year institutions, like the junior and community colleges, is immensely important to the profession. Community college instructors should work with companies who can use personnel fluent in particular foreign languages. National associations can help by locating such companies and alerting community colleges and other adult education groups to their needs. University departments should help colleagues in other fields who need to acquire a foreign language for advancing their research, or for initiating or maintaining overseas contacts, and provide specialized courses for advanced undergraduates and graduate students who need another language for their research or chosen career. Research is urgently needed into the type of language and content appropriate for foreign-language courses for students interested in business, advertising, public relations, law enforcement, community services, tourism, fashion, the sciences, architecture, the arts, engineering, work with international agencies, and so on.

The best long-term policy for changing community attitudes is undoubtedly to increase the number of interesting and effective school programs, thus reaching the decision makers of the future. The future of foreign-language teaching is in the hands of our present teachers and those they train. Let us not wait for others to promote us or find answers to our problems. In us lie the seeds of our own future.

Let's discuss

1 Discuss other changing relations and directions you have observed. Which of those listed seem most important to you in your teaching situation, and which concern you least?

2 In your teaching situation, or your preservice situation, which do you find to be the most confusing features, which the most threatening, and which the most demanding? How are you dealing with these problems?

3 What was your experience of a preservice internship or student teaching period? How do you think it could have been improved? (If you have not yet had this experience, what would you hope to learn from it, and how do you think this could be achieved?)

4 What are you finding (or what did you find) most interesting and most useful in your methods course? What, in your opinion, should receive more emphasis or more detailed treatment? (Discuss your response with your instructor to help in the evolution of the course.)

5 What would you add or subtract from the proposed content of the general and the specific-language methods courses described in this chapter? Which items do you think are no longer of great relevance?

6 What subjects would you like to see treated at an inservice or district workshop? Draw up a detailed program for a one-day workshop and for a two-day workshop on one of these subjects, keeping the approach varied and the participants actively involved.

7 Evaluate the textbook you are or will be using for an elementary (or intermediate) course, drawing from what you have learned in this book.[8]

Appendix: ACTFL provisional proficiency guidelines

The experts appointed by the American Council on the Teaching of Foreign Languages (ACTFL) to develop guidelines for generic and language-specific goals for language skills were Dale Lange (coordinating consultant), Pardee Lowe (speaking and listening), Howard Nostrand (culture), Alice Omaggio (writing), and June Phillips (reading).[1]

The following correspondence was established with the Interagency Language Roundtable (ILR) scales for speaking proficiency (formerly the Foreign Service Institute, or FSI, scales[2]).

ILR Scale	*ACTFL/ETS* Scale*
0	Novice – low
No practical proficiency	Novice – mid
0 +	Novice – high
1	Intermediate – low
Elementary proficiency	Intermediate – mid
1 +	Intermediate – high
2 Limited working proficiency	Advanced
2 +	Advanced plus
3 Professional proficiency	Superior
3 +	Superior
4 Distinguished proficiency	Superior
4 +	Superior
5 Native or bilingual proficiency	Superior

*Educational Testing Services (Princeton, N.J.)

208

The *Provisional Generic Descriptions* of the ACTFL Provisional Proficiency Guidelines, issued in the autumn of 1982, are set out as follows. The language-specific guidelines may be obtained from ACTFL.

Provisional generic descriptions: speaking

Novice – low	Unable to function in the spoken language. Oral production is limited to occasional isolated words. Essentially no communicative ability.
Novice – mid	Able to operate only in a very limited capacity within very predictable areas of need. Vocabulary limited to that necessary to express simple elementary needs and basic courtesy formulae. Syntax is fragmented, inflections and word endings frequently omitted, confused or distorted and the majority of utterances consist of isolated words or short formulae. Utterances rarely consist of more than two or three words and are marked by frequent long pauses and repetition of an interlocutor's words. Pronunciation is frequently unintelligible and is strongly influenced by first language. Can be understood only with difficulty, even by persons such as teachers who are used to speaking with non-native speakers or in interactions where the content strongly supports the utterance.
Novice – high	Able to satisfy immediate needs using learned utterances. Can ask questions or make statements with reasonable accuracy only where this involves short memorized utterances or formulae. There is no real autonomy of expression, although there may be some emerging signs of spontaneity and flexibility. There is a slight increase in utterance length but frequent long pauses and reception of interlocutor's words still occur. Most utterances are telegraphic and word endings are often omitted, confused or distorted. Vocabulary is limited to areas of immediate survival needs. Can differentiate most phonemes when produced in isolation but when they are combined in words or groups of words, errors are frequent and, even with repetition, may severely inhibit communication even with persons used to dealing with such learners. Little development in stress and intonation is evident.
Intermediate – low	Able to satisfy basic survival needs and minimum courtesy requirements. In areas of immediate need or on very familiar topics, can ask and answer simple questions, initiate and respond to simple state-

ments, and maintain very simple face-to-face conversations. When asked to do so, is able to formulate some questions with limited constructions and much inaccuracy. Almost every utterance contains fractured syntax and other grammatical errors. Vocabulary inadequate to express anything but the most elementary needs. Strong interference from native language occurs in articulation, stress and intonation. Misunderstandings frequently arise from limited vocabulary and grammar and erroneous phonology but, with repetition, can generally be understood by native speakers in regular contact with foreigners attempting to speak their language. Little precision in information conveyed owing to tentative state of grammatical development and little or no use of modifiers.

Intermediate – mid   Able to satisfy some survival needs and some limited social demands. Is able to formulate some questions when asked to do so. Vocabulary permits discussion of topics beyond basic survival needs such as personal history and leisure-time activities. Some evidence of grammatical accuracy in basic constructions, for example, subject-verb agreement, noun-adjective agreement, some notion of inflection.

Intermediate – high   Able to satisfy most survival needs and limited social demands. Shows some spontaneity in language production but fluency is very uneven. Can initiate and sustain a general conversation but has little understanding of the social conventions of conversation. Developing flexibility in a range of circumstances beyond immediate survival needs. Limited vocabulary range necessitates much hesitation and circumlocution. The commoner tense forms occur but errors are frequent in formation and selection. Can use most question forms. While some word order is established, errors still occur in more complex patterns. Cannot sustain coherent structures in longer utterances or unfamiliar situations. Ability to describe and give precise information is limited. Aware of basic cohesive features such as pronouns and verb inflections, but many are unreliable, especially if less immediate in reference. Extended discourse is largely a series of short, discrete utterances. Articulation is comprehensible to native speakers used to dealing with foreigners, and can combine most phonemes with reasonable comprehensibility, but still has difficulty in producing certain sounds, in certain positions, or in certain combinations, and speech will usually be labored. Still has to repeat utterances frequently to be understood by the general public. Able to produce some narration in either past or future.

Advanced Able to satisfy routine social demands and limited work requirements. Can handle with confidence but not with facility most social situations including introductions and casual conversations about current events, as well as work, family, and autobiographical information; can handle limited work requirements, needing help in handling any complications or difficulties. Has a speaking vocabulary sufficient to respond simply with some circumlocutions; accent, though often quite faulty, is intelligible; can usually handle elementary constructions quite accurately but does not have thorough or confident control of the grammar.

Advanced plus Able to satisfy most work requirements and show some ability to communicate on concrete topics relating to particular interests and special fields of competence. Generally strong in either grammar or vocabulary, but not in both. Weaknesses or unevenness in one of the foregoing or in pronunciation result in occasional miscommunication. Areas of weakness range from simple constructions such as plurals, articles, prepositions, and negatives to more complex structures such as tense usage, passive constructions, word order and relative clauses. Normally controls general vocabulary with some groping for everyday vocabulary still evident. Often shows remarkable fluency and ease of speech, but under tension or pressure language may break down.

Superior Able to speak the language with sufficient structural accuracy and vocabulary to participate effectively in most formal and informal conversations on practical, social, and professional topics. Can discuss particular interests and special fields of competence with reasonable ease. Vocabulary is broad enough that speaker rarely has to grope for a word; accent may be obviously foreign; control of grammar good; errors virtually never interfere with understanding and rarely disturb the native speaker.

Provisional generic descriptions: listening

Novice – low No practical understanding of the spoken language. Understanding limited to occasional isolated words, such as cognates, borrowed words, and high-fre-

211

quency social conventions. Essentially no ability to comprehend even short utterances.

Novice – mid Sufficient comprehension to understand some memorized words within predictable areas of need. Vocabulary for comprehension limited to simple elementary needs and basic courtesy formulae. Utterances understood rarely exceed more than two or three words at a time and ability to understand is characterized by long pauses for assimilation and by repeated requests on the listener's part for repetition, and/or a slower rate of speech. Confuses words that sound similar.

Novice – high Sufficient comprehension to understand a number of memorized utterances in areas of immediate need. Comprehends slightly longer utterances in situations where the context aids understanding, such as at the table, in a restaurant/store, in a train/bus. Phrases recognized have for the most part been memorized. Comprehends vocabulary common to daily needs. Comprehends simple questions/statements about family members, age, address, weather, time, daily activities and interests. Misunderstandings arise from failure to perceive critical sounds or endings. Understands even standard speech with difficulty but gets some main ideas. Often requires repetition and/or a slowed rate of speed for comprehension, even when listening to persons such as teachers who are used to speaking with non-natives.

Intermediate – low Sufficient comprehension to understand utterances about basic survival needs, minimum courtesy and travel requirements. In areas of immediate need or on very familiar topics, can understand non-memorized material, such as simple questions and answers, statements, and face-to-face conversations in the standard language. Comprehension areas include basic needs: meals, lodging, transportation, time, simple instructions (e.g., route directions) and routine commands (e.g., from customs officials, police). Understands main ideas. Misunderstandings frequently arise from lack of vocabulary or faulty processing of syntactic information often caused by strong interference from the native language or by the imperfect and partial acquisition of the target grammar.

Intermediate – mid Sufficient comprehension to understand simple conversations about some survival needs and some limited social conventions. Vocabulary permits understanding of topics beyond basic survival needs such as personal history and leisure time activities. Evidence of understanding basic constructions, for example, subject-verb agreement, noun-adjective agreement; evidence that some inflection is understood.

Intermediate – high
Sufficient comprehension to understand short conversations about most survival needs and limited social conventions. Increasingly able to understand topics beyond immediate survival needs. Shows spontaneity in understanding, but speed and consistency of understanding uneven. Limited vocabulary range necessitates repetition for understanding. Understands commoner tense forms and some word order patterns, including most question forms, but miscommunication still occurs with more complex patterns. Can get the gist of conversations, but cannot sustain comprehension in longer utterances or in unfamiliar situations. Understanding of descriptions and detailed information is limited. Aware of basic cohesive features such as pronouns and verb inflections, but many are unreliably understood, especially if other material intervenes. Understanding is largely limited to a series of short, discrete utterances. Still has to ask for utterances to be repeated. Some ability to understand the facts.

Advanced
Sufficient comprehension to understand conversations about routine social conventions and limited school or work requirements. Able to understand face-to-face speech in the standard language, delivered at a normal rate with some repetition and rewording, by a native speaker not used to dealing with foreigners. Understands everyday topics, common personal and family news, well-known current events, and routine matters involving school or work; descriptions and narration about current, past and future events; and essential points of discussion or speech at an elementary level on topics in special fields of interest.

Advanced plus
Sufficient comprehension to understand most routine social conventions, conversations on school or work requirements, and discussions on concrete topics related to particular interests and special fields of competence. Often shows remarkable ability and ease of understanding, but comprehension may break down under tension or pressure, including unfavorable listening conditions. Candidate may display weakness or deficiency due to inadequate vocabulary base or less than secure knowledge of grammar and syntax. Normally understands general vocabulary with some hesitant understanding of everyday

vocabulary still evident. Can sometimes detect emotional overtones. Some ability to understand between the lines, i.e., to make inferences.

Superior   Sufficient comprehension to understand the essentials of all speech in standard dialects, including technical discussions within a special field. Has sufficient understanding of face-to-face speech, delivered with normal clarity and speed in standard language, on general topics and areas of special interest; understands hypothesizing and supported opinions. Has broad enough vocabulary that rarely has to ask for paraphrasing or explanation. Can follow accurately the essentials of conversations between educated native speakers, reasonably clear telephone calls, radio broadcasts, standard news items, oral reports, some oral technical reports, and public addresses on non-technical subjects. May not understand native speakers if they speak very quickly or use some slang or unfamiliar dialect. Can often detect emotional overtones. Can understand "between the lines" (i.e., make inferences).

Provisional generic descriptions: reading

Novice – low   No functional ability in reading the foreign language.

Novice – mid   Sufficient understanding of the written language to interpret highly contextualized words or cognates within predictable areas. Vocabulary for comprehension limited to simple elementary needs such as names, addresses, dates, street signs, building names, short informative signs (e.g., no smoking, entrance/ exit) and formulaic vocabulary requesting same. Material understood rarely exceeds a single phrase and comprehension requires successive rereading and checking.

Novice – high   Sufficient comprehension of the written language to interpret set expressions in areas of immediate need. Can recognize all the letters in the printed version of an alphabetic system and high-frequency elements of a syllabary or a character system. Where vocabulary has been mastered can read for instruction and directional purposes standardized messages, phrases or expressions such as some items on menus, schedules, timetables, maps and signs indicating hours of operation, social codes, and traffic regulations. This material is read only for essential information. Detail is overlooked or misunderstood.

Intermediate – low	Sufficient comprehension to understand in printed form the simplest connected material, either authentic or specially prepared, dealing with basic survival and social needs. Able to understand both mastered material and recombinations of the mastered elements that achieve meanings at the same level. Understands main ideas in material whose structures and syntax parallel the native language. Can read messages, greetings, statements of social amenities or other simple language containing only the highest frequency grammatical patterns and vocabulary items including cognates (if appropriate). Misunderstandings arise when syntax diverges from that of the native language or when grammatical cues are overlooked.
Intermediate – mid	Sufficient comprehension to understand in printed form simple discourse for informative or social purposes. In response to perceived needs can read for information material such as announcements of public events, popular advertising, notes containing biographical information or narration of events, and straightforward newspaper headlines and story titles. Can guess at unfamiliar vocabulary if highly contextualized. Relies primarily on adverbs as time indicators. Has some difficulty with the cohesive factors in discourse, such as matching pronouns with referents. May have to read material several times before understanding.
Intermediate – high	Sufficient comprehension to understand a simple paragraph for personal communication, information or recreational purposes. Can read with understanding social notes, letters and invitations; can locate and derive main ideas of the introductory/summary paragraphs from high interest or familiar news or other informational sources; can read for pleasure specially prepared, or some uncomplicated authentic prose, such as fictional narratives or cultural information. Shows spontaneity in reading by ability to guess at meaning from context. Understands common time indicators and can interpret some cohesive factors such as objective pronouns and simple clause connectors. Begins to relate sentences in the discourse to advance meaning, but cannot sustain understanding of longer discourse on unfamiliar topics. Misinterpretation still occurs with more complex patterns.
Advanced	Sufficient comprehension to read simple authentic printed material or edited textual material within a

familiar context. Can read uncomplicated but authentic prose on familiar subjects containing description and narration such as news items describing frequently occurring events, simple biographic information, social notices, and standard business letters. Can read edited texts such as prose fiction and contemporary culture. The prose is predominantly in familiar sentence patterns. Can follow essential points of written discussion at level of main ideas and some supporting ones with topics in a field of interest or where background exists. Some misunderstandings. Able to read the facts but cannot draw inferences.

Advanced plus   Sufficient comprehension to understand most factual information in non-technical prose as well as some discussions on concrete topics related to special interests. Able to read for information and description, to follow sequence of events, and to react to that information. Is able to separate main ideas from lesser ones, and uses that division to advance understanding. Can locate and interpret main ideas and details in material written for the general public. Will begin to guess sensibly at new words by using linguistic context and prior knowledge. May react personally to material but does not yet detect subjective attitudes, values, or judgments in the writing.

Superior   Able to read standard newspaper items addressed to the general reader, routine correspondence reports and technical material in a field of interest at a normal rate of speed (at least 220 wpm). Readers can gain new knowledge from material on unfamiliar topics in areas of a general nature. Can interpret hypotheses, supported opinions and conjectures. Can also read short stories, novels, and other recreational literature accessible to the general public. Reading ability is not subject-matter dependent. Has broad enough general vocabulary that successful guessing resolves problems with complex structures and low-frequency idioms. Misreading is rare. Almost always produces correct interpretation. Able to read between the lines. May be unable to appreciate nuance or stylistics.

Provisional generic descriptions: writing

Novice – low   No functional ability in writing the foreign language.
Novice – mid   No practical communicative writing skills. Able to

copy isolated words or short phrases. Able to transcribe previously studied words or phrases.

Novice – high
Able to write simple fixed expressions and limited memorized material. Can supply information when requested on forms such as hotel registrations and travel documents. Can write names, numbers, dates, one's own nationality, addresses, and other simple biographic information, as well as learned vocabulary, short phrases, and simple lists. Can write all the symbols in an alphabetic or syllabic system of 50 of the most common characters. Can write simple memorized material with frequent misspellings and inaccuracies.

Intermediate – low
Has sufficient control of the writing system to meet limited practical needs. Can write short messages, such as simple questions or notes, postcards, phone messages, and the like within the scope of limited language experience. Can take simple notes on material dealing with very familiar topics although memory span is extremely limited. Can create statements or questions within the scope of limited language experience. Material produced consists of recombinations of learned vocabulary and structures into simple sentences. Vocabulary is inadequate to express anything but elementary needs. Writing tends to be a loosely organized collection of sentence fragments on a very familiar topic. Makes continual errors in spelling, grammar, and punctuation, but writing can be read and understood by a native speaker used to dealing with foreigners. Able to produce appropriately some fundamental sociolinguistic distinctions in formal and familiar style, such as appropriate subject pronouns, titles of address and basic social formulae.

Intermediate – mid
Sufficient control of writing system to meet some survival needs and some limited social demands. Able to compose short paragraphs or take simple notes on very familiar topics grounded in personal experience. Can discuss likes and dislikes, daily routine, everyday events, and the like. Can express past time, using content words and time expressions, or with sporadically accurate verbs. Evidence of good control of basic constructions and inflections such as subject-verb agreement, noun-adjective agreement, and straightforward syntactic constructions in present or future time, though errors occasionally occur. May make frequent errors, however, when venturing beyond current level of linguistic competence.

Intermediate – high

When resorting to a dictionary, often is unable to identify appropriate vocabulary, or uses dictionary entry in uninflected form.
Sufficient control of writing system to meet most survival needs and limited social demands. Can take notes in some detail on familiar topics, and respond to personal questions using elementary vocabulary and common structures. Can write simple letters, brief synopses and paraphrases, summaries of biographical data and work experience, and short compositions on familiar topics. Can create sentences and short paragraphs relating to most survival needs (food, lodging, transportation, immediate surroundings and situations) and limited social demands. Can relate personal history, discuss topics such as daily life, preferences, and other familiar material. Can express fairly accurately present and future time. Can produce some past verb forms, but not always accurately or with correct usage. Shows good control of elementary vocabulary and some control of basic syntactic patterns but major errors still occur when expressing more complex thoughts. Dictionary usage may still yield incorrect vocabulary of forms, although can use a dictionary to advantage to express simple ideas. Generally cannot use basic cohesive elements of discourse to advantage such as relative constructions, subject pronouns, connectors, etc. Writing, though faulty, is comprehensible to native speakers used to dealing with foreigners.

Advanced

Able to write routine social correspondence and simple discourse of at least several paragraphs on familiar topics. Can write simple social correspondence, take notes, and write cohesive summaries, resumes, and short narratives and descriptions on factual topics. Able to write about everyday topics using both description and narration. Has sufficient writing vocabulary to express himself/herself simply with some circumlocution. Can write about a very limited number of current events or daily situations and express personal preferences and observations in some detail, using basic structures. Still makes common errors in spelling and punctuation, but shows some control of the most common formats and punctuation conventions. Good control of the morphology of the language (in inflected languages) and of the most frequently used syntactic structures. Elementary constructions are usually handled quite accurately, and writing is understandable to a native speaker not used to reading the writing of foreigners. Uses a limited number of cohesive devices such as pronouns and repeated words with good accuracy. Able to join sentences in limited discourse, but has difficulty and makes frequent errors in producing complex sentences. Paragraphs are reasonably unified and coherent.

Advanced plus
Shows ability to write about most common topics with some precision and in some detail. Can write fairly detailed resumes and summaries and take quite accurate notes. Can write most social and informal business correspondence. Can describe and narrate personal experiences and explain simple points of view in prose discourse. Can write about concrete topics relating to particular interests and special fields of competence. Normally controls general vocabulary with some circumlocution. Often shows remarkable fluency and ease of expression, but under time constraints and pressure language may be inaccurate and/or incomprehensible. Generally strong in either grammar or vocabulary, but not in both. Weaknesses and unevennesses in one of the foregoing or in spelling result in occasional miscommunication. Areas of weakness range from simple constructions such as plurals, articles, prepositions, and negatives to more complex structures such as tense usage, passive constructions, word order, and relative clauses. Some misuse of vocabulary still evident. Shows a limited ability to use circumlocution. Uses dictionary to advantage to supply unknown words. Writing is understandable to native speakers not used to reading material written by non-natives, though the style is still obviously foreign.

Superior
Able to use the written language effectively in most formal and informal exchanges on practical, social, and professional topics. Can write most types of correspondence, such as memos and social and business letters, short research papers and statements of position in areas of special interest or in special fields. Can express hypotheses, conjectures, and present arguments or points of view accurately and effectively. Can write about areas of special interest and handle topics in special fields, in addition to most common topics. Good control of a full range of structures, spelling, and a wide general vocabulary allow the writer to convey his/her message accurately, though style may be foreign. Can use complex and compound sentence structures to express

ideas clearly and coherently. Uses dictionary with a high degree of accuracy to supply specialized vocabulary. Errors, though sometimes made when using more complex structures, are occasional, and rarely disturb the native speaker. Sporadic errors when using basic structures. Although sensitive to differences in formal and informal style, still cannot tailor writing precisely and accurately to a variety of audiences or styles.

Provisional generic descriptions: culture

Novice
Limited interaction. Behaves with considerateness. Is resourceful in nonverbal communication, but is unreliable in interpretation of nonverbal cues. Is limited in language, as indicated under the listening and speaking skills. Lacks generally the knowledge of culture patterns requisite for survival situations.

Intermediate
Survival competence. Can deal with familiar survival situations and interact with a culture bearer accustomed to foreigners. Uses behavior acquired for the purpose of greeting and leave-taking, expressing wants, asking directions, buying food, using transportation, tipping. Comprehends the response. Makes errors as the result of misunderstanding; miscommunicates, and misapplies assumptions about the culture.

Advanced
Limited social competence. Handles routine social situations successfully with a culture bearer accustomed to foreigners. Shows comprehension of common rules of etiquette, taboos and sensitivities, though home culture predominates. Can make polite requests, accept and refuse invitations, offer and receive gifts, apologize, make introductions, telephone, purchase and bargain, do routine banking. Can discuss a few aspects of the home and the foreign country, such as general current events and policies, as well as a field of personal interest. Does not offend the culture bearer, but some important misunderstandings and miscommunications occur, in interaction with one unaccustomed to foreigners. Is not competent to take part in a formal meeting, or in a group situation where several persons are speaking informally at the same time.

Superior
Working social and professional competence. Can participate in almost all social situations and those within one vocation. Handles unfamiliar types of situations with ease and sensitivity, including some

involving common taboos, or other emotionally charged subjects. Comprehends most nonverbal responses. Laughs at some culture-related humor. In productive skills, neither culture predominates; nevertheless, makes appropriate use of cultural references and expressions. Generally distinguishes between a formal and informal register. Discusses abstract ideas relating the foreign to the native culture. Is generally limited, however, in handling abstractions. Minor inaccuracies occur in perception of meaning and in the expression of the intended representation, but do not result in serious misunderstanding, even by a culture bearer unaccustomed to foreigners.

Near-native competence
Full social and professional competence. Fits behavior to audience, and the culture of the target language dominates almost entirely. Has internalized the concept that culture is relative and is always on the lookout to do the appropriate thing. Can counsel, persuade, negotiate, represent a point of view, interpret for dignitaries, describe and compare features of the two cultures. In such comparisons, can discuss geography, history, institutions, customs and behavior patterns, current events, and national policies. Perceives almost all unverbalized responses, and recognizes almost all allusions, including historical and literary commonplaces. Laughs at most culture-related humor. Controls a formal and informal register of behavior. Is inferior to the culture bearer only in background information related to the culture such as childhood experiences, detailed regional geography and past events of significance.

Native competence
Examinee is indistinguishable from a person brought up and educated in the culture.

Abbreviations used in notes and bibliography

ACTFL	American Council on the Teaching of Foreign Languages (Hastings-on-Hudson, New York)
ADFL	Association of Departments of Foreign Languages (MLA)
AL	*Applied Linguistics* (Oxford: Oxford University Press)
CAL	Center for Applied Linguistics (Washington, D.C.)
CMLR	*Canadian Modern Language Review* (Welland, Ontario)
ETS	Educational Testing Services (Princeton, N.J.)
FL	Foreign language
FLA	*Foreign Language Annals* (Journal of ACTFL)
FR	*French Review* (Journal of the American Association of Teachers of French)
GURT	Georgetown Roundtable on Languages and Linguistics (monograph series) (Washington, D.C.: Georgetown University Press)
ILR	Interagency Language Roundtable
IP	Information processing
IRAL	*International Review of Applied Linguistics in Language Teaching* (Heidelberg, Julius Gross Verlag)
L_1; L_2	First language; second language
LL	*Language Learning* (Ann Arbor, Michigan)
LSP	Language for Specific Purposes
LT	*Language Teaching* (Cambridge: Cambridge University Press); formerly *LTLA*
LTLA	*Language Teaching and Linguistics: Abstracts* (Cambridge, U.K.: Cambridge University Press), now *LT*
MLA	Modern Language Association (New York)
MLJ	*Modern Language Journal* (Madison: University of Wisconsin Press)
NEC	Northeast Conference on the Teaching of Foreign Languages (Middlebury, Vermont)
OISE	Ontario Institute for Studies in Education (Toronto)
TESOL	Teachers of English to Speakers of Other Languages (Washington, D.C.)
TQ	*TESOL Quarterly*
UP	*Die Unterrichtspraxis*

222

Notes

Preface

1 This model is reproduced in the *Practical Guides* and in chap. 3 of Rivers, *Communicating Naturally in a Second Language: Theory and Practice in Language Teaching* (Cambridge: Cambridge University Press, 1983). It may also be found in *TQ* 6(1972): 72; and *TQ* 7(1973): 25.
2 John Holt, *How Children Fail* (New York: Dell, 1970).
3 George Isaac Brown, *Human Teaching for Human Learning: An Introduction to Confluent Education* (New York: Viking Press, 1971), p. 6.
4 See p. 158 of this book.
5 These themes are developed at length in *Proceedings of the National Conference on Professional Priorities. November 1980. Boston, Massachusetts*, ed. D. L. Lange (Hastings-on-Hudson, N.Y.: ACTFL Materials Center, 1981).

1 The view on the way up

1 G. L. Trager, "The Field of Linguistics," Summer Institute of Linguistics, Occasional Papers, vol. 1 (Oklahoma City: SIL, 1949), p. 4.
2 This behaviorist approach to language acquisition is explained in detail in W. M. Rivers, *The Psychologist and the Foreign-Language Teacher* (Chicago: University of Chicago Press, 1964), chap. 7; and in W. M. Rivers, *Teaching Foreign-Language Skills*, 2d ed. (Chicago: University of Chicago Press, 1981), p. 75.
3 For a detailed description of the audiolingual method, see Rivers, *Teaching Foreign-Language Skills*, pp. 38–48.
4 For a fuller discussion of cognitive processes, see "The Second-Language Teacher and Cognitive Psychology," chap. 7 of W. M. Rivers, *Communicating Naturally in a Second Language: Theory and Practice in Language Teaching* (Cambridge: Cambridge University Press, 1983).
5 See N. Chomsky, "Linguistic Theory," in *Language Teaching: Broader Contexts,* ed. R. G. Mead, Jr. (Middlebury, Vt.: NEC, 1966), pp. 43–9.
6 See N. Chomsky, *Aspects of the Theory of Syntax* (Cambridge, Mass.: MIT Press, 1965), pp. 25–6.
7 For a fuller discussion of applications of Chomsky's theory, see "Linguistics, Psychology, and Language Teaching: An Overview," chap. 1 of Rivers, *Communicating Naturally*; or Rivers, *Teaching Foreign-Language Skills*, pp. 77–83.
8 See Rivers, *Teaching Foreign-Language Skills*, p. 49.

9 K. Chastain, *The Development of Modern Language Skills: Theory to Practice* (Philadelphia: The Center for Curriculum Development, 1971), p. 48, and *Developing Second-Language Skills: Theory to Practice*, 2d ed. (Chicago: Rand McNally, 1976), pp. 156–7.

10 H. Sweet, *The Practical Study of Languages* (1899; reprinted, London: Oxford University Press, 1964), pp. 75–6. See also Rivers, *Teaching Foreign-Language Skills*, pp. 52–3.

11 T. D. Terrell, "A Natural Approach to Second Language Acquisition and Learning," *MLJ* 61(1977): 325–37, and "The Natural Approach to Language Teaching: An Update," *MLJ* 66(1982): 121–32; and S. D. Krashen, *Second Language Acquisition and Second Language Learning* (Oxford: Pergamon Press, 1981).

12 C. A. Curran, *Counseling-Learning in Second Languages* (Apple River, Ill.: Apple River Press, 1976).

13 For the skill-getting and skill-using model, see chap. 3 of Rivers, *Communicating Naturally*; or pp. 3–5 of Rivers, *A Practical Guide to the Teaching of French* (New York: Oxford University Press, 1975), and parallel volumes for German (1975), Spanish (1976), English as a Second or Foreign Language (1978), and Hebrew (in press). Henceforth referred to as the *Practical Guides*.

14 See "A Relevant Curriculum: An Instrument for Polling Student Opinion," in *Foreign Languages and the "New" Student*, ed. J. A. Tursi (Middlebury, Vt.: NEC, 1970), pp. 8–30; University of Illinois Questionnaire on Interests in Foreign Languages 1973, and appended Harvard questionnaires 1976, in W. M. Rivers, *Speaking in Many Tongues*, expanded 2d ed. (Rowley, Mass.: Newbury House, 1976), pp. 184–223; Questionnaire on Foreign-Language Learners' Goals 1978, at end of chapter 2 of this book.

15 For further discussion of the results of the University of Illinois study 1973, see "The Non-Major: Tailoring the Course to Fit the Person – Not the Image," in Rivers, *Speaking in Many Tongues*, expanded 2d ed., pp. 169–83; or *ADFL Bulletin* 5, 2(1973): 12–18; or Jankowsky, ed., *Language and International Studies*. GURT. (Washington, D.C.: Georgetown University Press, 1973), pp. 85–97.

16 For national needs in these areas, see *Strength Through Wisdom: A Critique of U.S. Capability*. A Report to the President from the President's Commission on Foreign Language and International Studies (Washington, D.C.: Government Printing Office, 1979); and P. Simon, *The Tongue-Tied American: Confronting the Foreign Language Crisis* (New York: Continuum, 1980).

17 See W. C. Born, ed., *New Contents, New Teachers, New Publics* (Middlebury, Vt.: NEC, 1978), pp. 25–8.

18 The foreign-language requirement of Harvard College is the attainment of a score of 560 on the Harvard Placement Test, or on the College Entrance Examination Board Test before entry, or the successful completion of a full year of language study at Harvard (at either the elementary or intermediate level – the elementary course moves fast). This provides a choice between a proficiency or a study requirement. In *The Harvard*

Independent (Sept. 28–Oct. 4, 1978), D. Danielfour expressed a student view of the requirement classes: "With Harvard's excellent language labs and generally small language classes, it becomes worthwhile to take advantage of the requirement and achieve true proficiency in another language. And because of frequency of classes and accelerated pace of learning here, languages can be learned in amazingly short periods of time." See "Students Need Two Tongues," reprinted in *MLJ* 63(1979): 126–7. At the University of Illinois in 1973, 62 percent at elementary and intermediate levels enjoyed learning a language. In 1980 at Harvard this had risen to 82 percent at the same level. For student support or opposition to a requirement (Illinois data) see Rivers, "The Non-Major...," in *Speaking in Many Tongues*, expanded 2d ed. Harvard data obtainable from the author.

19 S. A. Sadow, "Marketing Your Innovative Language Program," in *Foreign Languages for the Professions: An Inter-Cultural Approach to Modern Communications*, ed. S. M. Turner (Boston: Northeastern University, 1981), p. 3. In this article, Sadow gives very practical step-by-step advice on investigating the interests and needs of students for nontraditional language programs, and on the design and execution of new programs when their feasibility is established.

20 For a discussion of three new methodologies that emphasize attention to the student factor in language learning, see "Student-Centered Trends: A Rationale," chap. 6 of Rivers, *Communicating Naturally*.

21 H. E. Palmer, *The Principles of Language-Study* (London: Oxford University Press, 1964), p. 141. Original publication date 1921.

2 Educational goals

1 For a discussion of the applicability of performance objectives to the language class, see "Individualized Instruction and Cooperative Learning: Some Theoretical Considerations," chap. 5 of Rivers, *Communicating Naturally in a Second Language: Theory and Practice in Language Teaching* (Cambridge: Cambridge University Press, 1983).

2 The ILR definitions for these six levels of proficiency parallel, with minor changes in wording, the Foreign Service Institute Rating Scales of Absolute Language Proficiency on which they are based. The FSI Scales for speaking and reading are reproduced in full in Appendix A of Rivers, *Teaching Foreign-Language Skills*, 2d ed. (Chicago: University of Chicago Press, 1981), pp. 497–9.

3 The Generic Descriptions only are reproduced in the Appendix to this book. Detailed descriptions for French, German, and Spanish are obtainable from ACTFL.

4 J. L. M. Trim et al., *Systems Development in Adult Language Learning* (Oxford: Pergamon Press, for the Council of Europe, 1980).

5 J. L. M. Trim, *Developing a Unit/Credit Scheme of Adult Language Learning* (Oxford: Pergamon Press, for the Council of Europe, 1980); J. A. van Ek and L. G. Alexander, *Threshold Level English* (Oxford: Pergamon Press, for the Council of Europe, 1980); J. A. van Ek, *The*

2   J. Bruner in Foreword to Luria, *Mind of a Mnemonist*, p. viii.

3   Luria, *Mind of a Mnemonist*, p. 65.

4   Ibid.

5   Ibid., pp. 68–9.

6   G. A. Miller, *Psychology: The Science of Mental Life* (Harmondsworth: Pelican Books, 1966), p. 192.

7   J. J. Jenkins, "Language and Memory," in *Communication, Language, and Meaning: Psychological Perspectives*, ed. G. A. Miller (New York: Basic Books, 1973), p. 170. Italics in the original.

8   The theoretical discussion underlying the practical recommendations in this chapter, with bibliographic references, will be found in B. S. Melvin and W. M. Rivers, "In One Ear and Out the Other: Implications of Memory Studies for Language Learning," in *On TESOL 1976*, ed. J. Fanselow and R. Crymes (Washington, D.C.: TESOL, 1976), pp. 155–64, and W. M. Rivers and B. S. Melvin, "Memory and Memorization in Comprehension and Production: Contributions of IP Theory," *CMLR* 33(1977): 497–502.

9   For a more detailed discussion of semantic or conceptual networks, see "Apples of Gold in Pictures of Silver: Where have all the Words Gone?" in Rivers, *Communicating Naturally in a Second Language: Theory and Practice in Language Teaching* (Cambridge: Cambridge University Press, 1983), chap. 9.

10 For activities for vocabulary acquisition consistent with the principles set out in this discussion, see Rivers, *Teaching Foreign-Language Skills*, 2d ed. (Chicago: University of Chicago Press, 1981), pp. 462–70. See also S. A. Sadow, *Idea Bank: Creative Activities for the Language Class* (Rowley, Mass.: Newbury House, 1982). For creative ways to exploit dialogue material, see chap. 1, "Structured Interaction," in the *Practical Guides*.

11 Ways of converting intensive practice exercises from Type A (manipulative) to Type B (creative) are discussed in chap. 4, "Oral Drills for the Learning of Grammar," in Rivers and Temperley, *A Practical Guide to the Teaching of English as a Second or Foreign Language* (New York: Oxford University Press, 1978), and in "From Linguistic Competence to Communicative Competence," *TQ* 7(1973): 25–34; reprinted in revised form as "Bridging the Gap to Autonomous Interaction," in Rivers, *Communicating Naturally*, chap. 4.

12 For normal purposes of language in communication, see Rivers and Temperley, *A Practical Guide*, chap. 2, "Autonomous Interaction," and "The Natural and the Normal in Language Learning," chap. 8, in Rivers, *Communicating Naturally*.

13 J. B. Carroll, "Learning Theory for the Classroom Teacher," in *The Challenge of Communication*. ACTFL Review of Foreign Language Education, vol. 6, ed. G. A. Jarvis (Skokie, Ill.: National Textbook Co., 1974b), pp. 113–49.

14 A. L. Blumenthal, *Language and Psychology* (New York: Wiley, 1970), p. 243.

5 Linguistic and psychological factors in speech perception

1   D. I. Slobin, *Psycholinguistics*, 2d ed. (Glenview, Ill.: Scott, Foresman, 1979), p. 37. Capitalization and italicization in the original.

2   For a full discussion of "Hearing and Comprehending," see Rivers, *Teaching Foreign-Language Skills*, 2d ed. (Chicago: University of Chicago Press, 1981), pp. 160–5.

3   I. M. Schlesinger, *Sentence Structure and the Reading Process* (The Hague: Mouton, 1968), chap. 6; and T. G. Bever, "Psychologically Real Grammar Emerges Because of its Role in Language Acquisition," in *Developmental Psycholinguistics: Theory and Applications*, ed D. P. Dato. GURT. (Washington, D.C.: Georgetown University Press, 1975), pp. 63–75.

4   I. M. Schlesinger, *Production and Comprehension of Utterances* (Hillsdale, N.J.: Erlbaum, 1977).

5   For further discussion of Bever's approach, see chap. 7 in Rivers, *Communicating Naturally in a Second Language: Theory and Practice in Language Teaching* (Cambridge: Cambridge University Press, 1983).

6   See N. Chomsky, *Aspects of the Theory of Syntax* (Cambridge, Mass.: MIT Press, 1965), p. 9.

7   Chomsky and others who employ the transformational-generative model have concerned themselves, in recent years, with the psychological reality of the model. See M. Halle, J. Bresnan, and G. A. Miller, eds., *Linguistic Theory and Psychological Reality* (Cambridge, Mass.: MIT Press, 1978).

8   For a full discussion with supporting experiments, see U. Neisser, *Cognitive Psychology* (New York: Appleton-Century-Crofts, 1967), chap. 7.

9   P. Lieberman, "On the Acoustic Basis of the Perception of Intonation by Linguists," *Word* 21(1965): 40–54.

10 Neisser, *Cognitive Psychology*, chap. 7, "Speech Perception."

11 Suggestions for activities and materials for these three stages are given in detail in the *Practical Guides*, chap. 3, "Listening."

12 G. A. Miller, "The Magical Number Seven, Plus or Minus Two," *Psychological Review* 63(1956): 81–97.

13 Analysis by synthesis is succinctly described in H. S. Cairns and C. E. Cairns, *Psycholinguistics: A Cognitive View of Language* (New York: Holt, Rinehart and Winston, 1976), pp. 141–2.

14 J. Fodor and M. Garrett, "Some Reflections on Competence and Performance," in *Psycholinguistics Papers: Proceedings of the 1966 Edinburgh Conference*, ed. J. Lyons and R. J. Wales (Edinburgh: Edinburgh University Press, 1966), pp. 148–51.

15 C. J. Fillmore, "Toward a Modern Theory of Case," in *Modern Studies in English: Readings in Transformational Grammar*, ed. D. A. Reibel and S. A. Schane (Englewood Cliffs, N.J.: Prentice-Hall, 1969), pp. 361–75.

16 A. L. Blumenthal's 1965 experiment is described in R. J. Wales and J. C. Marshall, "Linguistic Performance," in Lyons and Wales, *Psycholinguis-*

tics Papers, pp. 70–1. See also A. L. Blumenthal and R. Boakes, "Prompted Recall of Sentences," *Journal of Verbal Learning and Verbal Behavior* 6(1967): 674–6.

17 A detailed description of research projects in sustained listening preceding production and an evaluation and critique of this approach are provided in Rivers, *Teaching Foreign-Language Skills,* pp. 176–81. See also V. A. Postovsky, "Effects of Delay in Oral Practice at the Beginning of Second Language Learning," *MLJ* 58(1974): 229–39; J. O. Gary, "Why Speak if You Don't Need to? The Case for a Listening Approach to Beginning Foreign Language Learning," in *Second Language Acquisition Research: Issues and Implications,* ed. W. C. Ritchie (New York: Academic Press, 1978); and H. Winitz, ed., *The Comprehension Approach to Foreign Language Instruction* (Rowley, Mass.: Newbury House, 1981).

18 For a thorough discussion of *semantic-syntactic decoding* as developed by Schlesinger, see the *Practical Guides,* chap. 3.

19. Harvard Center for Cognitive Studies, *Sixth Annual Report 1965–66,* p. 18; *Seventh Annual Report 1966–67,* pp. 30–1.

20 For examples in different languages of the types of exercises proposed in this section (reducing to SAADs and storing the gist, etc.), see chap. 3 of the *Practical Guides.*

21 Harvard Center for Cognitive Studies, *Seventh Annual Report,* p. 32.

22 Examples of suitable exercises for these aspects of reading are given in chaps. 6 and 7 of the *Practical Guides.*

6 Reading fluently

1 For a detailed discussion of first- and second-language learning as the same or different processes, see "Foreign-Language Acquisition: Where the Real Problems Lie," chap. 12 in Rivers, *Communicating Naturally in a Second Language: Theory and Practice in Language Teaching* (Cambridge: Cambridge University Press, 1983).

2 See C. E. Snow and M. Hoefnagel-Höhle, "The Critical Period for Language Acquisition: Evidence from Second-Language Learning," in *Child-Adult Differences in Second Language Acquisition,* ed. S. D. Krashen, R. C. Scarcella, and M. H. Long (Rowley, Mass.: Newbury House, 1982), pp. 93–111; and S. D. Krashen and H. W. Seliger, "The Essential Contributions of Formal Instruction in Adult Second Language Learning," *TQ* 9(1975): 172-83.

3 The original "critical period" hypothesis stems from W. Penfield and L. Roberts, *Speech and Brain-Mechanisms* (Princeton, N.J.: Princeton University Press, 1959); and E. Lenneberg, *Biological Foundations of Language* (New York: Wiley, 1967). For a detailed discussion of this hypothesis, see S. D. Krashen, "The Critical Period for Language Acquisition and Its Possible Bases," in *Developmental Psycholinguistics and Communicative Disorders,* ed. D. Aaronson and R. W. Rieber (New York: New York Academy of Sciences, 1975), pp. 211–24; and Rivers, *Teaching*

Foreign-Language Skills, 2d ed. (Chicago: Chicago University Press, 1981), pp. 445–52.

4 Snow and Hoefnagel-Höhle, "The Critical Period...."

5 Penfield and Roberts, *Speech and Brain-Mechanisms*; and Lenneberg, *Biological Foundations of Language*.

6 See E. J. Rosansky, "The Critical Period for the Acquisition of Language: Some Cognitive Developmental Considerations," *Working Papers in Bilingualism* 6(1975): 93–100 (Toronto: OISE); and S. D. Krashen, "The Critical Period...," in Aaronson and Rieber, p. 220.

7 B. Inhelder and J. Piaget, *The Growth of Logical Thinking from Childhood to Adolescence* (New York: Basic Books, 1958).

8 It can be shown that a concept such as the agreement of the past participle in French in all its ramifications involves nearly all of these logical operations (Rivers 1960, unpublished paper, from which this paragraph is drawn). This explains why certain aspects of grammar are difficult for a young child to grasp through explanation. Even French children have to be taught meticulously and thoroughly drilled in the complete series of these agreements, many of which are written language phenomena.

9 Snow and Hoefnagel-Höhle, "The Critical Period...."

10 J. H. Schumann, *The Pidginization Process: A Model for Second Language Acquisition* (Rowley, Mass.: Newbury House, 1978), chap. 7; and Schumann, "Affective Factors and the Problem of Age in Second Language Acquisition," *LL* 25(1975): 209–35; and "Social Distance as a Factor in Second Language Acquisition," *LL* 26(1976): 135–43.

11 See the many studies of second-language learning by children in E. Hatch, ed., *Second Language Acquisition: A Book of Readings* (Rowley, Mass.: Newbury House, 1978).

12 For extracting messages from oral material, see chap. 5 of this book.

13 T. G. Bever, "Psychologically Real Grammar Emerges because of its Role in Language Acquisition," in *Developmental Psycholinguistics: Theory and Applications*, ed. D. P. Dato. GURT. (Washington, D.C.: Georgetown University Press, 1975), p. 66.

14 Ibid.

15 For examples of authentic listening materials, see chap. 3, "Listening," in the *Practical Guides*.

16 J. B. Carroll, "Learning Theory for the Classroom Teacher," in Jarvis (1974b), pp. 140–1.

17 Bever, "Psychologically Real Grammar...," pp. 63–75.

18 See also J. B. Carroll, "Conscious and Automatic Processes in Language Learning," *CMLR* 37(1981), pp. 462–74.

19 Learning to read a new script is discussed in Rivers and Temperley, *A Practical Guide to the Teaching of English as a Second or Foreign Language* (New York: Oxford University Press, 1978), pp. 196–7. Of course, learning to read an ideographic system like the characters used by the Chinese and Japanese is a much more formidable undertaking than learning a new alphabetic system.

20 K. S. Goodman, "Reading: A Psycholinguistic Guessing Game," *Journal of the Reading Specialist* 6(1967): 126–35.

21 M. C. Robeck and J. A. Wilson, *Psychology of Reading: Foundations of Instruction* (New York: Wiley, 1974), p. 33.

22 F. Smith, ed., *Psycholinguistics and Reading* (New York: Holt, Rinehart and Winston, 1973), p. v. Italics not in the original. Smith bases his "insights" on the theoretical and experimental work of G. A. Miller, K. S. Goodman, P. A. Kolers, D. L. Holmes, C. Chomsky, P. Rozin, and J. Torrey.

23 P. A. Kolers, "Three Stages of Reading," in Smith, pp. 47–8. Original publication in *Basic Studies on Reading*, ed. H. Levin and J. Williams (New York: Basic Books, 1970).

24 For the linguistic use of the term "redundancy," see Rivers, *Teaching Foreign-Language Skills*, pp. 53–4.

25 D. R. Olson, "Language Use for Communicating, Instructing, and Thinking," in *Language Comprehension and the Acquisition of Knowledge*, ed. J. B. Carroll and R. O. Freedle (Washington, D.C.: V. H. Winston and Sons, 1972), p. 143.

26 G. A. Miller and P. N. Johnson-Laird, *Language and Perception* (Cambridge, Mass.: Harvard University Press, 1976), p. 704.

27 For guidance in choosing materials and constructing exercises for developing confidence in reading, see F. Grellet, *Developing Reading Skills: A Practical Guide to Reading Comprehension Exercises* (Cambridge: Cambridge University Press, 1981).

28 J. B. Carroll, "Defining Language Comprehension: Some Speculations," in Carroll and Freedle, p. 3.

29 J. Chall, "Learning to Read," in *Communication, Language, and Meaning*, ed. G. A. Miller (New York: Basic Books, 1973), p. 119.

30 F. Smith, *Psycholinguistics and Reading*, p. 7.

31 For a discussion of conceptual networks, see "If Only I Could Remember it all!" chap. 4 of this book.

32 Models of this type are sometimes referred to as analysis by synthesis models (see pp. 82–3 of this book). Gibson and Levin, *The Psychology of Reading* (Cambridge, Mass.: MIT Press, 1975), pp. 449–53, discuss the pros and cons of this approach. K. Goodman, "Reading:...," calls his model "a psycholinguistic guessing game" that "involves an interaction between thought and language." A. R. Luria, *Traumatic Aphasia* (The Hague: Mouton, 1970), describes normal reading in similar terms.

33 T. G. Sticht, "Learning by Listening," in Carroll and Freedle, p. 294. Italics not in the original.

34 J. B. Carroll, "Defining Language Comprehension," in Carroll and Freedle, p. 8.

35 T. G. Bever, "Perceptions, Thought, and Language," in Carroll and Freedle, p. 101.

36 For examples of suitable materials, activities, and tests for various levels of reading, see Rivers, *Teaching Foreign-Language Skills*, chap. 9; and chaps. 6 and 7 of the *Practical Guides*.

7 Motivating through classroom techniques

1 J. Frymier, "Motivation: The Mainspring and Gyroscope of Learning," *Theory into Practice* 9(1970): 23. Italics in the original.
2 T. Johnson, R. Feigenbaum, and M. Weiby, "Some Determinants and Consequences of the Teacher's Perception of Causation." Unpublished manuscript, University of Wisconsin, 1964, cited by W. B. Waetjen in "The Teacher and Motivation," *Theory into Practice* 9(1970): 13–14.
3 For a discussion of making even exercises resemble communication activities, see "Bridging the Gap to Autonomous Interaction," chap. 4 in Rivers, *Communicating Naturally in a Second Language: Theory and Practice in Language Teaching* (Cambridge: Cambridge University Press, 1983).
4 For a discussion of pidginization, see J. H. Schumann, *The Pidginization Process: A Model for Second Language Acquisition* (Rowley, Mass.: Newbury House, 1978).
5 John Holt, *How Children Fail* (New York: Dell, 1970), p. 42.
6 N. Postman and C. Weingartner, *Teaching as a Subversive Activity* (New York: Delacorte, 1969), p. 18. Italics not in the original. This is also the emphasis of Lozanov, who speaks of the peripheral perceptions of the students and tries to create a relaxing environment for language learning in the classroom. See G. Lozanov, *Suggestology and Outlines of Suggestopedy* (New York: Gordon and Breach, 1978).
7 D. P. Ausubel, *Educational Psychology: A Cognitive View* (New York: Holt, Rinehart and Winston, 1968), pp. 363–93.
8 Ibid., pp. 367–8.
9 R. C. Gardner and W. E. Lambert, *Attitudes and Motivation in Second-Language Learning* (Rowley, Mass.: Newbury House, 1972), pp. 11–16. Gardner and Lambert deliberately avoided the inclusion of *the teacher variable* in their studies.
10 R. C. Gardner, "Attitudes and Motivation: Their Role in Second Language Acquisition," in *Focus on the Learner: Pragmatic Perspectives for the Language Teacher*, ed. J. W. Oller, Jr. and J. C. Richards (Rowley, Mass.: Newbury House, 1973). He attributed the attitudes of the students toward members of the other-language community in large measure to parental influence.
11 Y. M. Lukmani, "Motivation to Learn and Language Proficiency," *LL* 22(1972): 261–73.
12 R. C. Gardner, P. C. Smythe, R. Clement, and L. Gliksman, "Second-Language Learning: A Social Psychological Perspective," *CMLR* 32(1976): 199. Italicized in the original.
13 R. C. Gardner, P. C. Smythe, and G. R. Brunet, "Intensive Second Language Study: Effects on Attitudes, Motivation and French Achievement," *LL* 27(1977): 243–61.
14 Schumann, *The Pidginization Process*, pp. 86–99. Also discussed in Rivers, *Teaching Foreign-Language Skills*, 2d ed. (Chicago: University

of Chicago Press, 1981), pp. 451–2, where useful further reading is indicated in the footnotes.

15 "Social distance" here does not refer to class distinctions (although these can play a role). Social distance can refer to the fact that the language learners and available native speakers attend different schools, go to different churches, enjoy different types of leisure activities (sports, music, or social gatherings), so that opportunities to meet each other are rare without some major effort on the learner's part and some reciprocal response on the part of the native speakers.

16 The complexities of motivation in bilingual situations have been the subject of much research and are related to such sociological factors as dominance, enclosure, and acculturation. See C. B. Paulston, *Bilingual Education: Theories and Issues* (Rowley, Mass.: Newbury House, 1980); J. H. Schumann, "Social Distance as a Factor in Second Language Acquisition," *LL* 26(1976): 135–43; and Schumann, *The Pidginization Process*, chap. 7, "Social and Psychological Distance as Factors in Second Language Acquisition," pp. 69–100.

17 Implications from motivation theory for classroom practice are also dealt with at length in Rivers, *The Psychologist and the Foreign-Language Teacher* (Chicago: University of Chicago Press, 1964), chap. 9.

18 For a fuller discussion of making all exercises serve the purposes of communication, see W. M. Rivers, "Bridging the Gap to Autonomous Interaction," chap. 4 in Rivers, *Communicating Naturally*.

19 Initiated by Linda B. Rivers, at Neenah School, in Hyderabad, India, for first-grade children learning English.

20 See J. J. Asher, "The Learning Strategy of the Total Physical Response: A Review," *MLJ* 50(1966): 79–84.

21 For the Natural Approach, see T. D. Terrell, "A Natural Approach to Second Language Acquisition and Learning," *MLJ* 61(1977): 325–37; and "The Natural Approach to Language Teaching: An Update," *MLJ* 66(1982): 121-32.

22 For Direct Method, see Rivers, *Teaching Foreign-Language Skills*, chap. 2.

23 Ibid.

24 Ibid., chap 8.

25 For further discussion of possible approaches to different types of students, see "Teacher-Student Relations: Coercion or Cooperation?" chap. 8 of this book.

26 Described in C. E. Silberman, *Crisis in the Classroom* (New York: Random House, 1970).

27 D. A. McCarthy, "Sex Differences in Language Development," in *Psychological Studies of Human Development*, ed. R. G. Kuhlen and G. G. Thompson (New York: Appleton-Century-Crofts, 1970), pp. 349–53. We will not enter here into whether this observed difference is culturally fostered.

28 R. L. Politzer and L. Weiss, "Characteristics and Behaviors of the Successful Foreign Language Teacher." Stanford Center for Research and

Development in Teaching, Technical Report No. 5 (Palo Alto, April 1969), pp. 69–70.

29 Ausubel, *Educational Psychology*, p. 393.

30 Ibid., p. 365.

31 Ibid., p. 385.

32 For a discussion of achievement motivation, see A. S. Alschuler, D. Tabor, and J. McIntyre, *Teaching Achievement Motivation: Theory and Practice in Psychological Education* (Middletown, Conn.: Education Ventures, 1971); for an in-depth discussion of the subject, see J. R. Cook, *A Theoretical Approach for Training Second Language Teachers in Motivation Based on Atkinson's Achievement Motivation and Bandura's Social Learning Theories*. Ph.D. thesis for the University of Texas at Austin (Ann Arbor, Mich.: University Microfilms International, 1980: RTA 81-00893).

33 Quoted in Silberman, *Crisis in the Classroom*, p. 159.

8 Teacher-student relations

1 R. Coles, *Teachers and the Children of Poverty* (Washington, D.C.: The Potomac Institute, 1970).

2 Harry Reinert, "Student Attitudes Toward Foreign Language: No Sale!" *MLJ* 54(1970): 107.

3 Otto K. Liedke, "A Historical View of the Controversy between the Ancient and the Modern Languages in American Higher Education," *German Quarterly* 17(1944): 1–13, reprinted in *Twentieth Century Modern Language Teaching: Sources and Readings*, ed. M. Newmark (New York, Philosophical Library, 1948), pp. 11–21.

4 Quoted by A. E. Lean in *And Merely Teach* (Carbondale: Southern Illinois University Press, 1968), p. 58. Italics in the original.

5 E. J. Murray, *Motivation and Emotion* (Englewood Cliffs, N.J.: Prentice-Hall, 1964), pp. 74–82.

6 "Individualized approach," as used here, should not be confused with some models of individualized instruction that have come very close to individual independent study. "Individualized" here means "adapted to the needs of the individual." This may be within the context of a normal class, in which students have some latitude in choice of type of assignment and a flexible grading system takes this into account. See also "Individualized Instruction and Cooperative Learning: Some Theoretical Considerations," in Rivers, *Communicating Naturally in a Second Language: Theory and Practice in Language Teaching* (Cambridge: Cambridge University Press, 1983), chap. 5.

7 See H. Sebald, *Adolescence: A Sociological Analysis* (New York: Appleton-Century-Crofts, 1968).

8 See also chap. 2 of this book, section on "Career Education."

9 For further discussion of teacher training, see chap. 14 of this book.

10 After preparing your own statement you may like to compare it with

similar statements appended to chap. 1 of Rivers, *Teaching Foreign-Language Skills*, 2d ed. (Chicago: University of Chicago Press, 1981).

9 Understanding the learner in the language laboratory

1 W. R. Parker, *The National Interest in Foreign Languages*, 3d ed. (Washington, D.C.: Government Printing Office, 1962), p. 67.
2 E. Hocking, *Language Laboratory and Language Learning* (Washington, D.C.: Department of Audiovisual Instruction, National Education Association of the United States, 1964), p. 11.
3 Ibid., pp. 19–20.
4 Ibid., p. 21.
5 For cognitive styles, see W. M. Rivers and B. J. Melvin, "Language Learners as Individuals: Discovering their Needs, Wants, and Learning Styles," in *The Second Language Classroom: Directions for the 1980's*, ed. J. E. Alatis, H. B. Altman, and P. M. Alatis (New York: Oxford University Press, 1981), pp. 87–91.
6 Discussed in "Bridging the Gap to Autonomous Interaction" in Rivers, *Communicating Naturally in a Second Language: Theory and Practice in Language Teaching* (Cambridge: Cambridge University Press, 1983), chap. 4.
7 Rivers and Melvin, "Language Learners as Individuals," pp. 84–6.
8 Rivers, *Teaching Foreign-Language Skills*, 2d ed. (Chicago: University of Chicago Press, 1981), pp. 55–9.
9 The Silent Way, Counseling-Learning/Community Language Learning, and Suggestopaedia are discussed in depth in E. W. Stevick, *Teaching Languages: A Way and Ways* (Rowley, Mass.: Newbury House, 1980).
10 For more information, see J. A. van Ek, *The Threshold Level for Modern Language Learning in Schools* (London: Longman, 1977). Original publication: Strasbourg: Council of Europe, 1976.
11 An attempt to draw together these three trends has been made by the staff of the Modern Language Centre of OISE. See H. H. Stern, "Communicative Language Teaching and Learning: Toward a Synthesis," in Alatis, Altman, and Alatis, pp. 133–48; and "Directions in Foreign Language Curriculum Development," in *Proceedings of the National Conference on Professional Priorities. November 1980. Boston, Massachusetts*, ed. D. L. Lange (Hastings-on-Hudson, N.Y.: ACTFL Materials Center, 1981), pp. 12–17.
12 A dictocomp is an exercise in which students listen to the reading of a short passage (anecdote, explanation of facts, or conversation) and then write an account of it in their own words, with a short list of key words as a memory aid.
13 Hocking, *Language Laboratory*, p. 29.

10 Testing and student learning

1 A. E. Pilliner, "Subjective and Objective Testing," in *Language Testing Symposium: A Psycholinguistic Approach*, ed. A. Davies (London: Oxford University Press, 1968), p. 31.

2   J. B. Carroll, "Foreign Language Testing: Will the Persistent Problems Persist?" in *Testing in Second Language Teaching: New Dimensions,* ed. M. C. O'Brien (Dublin: Association of Teachers of English as a Second or Other Language, and Dublin University Press, 1973), p. 15.

3   G. A. Miller, E. Galanter, and K. H. Pribram, *Plans and the Structure of Behavior* (New York: Holt, Rinehart and Winston, 1960). The TOTE unit is described and discussed on pp. 25–38.

4   Ibid., p. 29.

5   Ibid., pp. 25–6.

6   Ibid., p. 31.

7   In the United States, Foreign Service Institute Absolute Language Proficiency Ratings are sometimes used for such certification. These are reproduced in Appendix A of Rivers, *Teaching Foreign-Language Skills,* 2d ed. (Chicago: University of Chicago Press, 1981), pp. 497–9.

8   Detailed language-specific guidelines are obtainable from the ACTFL Materials Center.

9   This subject is developed in relation to undergraduate-level courses in "The Non-Major: Tailoring the Course to Fit the Person – Not the Image," in Rivers, *Speaking in Many Tongues,* expanded 2d ed. (Rowley, Mass.: Newbury House, 1976), pp. 169–83; and *ADFL Bulletin 5,* 2(1973):12–18; and Jankowsky, ed. *Language and International Studies.* GURT. (Washington, D.C.: Georgetown University Press, 1973), pp. 85–97.

10 W. M. Rivers, "Techniques for Developing Proficiency in the Spoken Language in an Individualized Foreign Language Program," in *Individualizing Foreign Language Instruction,* ed. H. B. Altman and R. L. Politzer (Rowley, Mass.: Newbury House, 1971), p. 165.

11 J. Veatch, "Individualizing," in *Individualization of Instruction: A Teaching Strategy,* ed. V. M. Howes (New York: Macmillan, 1970), pp. 91–2.

12 For further details of this investigation, see Rivers, "The Non-Major. . . ."

13 The author worked in a school where the grades A, B, C, D, E were the only rankings allotted, but pluses and minuses were used to indicate personal achievement or lack of effort. In this system a C+ was more meritorious than an A–, since the former meant the student had worked hard to achieve the grade, whereas the latter indicated that the student's work did not reflect her full potential. Grades were never comparative, and students applauded each other's progress, while caring about their own degree of improvement from test to test rather than the number of other students they had surpassed on any one test. See June Epstein, *A Golden String: The Story of Dorothy J. Ross* (Collingwood, Australia: Greenhouse Publications, 1981). It was D. J. Ross who sowed the seed of this chapter in the mind of the author when, in 1955, she asked: "Why do we test anyway?"

14 E. D. Allen and R. M. Valette, *Modern Language Classroom Techniques* (New York: Harcourt Brace Jovanovich, 1972), pp. 21, 37.

15 I have discussed how we may move in this direction from the earliest stages in "Talking off the Tops of their Heads" and "Bridging the Gap to Autonomous Interaction," chaps. 3 and 4 in Rivers, *Communicating*

Naturally in a Second Language: Theory and Practice in Language Teaching (Cambridge: Cambridge University Press, 1983).

16 In R. M. Valette and R. S. Disick, *Modern Language Performance Objectives and Individualization* (New York: Harcourt Brace Jovanovich, 1972), the distinction is made between "formal performance objectives" and "expressive performance objectives," the latter being "open-ended" with the conditions "less precise" (p. 26), "the actual form such student behavior will assume [being] not as readily predictable" (p. 54).

17 Robert Hutchins was the conservative President of the University of Chicago who introduced a structured, non-elective curriculum based on the great books of the past to that university in the 1930s and to St. John's College, Annapolis, of which he was a trustee.

18 Ivan Illich is a radical educator who despairs of conventional schooling. In an influential book, *Deschooling Society* (New York: Harper & Row, 1970), he proposed replacing school systems with networks of resources that would bring together things, people with special skills, and learners, so that the latter could learn what they wanted and felt they needed to learn.

19 See Rivers, *The Psychologist and the Foreign-Language Teacher* (Chicago: University of Chicago Press, 1964), chap. 6, "Two Levels of Language."

20 R. M. Valette, *Directions in Foreign Language Testing* (New York: MLA/ERIC, 1969), p. 31.

21 Many of the activities described in "Talking off the Tops of their Heads," chap. 3 of Rivers, *Communicating Naturally*, could be used as tests of this type. See also the *Practical Guides*, chap. 2.

22 The ACTFL Provisional Proficiency Guidelines in the Appendix to this book give indications of the level at which performance of such tasks may be ranked, should we wish to do so. They are guidelines for examiners, rather than for test constructors, in that they point out what aspects of production are typical of various levels of language control. They do, however, indicate at the same time the kinds of tasks students at different levels may be expected to perform. (The tasks are elaborated in more detail in the language-specific guidelines.)

23 J. B. Carroll, "The Psychology of Language Testing," in Davies, pp. 56–8.

11 From the pyramid to the commune

1 The terms "major" and "concentrator" will be used interchangeably; some universities use one term, some the other, for students committed to the full undergraduate program supplied by the department.

2 Many students "who have no intention of continuing" are unable to do so, because of the weight of preconcentration demands from their major departments. Under the commune system, where courses are complete in themselves, rather than essentially linked in an ascending pyramid, these students often return to take a more advanced course when major com-

mitments permit it, because their earlier experience of the language has been satisfying and stimulating.

3 For ways of making language learning communicative even at elementary and intermediate levels, see G. M. Russo, *Expanding Communication: Teaching Foreign Languages at the College Level* (New York: Harcourt Brace Jovanovich, 1982).

4 For a useful discussion of this subject, see A. Valdman, "The Incorporation of the Notion of Communicative Competence in the Design of the Introductory Foreign Language Course Syllabus," in *Proceedings of the National Conference on Professional Priorities November 1980. Boston, Massachusetts*, ed. D. L. Lange (Hastings-on-Hudson, N.Y.: ACTFL Materials Center), pp. 18–23. Valdman deals with the problem under the headings of cyclical progression, notional focus, discursive authenticity, and simplification and reduction.

5 For "Oral Survival" courses, see Rivers, *Teaching Foreign-Language Skills*, 2d ed. (Chicago: University of Chicago Press, 1981), pp. 242–4.

6 For a further discussion of the undergraduate curriculum, see "The Revolution Now," chap. 12 of this book.

7 *The Advisor* (Teacher-Course Evaluation, University of Illinois at Urbana-Champaign, 1970–1), p. 125.

8 For a detailed discussion of translation as a teaching-learning device and as a specialized study, see the *Practical Guides*, chap. 9.

9 At Harvard, where a fully developed series of living language courses in French, allowing for fifteen separate entry levels and a diversity of content, has been in place for nine years (and is still evolving), enrollments increased in nonrequirement-level courses by 90 percent (between 1973–4 and 1981–2).

12 The revolution now

1 For the sake of brevity, the term "(foreign-)language departments" will be used throughout. The term is intended to include departments of foreign languages and literatures.

2 From 1974 to 1980, the Department of Romance Languages and Literatures registered a 52 percent increase in enrollment in language courses in the five Romance languages taught. The increase was largely in courses for nonmajors (or nonconcentrators), the number of requirement students remaining approximately constant from year to year.

3 Quoted in the *Chronicle of Higher Education*, August 25, 1980, in the Dispatch Case column.

4 Alvin Toffler, *Future Shock* (New York: Bantam Books, 1970), pp. 359–61.

5 Ibid., p. 359.

6 Ibid. Italics in the original.

7 Ibid., p. 360, p. 359.

8 Ibid., p. 361.

9 Ibid., p. 362.

10 The political and educational response to societal needs for language teaching to adults, under the auspices of the Council of Europe, is described in detail in W. M. Rivers, "Language Learners as Individuals: Discovering their Needs and Wants," chap. 10 of Rivers, *Communicating Naturally in a Second Language: Theory and Practice in Language Teaching* (Cambridge: Cambridge University Press, 1983).

11 See P. Simon, *The Tongue-Tied American: Confronting the Foreign Language Crisis* (New York: Continuum, 1980). Representative Paul Simon of Illinois was a leading proponent and member of the President's Commission on Foreign Language and International Studies.

12 For a fuller discussion of the needs and interests of nonmajors (or nonconcentrators), see "The Non-Major: Tailoring the Course to Fit the Person – Not the Image," in Rivers, *Speaking in Many Tongues*, expanded 2d ed. (Rowley, Mass.: Newbury House, 1976), pp. 169–83; and *ADFL Bulletin 5*, 2(1973):12–18; and Jankowsky, ed., *Language and International Studies*. GURT. (Washington, D.C.: Georgetown University Press, 1973), pp. 85–97. See also the University of Illinois Questionnaire on Interests in Foreign Languages," in Rivers, *Speaking in Many Tongues*, 2d ed., pp. 184–220.

13 For some discussion of courses developed at Harvard University for nonconcentrators or nonmajors, see chap. 1 of this book; and S. Villani, "Communication in an Experimental Foreign-Language Class," *CMLR* 33(1977): 373–8.

14 *Strength Through Wisdom: A Critique of U.S. Capability.* A Report to the President from the President's Commission on Foreign Language and International Studies (Washington, D.C.: Government Printing Office, 1979), pp. 7–8, 11.

15 G. L. N. Robinson, *Issues in Second Language and Cross-Cultural Education: The Forest Through the Trees* (Boston: Heinle and Heinle, 1980), p. 150.

16 For suggestions for teaching for cultural understanding, see H. N. Seelye, *Teaching Culture: Strategies for Foreign Language Educators* (Skokie, Ill.: National Textbook Co., 1974); and H. L. Nostrand, "Empathy for a Second Culture: Motivation and Techniques," in *Responding to New Realities*. ACTFL Review of Foreign Language Education, vol. 5, ed. G. A. Jarvis (Skokie, Ill.: National Textbook Co., 1974a).

17 An excellent example is *Contemporary French Civilization* (Department of Modern Languages, Montana State University, Bozeman, Mont. 59717).

18 This is also strongly recommended by the President's Commission, which allotted one of the six sections of its report to International Educational Exchanges. See *Strength Through Wisdom*, p. 9.

19 At Harvard University, Professor Laurence Wylie taught a highly successful course of this type, called "Communication with the French." Film clips of communicative situations were analyzed to achieve an understanding of the nature and relationship of such elements as verbal expression, spatial relationships, touch, body posture and movement, formal and unconscious gesture, facial expression, and eye behavior in relation to the cultural and psychological context. Students then learned

to reproduce each situation as a total communication, using video to improve their role playing. Professor Wylie worked at Harvard in association with three departments: Romance Languages and Literatures, Psychology and Social Relations, and Anthropology.

20 See also "From the Pyramid to the Commune: The Evolution of the Foreign-Language Department," chap. 11 of this book. These types of courses have been very successful at Harvard and accounted for 70 percent of the 36 percent increase in French language enrollments between 1974 and 1980.

21 For specialized programs at Northeastern University, Boston, see chap. 1 of this book, p. 10.

22 For further details, see R. Richterich and J.-L. Chancerel, *Identifying the Needs of Adults Learning a Foreign Language* (Oxford: Pergamon Press, 1980); and J. L. Trim et al., *Systems Development in Adult Language Learning* (Oxford: Pergamon Press, for the Council of Europe, 1980). For a short account, see W. M. Rivers and M. S. Temperley, *A Practical Guide to the Teaching of English as a Second or Foreign Language* (New York: Oxford University Press, 1978), pp. 56–7.

23 For a detailed description of the teacher-training program for all teaching fellows (graduate students) and teaching assistants in the Department of Romance Languages and Literatures at Harvard University, see W. C. Born, ed., *New Contents, New Teachers, New Publics* (Middlebury, Vt.: NEC, 1978), p. 105, where it is cited as the Selected Teaching Fellow Training Model; reproduced in M. Mueller, "Leadership, Development Therapy: The Course Head's Problems and Pleasures," *ADFL Bulletin* (March, 1983). Since 1978, more videotaping sessions have been added for each trainee.

24 See chap. 13 of this book, pp. 163–4.

13 Conservation and innovation

1 Robert Frost, "Precaution," *Complete Poems of Robert Frost* (New York: Henry Holt and Company, 1948).

2 J. Robert Moskin, Interview with Günther Grass, "Günther Grass and the Murderer at the Desk," *Intellectual Digest* (April, 1972), p. 20.

3 The problems of adapting to new attitudes among youth and rapid change in society are discussed at length in "Foreign Languages in a Time of Change," in Rivers, *Speaking in Many Tongues*, expanded 2d ed. (Rowley, Mass.: Newbury House, 1976), pp. 145–56.

4 Quoted from "Basic Information on the FL Requirement," issued by the Scanlan Committee, University of Illinois at Urbana, 1972 (mimeograph).

5 *Julius Caesar*, act 1, scene 2, with adaptations.

6 Sr. M. Celeste, "The Status of Foreign Languages in Junior Colleges in Illinois, 1971," in *Changing Patterns in Foreign Language Programs*, ed. Rivers et al. (Rowley, Mass.: Newbury House, 1972), pp. 172–6.

7 The complex question of student motivation is discussed in "Motivating through Classroom Techniques," chap. 7 of this book.

8 The Two-Stage Approach is appropriate wherever foreign-language study

is begun – in elementary school, junior high school, high school, or at the undergraduate level.

14 Students, teachers, and the future

1 *The Rambler*, No. 178.
2 Suggestions for identifying the type of program the local community needs and wants are given in chap. 2 of this book, pp. 43–4.
3 See "The Revolution Now," chap. 12 of this book.
4 Teacher trainers should, as a minimum, have access to *FLA, MLJ, ADFL Bulletin, LL, AL, LT*, and specific language journals like *TQ, FR*, and *UP*.
5 One such program is described in full in S. and A. Shinall, "To Teach or Not to Teach: Is Para-Teaching the Answer?" *FR* 46(1973): 766–2.
6 Models of professional training for language teachers, with identification of some model programs, are discussed in "New Teachers: Developing Flexible Foreign-Language Teachers," in *New Contents, New Teachers, New Publics*, ed. W. C. Born (Middlebury, Vt.: NEC, 1978). For preparation of college teachers, see W. M. Rivers, "Preparing College and University Instructors for a Lifetime of Teaching: A Luxury or a Necessity," in J. E. Alatis, H. H. Stern, and P. Strevens, eds., *Applied Linguistics and the Preparation of Second-Language Teachers: Toward a Rationale*, GURT, 1983 (Washington, D.C.: Georgetown University Press, in press). Results of a questionnaire (Rivers, 1983) are included.
7 Much useful material of this kind is available from the ACTFL Materials Center, and from the Northeast Conference, Box 623, Middlebury, Vt. 05753.
8 For detailed guidance in textbook evaluation, see Rivers, *Teaching Foreign-Language Skills*, 2d ed. (Chicago: University of Chicago Press, 1981), pp. 475–82.

Appendix

1 The project for establishing the guidelines, entitled "A Design for Measuring and Communicating Foreign Language Proficiency," was funded by a grant (#G008 103203) from the International Research and Studies Program of the U.S. Department of Education.
2 For the original Foreign Service Institute (FSI) scales for speaking and reading, with full descriptions of expectations at each level, see *Absolute Language Proficiency Ratings*, Appendix A of W. M. Rivers, *Teaching Foreign-Language Skills*, 2d ed. (Chicago: University of Chicago Press, 1981), pp. 497–9.

Bibliography

Aaronson, Doris, and Rieber, Robert W., eds. 1975. *Developmental Psycho-linguistics and Communicative Disorders.* New York: New York Academy of Sciences.

Alatis, James E., Altman, Howard B., and Alatis, Penelope M., eds. 1981. *The Second Language Classroom: Directions for the 1980's.* New York: Oxford University Press.

Allen, Edward D., and Valette, Rebecca M. 1972. *Modern Language Classroom Techniques.* New York: Harcourt Brace Jovanovich.

——— 1977. *Classroom Techniques: Foreign Languages and English as a Second Language.* New York: Harcourt Brace Jovanovich.

Alschuler, Alfred S., Tabor, Diane, and McIntyre, James. 1971. *Teaching Achievement Motivation: Theory and Practice in Psychological Education.* Middletown, Conn.: Education Ventures.

Altman, Howard B., and Politzer, Robert L., eds. 1971. *Individualizing Foreign Language Instruction.* Rowley, Mass.: Newbury House.

Ausubel, David P. 1968. *Educational Psychology: A Cognitive View.* New York: Holt, Rinehart and Winston.

Bloom, Lois. 1970. *Language Development: Form and Function in Emerging Grammars.* Cambridge, Mass.: MIT Press.

Blumenthal, Arthur L. 1970. *Language and Psychology.* New York: Wiley.

Born, Warren C., ed. 1974. *Toward Student-Centered Foreign Language Programs.* Middlebury, Vt.: NEC.

——— ed. 1975. *Goals Clarification: Curriculum, Teaching, Evaluation.* Middlebury, Vt.: NEC.

——— ed. 1978. *New Contents, New Teachers, New Publics.* Middlebury, Vt.: NEC.

——— ed. 1979. *The Foreign Language Learner in Today's Classroom Environment.* Middlebury, Vt.: NEC.

Brown, Roger. 1973. *A First Language: The Early Stages.* Cambridge, Mass.: Harvard University Press.

Burt, Marina K., Dulay, Heidi C., and Finocchiaro, Mary, eds. 1977. *Viewpoints on English as a Second Language.* In Honor of James E. Alatis. New York: Regents Publishing Company.

Cairns, Helen S., and Cairns, Charles E. 1976. *Psycholinguistics: A Cognitive View of Language.* New York: Holt, Rinehart and Winston.

Carroll, John B., and Freedle, Roy O., eds. 1972. *Language Comprehension and the Acquisition of Knowledge.* Washington, D.C.: V.H. Winston and Sons.

243

Bibliography

Charnofsky, Stanley. 1971. *Educating the Powerless*. Belmont, Calif.: Wadsworth.

Chastain, Kenneth. 1976. *Developing Second-Language Skills: Theory to Practice*, 2d. ed. Chicago: Rand McNally. (A revision of *The Development of Modern Language Skills: Theory to Practice*. Philadelphia: The Center for Curriculum Development, 1971.)

Chomsky, Noam. 1965. *Aspects of the Theory of Syntax*. Cambridge, Mass.: MIT Press.

1966. *Topics in the Theory of Generative Grammar*. The Hague: Mouton.

Coles, Robert. 1970. *Teachers and the Children of Poverty*. Washington, D.C.: The Potomac Institute.

Coste, Daniel, Courtillon, Janine, Ferenczi, Victor, Martins-Baltar, Michel, and Papo, Eliane. 1976. *Un niveau-seuil*. Strasbourg: Council of Europe.

Curran, Charles A. C. 1976. *Counseling-Learning in Second Languages*. Apple River, Ill.: Apple River Press.

Dato, Daniel P., ed. 1975. *Developmental Psycholinguistics: Theory and Applications*. GURT. Washington, D.C.: Georgetown University Press.

Davies, Alan, ed. 1968. *Language Testing Symposium: A Psycholinguistic Approach*. London: Oxford University Press.

Deese, James. 1965. *The Structure of Associations in Language and Thought*. Baltimore: Johns Hopkins Press.

Dragonas, Phyllis J. 1983. *The High School Goes Abroad: International Home-Stay Exchange Programs*. Washington, D.C.: CAL.

Epstein, June. 1981. *A Golden String: The Story of Dorothy J. Ross*. Collingwood, Australia: Greenhouse Publications.

Fanselow, John F., and Crymes, Ruth, eds. 1976. *On TESOL 1976*. Washington, D.C.: TESOL.

Gardner, R. C., and Lambert, Wallace E. 1972. *Attitudes and Motivation in Second-Language Learning*. Rowley, Mass.: Newbury House.

Gibson, Eleanor J., and Levin, Harry. 1975. *The Psychology of Reading*. Cambridge, Mass.: MIT Press.

Halle, Morris, Bresnan, Joan, and Miller, George A., eds. 1978. *Linguistic Theory and Psychological Reality*. Cambridge, Mass.: MIT Press.

Halliday, Michael A. K. 1973. *Explorations in the Functions of Language*. London: Edward Arnold.

Harris, David P. 1969. *Testing English as a Second Language*. New York: McGraw-Hill.

Hatch, Evelyn, ed. 1978. *Second Language Acquisition: A Book of Readings*. Rowley, Mass.: Newbury House.

Hocking, Elton. 1964. *Language Laboratory and Language Learning*. Washington, D.C.: Department of Audiovisual Instruction, National Education Association of the United States.

Holt, John. 1970. *How Children Fail*. New York: Dell.

Howes, Virgil M., ed. 1970. *Individualization of Instruction: A Teaching Strategy*. New York: Macmillan.

Illich, Ivan. 1970. *Deschooling Society*. New York: Harper & Row.

Inhelder, Bärbel, and Piaget, Jean. 1958. *The Growth of Logical Thinking from Childhood to Adolescence.* New York: Basic Books.

Jankowsky, Kurt, ed. 1973. *Language and International Studies.* GURT. Washington, D.C.: Georgetown University Press.

Jarvis, Gilbert A., ed. 1974a. *Responding to New Realities.* ACTFL Review of Foreign Language Education, vol. 5. Skokie, Ill.: National Textbook Co.

——— ed. 1974b. *The Challenge of Communication.* ACTFL Review of Foreign Language Education, vol. 6. Skokie, Ill.: National Textbook Co.

——— ed. 1975. *Perspective: A New Freedom.* ACTFL Review of Foreign Language Education, vol. 7. Skokie, Ill.: National Textbook Co.

——— ed. 1978. *An Integrative Approach to Foreign Language Teaching: Choosing Among the Options.* ACTFL Foreign Language Education Series, vol. 8. Skokie, Ill.: National Textbook Co.

Katona, George. 1940. *Organizing and Memorizing.* New York: Columbia University Press.

Krashen, Stephen D. 1981. *Second Language Acquisition and Second Language Learning.* Oxford: Pergamon Press.

Krashen, Stephen D., Scarcella, Robin C., and Long, Michael H., eds. 1982. *Child-Adult Differences in Second Language Acquisition.* Rowley, Mass.: Newbury House.

Kuhlen, R. G., and Thompson, G. G., eds. 1970. *Psychological Studies of Human Development.* New York: Appleton-Century-Crofts.

Lacy, G. n.d. *Developing Defensible Differentiated Programs for the Gifted.* Albany: New York State Education Department.

Lado, Robert. 1961. *Language Testing.* London: Longman.

Lange, Dale L., ed. 1970. *Pluralism in Foreign Language Education.* Britannica Review of Foreign Language Education, vol. 3. Chicago: Encyclopaedia Britannica.

——— ed. 1981. *Proceedings of the National Conference on Professional Priorities. November 1980. Boston, Massachusetts.* Hastings-on-Hudson, N.Y.: ACTFL Materials Center.

Lean, Arthur E. 1968. *And Merely Teach.* Carbondale: Southern Illinois University Press.

Lenneberg, Eric H. 1967. *Biological Foundations of Language.* New York: Wiley.

Levin, Harry, and Williams, J., eds. 1970. *Basic Studies on Reading.* New York: Basic Books.

Lozanov, Georgi. 1978. *Suggestology and Outlines of Suggestopedy.* New York: Gordon and Breach.

Luria, A. R. 1968. *The Mind of A Mnemonist: A Little Book About a Vast Memory,* trans. L. Solotaroff. New York: Basic Books.

——— 1970. *Traumatic Aphasia.* The Hague: Mouton.

Lyons, John, and Wales, R. J., eds. 1966. *Psycholinguistics Papers: Proceedings of the 1966 Edinburgh Conference.* Edinburgh: Edinburgh University Press.

Maley, Alan, and Duff, Alan. 1978. *Drama Techniques in Language Learning.* Cambridge: Cambridge University Press.

Bibliography

Mead, Robert G., Jr., ed. 1966. *Language Teaching: Broader Contexts.* Middlebury, Vt.: NEC.

Miller, George A. 1966. *Psychology: The Science of Mental Life.* Harmondsworth: Pelican Books.

    1967. *Psychology and Communication.* New York: Basic Books.

    ed. 1973. *Communication, Language, and Meaning: Psychological Perspectives.* New York: Basic Books.

Miller, George A., Galanter, E., and Pribram, K. 1960. *Plans and the Structure of Behavior.* New York: Holt, Rinehart and Winston.

Miller, George A., and Johnson-Laird, P. N. 1976. *Language and Perception.* Cambridge, Mass.: Harvard University Press.

Modern Languages for Everyone. 1978. Albany, N.Y.: Bureau of General Education Curriculum Development, State Education Department.

Moskowitz, Gertrude. 1978. *Caring and Sharing in the Foreign Language Class: A Sourcebook on Humanistic Techniques.* Rowley, Mass.: Newbury House.

Murray, Edward J. 1964. *Motivation and Emotion.* Englewood Cliffs, N.J.: Prentice-Hall.

Naiman, N, Fröhlich, M., Stern, H. H., and Todesco, A. 1978. *The Good Language Learner.* Research in Education Series, vol. 7. Toronto: OISE.

Neisser, Ulrich. 1967. *Cognitive Psychology.* New York: Appleton-Century-Crofts.

Newmark, Maxim, ed. 1948. *Twentieth Century Modern Language Teaching: Sources and Readings.* New York: Philosophical Library.

O'Brien, Maureen C., ed. 1973. *Testing in Second Language Teaching: New Dimensions.* Dublin: Association of Teachers of English as a Second or Other Language, and Dublin University Press.

Oller, John W., Jr. 1969. *Language Tests at School: A Pragmatic Approach.* London: Longman.

Oller, John W., Jr., and Richards, Jack C., eds. 1973. *Focus on the Learner: Pragmatic Perspectives for the Language Teacher.* Rowley, Mass.: Newbury House.

Palmer, Harold E. 1964. *The Principles of Language-Study.* Reprint of 1921 edition. London: Oxford University Press. Original Publication date 1921.

Parker, William Riley. 1962. *The National Interest in Foreign Languages,* 3d ed. Washington, D.C.: Government Printing Office.

Paul, James L., Turnbull, Ann, and Cruickshank, William M. 1977. *Mainstreaming: A Practical Guide.* Syracuse, N.Y.: Syracuse University Press.

Paulston, Christina Bratt. 1980. *Bilingual Education: Theories and Issues.* Rowley, Mass.: Newbury House.

Penfield, Wilder, and Roberts, Lamar. 1959. *Speech and Brain-Mechanisms.* Princeton, N.J.: Princeton University Press.

Pimsleur, Paul, and Quinn, Terence, eds. 1971. *The Psychology of Second Language Learning.* Cambridge: Cambridge University Press.

Reibel, David A., and Schane, Sanford A., eds. 1969. *Modern Studies in English: Readings in Transformational Grammar*. Englewood Cliffs, N.J.: Prentice-Hall.

Richterich, René, and Chancerel, Jean-Louis. 1980. *Identifying the Needs of Adults Learning a Foreign Language*. Oxford: Pergamon Press, for the Council of Europe. Originally published 1977 by the Council of Europe, Strasbourg.

Ritchie, W. C., ed. 1978. *Second Language Acquisition Research: Issues and Implications*. New York: Academic Press.

Rivers, Wilga M. 1964. *The Psychologist and the Foreign-Language Teacher*. Chicago: University of Chicago Press.

    1975. *A Practical Guide to the Teaching of French*. New York: Oxford University Press.

    1976. *Speaking in Many Tongues*, expanded 2d ed. Rowley, Mass.: Newbury House.

    1981. *Teaching Foreign-Language Skills*, 2d ed. Chicago: University of Chicago Press.

    1983. *Communicating Naturally in a Second Language: Theory and Practice in Language Teaching*. Cambridge: Cambridge University Press.

Rivers, Wilga M., Allen, Louise H., Savignon, Sandra J., and Scanlan, Richard T., eds. 1972. *Changing Patterns in Foreign Language Programs*. Rowley, Mass.: Newbury House.

Rivers, Wilga M., Azevedo, Milton M., Heflin, William H., Jr., and Hyman-Opler, Ruth. 1976. *A Practical Guide to the Teaching of Spanish*. New York: Oxford University Press.

Rivers, Wilga M., Dell'Orto, Kathleen, and Dell'Orto, Vincent. 1975. *A Practical Guide to the Teaching of German*. New York: Oxford University Press.

Rivers, Wilga M., and Nahir, Moshe. (in press). *A Practical Guide to the Teaching of Hebrew*.

Rivers, Wilga M., and Temperley, Mary S. 1978. *A Practical Guide to the Teaching of English as a Second or Foreign Language*. New York: Oxford University Press.

Robeck, Mildred C., and Wilson, John A. R. 1974. *Psychology of Reading: Foundations of Instruction*. New York: Wiley.

Robinson, Gail L. Nemetz. 1980. *Issues in Second Language and Cross-Cultural Education: The Forest Through the Trees*. Boston: Heinle and Heinle.

Rubin, Louis, ed. 1975. *The Future of Education: Perspectives on Tomorrow's Schooling*. Boston: Allyn & Bacon.

    ed. 1978. *Educational Reform for a Changing Society: Anticipating Tomorrow's Schools*. Boston: Allyn & Bacon.

Russo, Gloria M. 1982. *Expanding Communication: Teaching Foreign Languages at the College Level*. New York: Harcourt Brace Jovanovich.

Sadow, Stephen A. 1982. *Idea Bank: Creative Activities for the Language Class*. Rowley, Mass.: Newbury House.

Schlesinger, I. M. 1968. *Sentence Structure and the Reading Process*. The Hague: Mouton.
   1977. *Production and Comprehension of Utterances*. Hillsdale, N.J.: Erlbaum.
Schumann, John H. 1978. *The Pidginization Process: A Model for Second Language Acquisition*. Rowley, Mass.: Newbury House.
Sebald, Hans. 1968. *Adolescence: A Sociological Analysis*. New York: Appleton-Century-Crofts.
Seelye, H. Ned. 1974. *Teaching Culture: Strategies for Foreign Language Educators*. Skokie, Ill.: National Textbook Co.
Silberman, Charles E. 1970. *Crisis in the Classroom*. New York: Random House.
Simon, Paul. 1980. *The Tongue-Tied American: Confronting the Foreign Language Crisis*. New York: Continuum.
Sims, W. D., and Hammond, S. B. 1981. *Award-Winning Foreign Language Programs: Prescriptions for Success*. In conjunction with ACTFL. Skokie, Ill.: National Textbook Co.
Skinner, Burrhus F. 1968. *The Technology of Teaching*. New York: Appleton-Century-Crofts.
Slobin, Dan I. 1979. *Psycholinguistics*, 2d ed. Glenview, Ill.: Scott, Foresman.
Smith, Frank, ed. 1973. *Psycholinguistics and Reading*. New York: Holt, Rinehart and Winston.
Smith, Frank, and Miller, George A., eds. 1966. *Genesis of Language*. Cambridge, Mass.: MIT Press.
Steiner, Florence. 1975. *Performing with Objectives*. Rowley, Mass.: Newbury House.
Stevick, Earl W. 1980. *Teaching Languages: A Way and Ways*. Rowley, Mass.: Newbury House
   1982. *Teaching and Learning Languages*. Cambridge: Cambridge University Press.
Strength Through Wisdom: A Critique of U.S. Capability. A Report to the President from the President's Commission on Foreign Language and International Studies. 1979. Washington, D.C.: Government Printing Office.
Sweet, Henry. 1899. *The Practical Study of Languages*. Reprint. London: Oxford University Press, 1964.
Toffler, Alvin. 1970. *Future Shock*. New York: Bantam Books.
Trim, John L. M. 1980. *Developing a Unit/Credit Scheme of Adult Language Learning*. Oxford: Pergamon Press, for the Council of Europe. Originally published 1978 by the Council of Europe, Strasbourg.
Trim, John L., Richterich, René, van Ek, Jan A., and Wilkins, David A. 1980. *Systems Development in Adult Language Learning: A Unit-Credit System for Modern Language Learning by Adults*. Oxford: Pergamon Press, for the Council of Europe. Originally published 1973 by the Council of Europe, Strasbourg.
Turner, Solveig M., ed. 1981. *Foreign Languages for the Professions: An Inter-Cultural Approach to Modern Communications*. Boston: Northeastern University.

Valette, Rebecca M. 1969. *Directions in Foreign Language Testing*. New York: MLA/ERIC.

Valette, Rebecca M. 1977. *Modern Language Testing*, 2d ed. New York: Harcourt Brace Jovanovich.

Valette, Rebecca M., and Disick, Renee S. 1972. *Modern Language Performance Objectives and Individualization*. New York: Harcourt Brace Jovanovich.

Van Ek, Jan A. 1977. *The Threshold Level for Modern Language Learning in Schools*. London: Longman. Originally published 1976 by the Council of Europe, Strasbourg.

Van Ek, Jan A., and Alexander, L. G. 1980. *Threshold Level English*. Oxford: Pergamon Press, for the Council of Europe.

Wardhaugh, Ronald. 1976. *The Contexts of Language*. Rowley, Mass.: Newbury House.

Winitz, Harris, ed. 1981. *The Comprehension Approach to Foreign Language Instruction*. Rowley, Mass.: Newbury House.

Wright, Andrew, Betteridge, David, and Buckby, Michael. 1979. *Games for Language Learning*. Cambridge: Cambridge University Press.

Index

accent, foreign, 114
accountability, 14, 15, 52
acquisition of language, *see* first-language
(L$_1$) acquisition; second-language
(L$_2$) acquisition
ACTFL Provisional Proficiency Guidelines, 17, 208–21, 225 n3, 238 n22,
144; scale for, 208
adolescent and adult learners, 22–3,
92, 94–6, 97–8, 99–100; investigation of needs of, 17–18, 20; *see also*
adult education; Council of Europe approach; critical period for
language acquisition; L$_1$ = L$_2$ acquisition controversy
adult education, 169, 171, 190, 206–7;
lifelong learning in, 14, 18, 22, 53
adult learners, *see* adolescent and adult
learners
advanced level, *see* college and university foreign language teaching; concentrators; nonmajors
affective element, 10, 80, 85, 113; in
classroom, 24, 109; in language-
learning laboratory (LLL), 133, 138;
and second culture, 175; *see also*
humanistic approach
analogy, 4, 59–60, 65, 67, 74
analysis by synthesis, 82–3, 232 n32
anxiety, *see* affective element
aphasia, 70
Asher, J.J., *see* Total Physical Response
(TPR)
associations, 61–2, 71, 82
attention, 66, 74, 80, 111, 133; span
of, 134
attitudes: toward language learning,
188; toward speakers of the
language, 112–13, 233 n10
audiolingual approach, 3–4, 58, 116,
194; *see also* confirmation of correct
response; dialogues; exercises
and drills, of structural patterns
audiovisual laboratory, *see* language-
learning laboratory (LLL)
aural-oral approach, *see* audiolingual
approach
Ausubel, D.P., 118
authentic materials, 4, 75, 76, 157,
231 n15; for reading and listening, 88, 97–8; in language-learning
laboratory (LLL), 137, 140

basic course, 18, 20, 178; *see also*
threshold level course
basics in foreign-language teaching, 14,
15, 18, 52
behavioral objectives, *see* performance
objectives
behaviorism, *see* Skinner, B.F.
Bever, T.G., 79, 97; analysis of concepts of, 106; psychogrammar
of, 98–9
bilingual programs, 21–22, 27–8, 116,
193, 206, 234 n16
Bloom, L., 57
Blumenthal, A.L., 76, 229–30 n16
body language, *see* nonverbal
communication
Boakes, R., 229–30 n16
Bruner, J.S., 69
Brunet, G.R., 113
business, language for, 9–10, 162, 178;
see also career education

career education, 14, 18, 19–20, 22–3,
35–6, 38, 49, 52–3, 121, 128,
158, 206–7; at college level, 10,
169, 170, 177–9; *see also* Northeastern University (Boston) program;
objectives of language study
Carroll, J.B., 102–3, 105; 231 n18;
and testing, 141–2, 151; two-
stream proposal of, 75–6, 97–8, 106
case for foreign-language study, 19,
24–8, 31–3, 76, 122, 128, 177, 193,
235–6 n10; at college level, 173,
183–4; *see also* objectives of language study
cassettes and tapes, 176; audio, 59,
135; video, 29, 117, 137, 161,
188, 240–1 n19; videotaping in
teacher training, 202, 203
Chall, J., 103
child language learning, *see* first-language
(L$_1$) acquisition; Piaget, J., stages of
cognitive development of
Chomsky, C., 232 n22
Chomsky, N., 60, 62–3, 64, 67, 223
n7, 229 n7; competence in, 4–5, 60;
performance in, 5, 64, 79, 80;
see also deep structure; hypothesis
testing; innateness; language acquisition device (LAD); rule-governed
behavior; surface structure

250

252

Galanter, E., 62, 142
Galyean, B., 53
games and competitions, 66, 115
Gardner, R.C., 112–13, 233 n10
Gary, J. Olmsted, 230 n17
Garrett, M., 229 n14
Gattegno, C., *see* Silent Way
general education, foreign languages in, 38, 121–7
Gestalt, *see* transposition (Gestalt)
gestures, *see* nonverbal communication
gisting, 84, 90
Gliksman, L., 233 n12
global education, 15, 28–9, 54; *see also* international perspective
Goodlad, J.L., 118
Goodman, K.S., 89; psycholinguistic guessing game of, 100
Gouin, F., 136
grammar, 74–5, 160–1, 165; through activity, 149, 162, 188; in audio-lingual approach, 3; combinatorial productivity of, 62; in cognitive code-learning approach, 5; in first-language (L_1) acquisition, 56–7; for functional communication, 157; in grammar-translation approach, 2–3; in natural language learning, 6; for production, 97; and reading, 103–4; for recognition, 97; review of, 156, 160; system of, 72, 99; *see also* communication, syntax in; listening, syntax in; rules, inter-nalization of; semantics, syntactic relations and; structuralism; sys-tem of language; transformational-generative grammar
grammars, interim, 5, 57
grammar-translation approach, 2–3, 5, 63
Grass, G., 183
Grittner, F.M., 54
group work, 23, 66, 111, 128, 146, 147, 163

habit: in associations, 61; formation of, 3, 4, 132; language as, 122; in language learning, 58–9, 62; *see also* generalization; reinforcement; Skinner, B.F., stimulus-response (S-R) learning
handicapped students, *see* mainstreaming; students, handicapped
Harris, D.P., 141
Harvard program, 8–10, 224 n18, 239 nn2,9, 240 nn13,19, 241 nn20,23

Hayden, R.L., 54
Hayes, A.S., 132
Hocking, E., 139
Hoefnagel-Höhle, M., 93, 94
Hoffding function, 227 n11
Holmes, D.L., 232 n22
Holt, J., 109
home-stay exchange programs, *see* exchange and study-abroad programs
hors d'oeuvre approach, *see* two-stage approach
Hosenfeld, C., 53
Huebener, T., 19
humanistic approach, 14, 23–5, 33, 37, 50, 53, 155, 193; *see also* objectives of language study, of learners
humanities, role of, 15, 31–3, 55; at college level, 170, 179–80
Hutchins, R., 149, 238 n17
hypothesis testing, 4, 5, 75–6; *see also* language acquisition device (LAD)

Illich, I., 149, 238 n18
illiterates, 94–5
imitation, 4, 58
immigrants, languages of, 129, 193
independent study, 30, 145–6, 147
individual differences, 53, 111, 127–8, 134–5, 145–6, 147, 158, 193
individualized instruction, 6–7, 23, 30, 110–11, 127, 145–7, 190, 235 n6; evaluation in, 237 n13; in teacher training, 202; *see also* students, as individuals
induction in learning, 6, 74, 99
inferencing, 4, 85, 86, 94, 97; in reading, 101–4, 105–6
information processing, 70, 80, 82–3, 86
Inhelder, B., 93
innateness, *see* language acquisition device (LAD)
interaction, communicative, 24, 75, 127, 149, 188; activities for, 6; personal element in, 65, 67, 227 n22; *see also* communication; cre-ative language use; natural lan-guage use; normal purposes of language; production of speech; speaking
Interagency Language Roundtable (ILR), 17, 144, 208; *see also* ACTFL Provisional Proficiency Guidelines; Foreign Service Institute Rating Scales of Absolute Language Proficiency

intercommunity understanding, 170, 173–6
interdisciplinary approach, 8, 28, 172, 176, 182
interference, see transfer, negative
interim grammars, 5; in first-language (L₁) acquisition, 57
interlanguage, 5
International High Schools, see magnet schools
international perspective, 15, 28–9, 36, 54; at college level, 170, 171–3; see also global education
internship, see teacher training, preservice
interpersonal relations, 15, 16, 25–6, 37, 54
interpreting, see translation and interpreting
intonation, 81, 177

Jenkins, J.J., 228 n7
Johnson, S., 191
Johnson, T., 233 n2
Johnson-Laird, P.N., 102
Juilland, A., 55
junior colleges, see two-year undergraduate institutions

Katona, G., 64–5
kinesics, see nonverbal communication
Kolers, P.A., 101, 232 n22
Krashen, S., 93, 230 nn2,3

L₁ = L₂ acquisition controversy, 92–3, 98–9, 230 n1; see also critical period for language acquisition; first-language (L₁) acquisition; second-language (L₂) acquisition
Lado, R., 141
Lambert, W.C. 112
Lange, D.L., 208
language: choice of, 128–9, 130; nature of, 3, 4, 72, 73
language acquisition device (LAD), 4–5
language for specific purposes (LSP), 20, 50, 177–8, 206; and reading, 103, 106–7
language-learning laboratory (LLL), 31, 60, 138; in audiolingual approach, 4; director of, 131, 133, 136–9; history of, 132–4; and the instructor, 138–9; the learner in, 132–3, 134–5; listening in, 87; teaching in, 135–7; see also cassettes and tapes; computer-assisted in-

struction (CAI); discs; media, use of
Lavergneau, R.L., 52
Law of Effect, see Thorndike, E.B.
Leestma, R., 54
Lenneberg, E.H., 93
Lester, K.A., 53
liberal education, foreign languages in, 15, 32–3, 38, 50, 55, 155, 157, 167, 176–7, 183; see also general education; humanities, role of
Lieberman, P., 81
Liedke, O.K., 235 n3
linguistic approach, 37–8, 128, 176–7; at college level, 170
linguistic theories, see sociolinguistics; structuralism; transformational-generative grammar
listening, 48, 75–6, 79–84, 229 n2; ACTFL guidelines for proficiency in, 211–14; in audiolingual approach, 3; in cognitive code-learning, 5; initial, 84–6, 230 n17; materials for, 78, 84, 102, 135; with reading, 90; research in, 96–7; stages of, 86–8; syntax in, 82, 84, 86, 87, 90, 96; tasks in, 105; teaching of, 86–8; testing of, 105–6; see also perception
literature, 2, 33, 38, 157, 158, 162, 179–80; teachers of, 162, 163; see also humanities, role of
living language courses, see college and university foreign-language teaching
Lowe, P., 208
Lowell, J.R., 11
Lozanov, G., see Suggestopaedia
Lukmani, Y.M., 233 n11
Luria, A.R., 69

macro-language use, 149–53
magazines, 29, 173, 187
magnet schools, 22
mainstreaming, 14, 21, 53, 126–7; see also students, handicapped
majors, see concentrators
manipulation level, see two levels of language control
Marcel, C., 136
Marshall, J.C., 229 n16
masks and puppets, 24
matching, see analysis by synthesis
McCarthy, D.A., 234 n27
McNeece, L.S., 227 n20
McNeill, D., 226 n1

meaning: in language learning, 74, 75, 76, 134; in language use, 73; in listening, 81, 82; in reading, 101–2, 104–6; *see also* semantics

media, use of, 136, 139; *see also* cassettes and tapes; computer-assisted instruction (CAI); discs; language-learning laboratory (LLL)

Melvin, B.S., 69, 228 n8, 236 n5

memorization, 58, 62, 66, 70–2, 135; in audiolingual approach, 3; in grammar-translation approach, 2; of vocabulary, 2, 71

memory, 69–70, 71–2, 73–5, 80, 228 n8; concepts in, 73; echoic, 82, 86; long-term, 73, 74; in reading, 94, 105–6; recognition in, 62; retention in, 81, 82, 87–8; short-term, 86–7; span of, 134; storage and retrieval in, 70, 75, 84, 160; *see also* networks, conceptual; memorization

methods courses, *see* teacher training, methods courses for

micro-language learning, 149–50, 152–3

microteaching, *see* teacher training, videotaping in

Miller, G.A., 54, 62, 63, 70, 77, 82, 100, 142

minority students, 21, 127

Monsees, A., 53

Montaigne, M. de, 45

Morain, G., 54

Moravcsik, J., 55

Moskowitz, G., 51

motivation, 94, 124, 127, 129, 184, 188, 234 nn16–17; achievement as, 110, 111, 118, 235 n32; autonomous impulses in, 111; in the classroom, 108–9, 114–17; through course content, 158; definition of, 108; ego-involvement as, 111–12, 118; experiments in, 108; hedonistic, 111; individual nature of, 108, 110, 112; integrative and instrumental, 112–13; intrinsic, 111; in language learning laboratory (LLL), 133–4; for reading, 95

Mueller, M., 241 n23

multicultural education, 15, 16, 26–8, 36, 38, 54; at college level, 169, 170, 173–6; *see also* culture, second; culture shock

National Council on Foreign Language and International Studies, 169

native language, use of, 124, 176

native speakers, use of, 76, 109, 113, 137, 140; at college level, 157, 160, 175, 177; in cultural understanding, 174

natural language learning, 5, 116, 234 n21

natural language use, 150, 151–2; *see also* creative language use; normal purposes of language

Neisser, U., 81, 90;

networks, conceptual, 72–4, 104

neuropsychology, 70, 93

newscasts, 76, 139, 151

newspapers, 29, 173, 187

New York State curriculum guide (1978), 18

nonmajors, 50, 159, 171, 181, 238 n2, 239 n2, 240 nn12–13

nonverbal communication, 26, 54, 83, 137, 177, 240–1 n19; in second culture, 25–6

normal purposes of language, 62, 75, 149, 228 n12; *see also* task-oriented language learning

normal speech, characteristics of, 98

Northeastern University (Boston) program, 10, 225 n19

Nostrand, H.L., 208

notional-functional approach, *see* functional-notional approach

objectives of language study, 2, 13; at college level, 21, 167, 171–81; how to identify, 43–7; of learners, 34–43, 52, 135, 144, 145, 147, 237 n9; statements of, 18, 19, 20, 22, 23, 25, 26, 28, 29, 31, 33, 35, 36, 37, 38, 47–51; ten trends in, 13–15; *see also* diversification of content; performance objectives; questionnaires, Rivers (1978); reading, objectives in; students, interests of, needs of

Olson, D.R., 102

Omaggio, A., 208

oral survival and communication-oriented courses, 9, 23, 26, 158, 160, 161, 177, 182, 239 n5, 240 n13; *see also* communication; college and university foreign-language teaching, living language courses in

order of skills, 136

second-language (L$_2$) acquisition, 73, 109, 134, 231 n11; influence of L$_1$ on L$_2$, 74; *see also* critical period for language acquisition; L$_1$ = L$_2$ acquisition controversy

Seliger, H.W., 230 n2

semantic networks, *see* networks, conceptual

semantics, 72, 106, 149; in L$_1$ acquisition, 57; in production of speech, 98–9; syntactic relations and, 84; *see also* meaning; networks, conceptual

semantic-syntactic decoding, 230 n18

Shinall, A., 242 n5

Shinall, S., 242 n5

Silent Way, 136, 195, 225 n20, 236 n9

Simon, P., 240 n11

simulation games, *see* role playing

situations, 18, 64, 83, 116; communicative, 113, 115, 137; *see also* context; dialogues

skill-getting and skill-using, 6, 95, 122, 224 n13; *see also* order of skills

skill-learning approach, 57–60

Skinner, B.F., 58–9, 226 nn4–5; *see also* habit; reinforcement; stimulus-response (S-R) learning

skits, *see* drama techniques

Slobin, D.I., 78, 91

Smith, F., 100, 103

Smythe, P.C., 113

Snow, C., 93, 94

social and psychological distance, 94–5, 113–14, 234 n15

societal pressures, 34, 131, 141, 240 n10, 241 n3; on college programs, 166, 167–70; on curriculum, 13, 15

songs and music, 24, 33, 76, 115, 127–8, 137, 173

sound-symbol correspondences, 71, 100, 104–5

sound system, 72, 149; *see also* accent, foreign; stress and intonation

speaking: ACTL guidelines for proficiency in, 209–11; as goal, 108–9; *see also* communication; creative language use; interaction, communicative; natural language use; normal purposes of language; production of speech

Stanislavski method, 227 n20

Starr, S.F., 226 n10

stereotypes, *see* culture, second

Stern, H.H., 236 n11

Stevick, E.W., 236 n9

Sticht, T.G., 105

stimulus-response (S-R) learning, 71, 72, 132–3; *see also* habit; reinforcement; Skinner, B.F.

Strasheim, L.A., 54

strategies of learners, 2–3, 134–5, 158, 236 n5; *see also* individual differences

strategy and tactics, 63–4

stress and intonation, 81, 104; *see also* pronunciation

structuralism, 3

students: at advanced level, 8–9; attitude to foreign language of, 120; in classroom, 109, 112; and decision making, 117, 125, 148, 189, 197; disadvantaged, 127–8; gifted, 15, 29–31, 54; handicapped, 126–7; as individuals, 5–6, 15, 149, 155–6; interests of, 34, 111, 117–18, 126, 150–1, 177; needs of, 6–7, 21, 162, 180; perceptions of, 111–12, 116, 117, 122, 166, 169, 184; selection of, 124–5; in two-year undergraduate institutions, 184, 186–7, 190; *see also* equality of opportunity; individualized instruction; mainstreaming; motivation; objectives of language study; student-teacher relations, testing student-centered

student-teacher relations, 10–11, 39, 75, 120–9, 192, 194, 196; changing, 192; in testing, 143

study-abroad programs, *see* exchange and study-abroad programs

Suggestopaedia, 136, 195, 225 n20, 233 n6, 236 n9

surface structure, 60, 64, 84, 88, 97; *see also* Chomsky, N.

Sweet, H., 5

syllabus: experiential, 136–7; functional, 136, 140; structural, 136; *see also* curriculum

syntax, *see* grammar

system of language, 65, 67, 81, 82; *see also* grammar; rules

systems approach, *see* threshold level course

Tamarkin, T., 53

task-oriented language learning, 160, 161, 177; in listening, 105; in reading, 105, 107; *see also* normal purposes of language; reading, and purposeful activity; testing, task-oriented

teacher: in classroom, 21, 111, 112, 123; and cultural understanding, 27, 29; as decision maker, 195; as experimenter, 118, 158; as individual, 146, 158; and present state of the field, 194–7; as professional, 13, 15, 33, 34, 44–5, 128, 146, 194, 204–5; and public awareness, 206; training of, 122–3, 124, 128–9, 198; in two-year undergraduate institutions, 185–6; role of, 2, 4, 19, 24, 47, 97, 116, 117, 120, 127; *see also* student-teacher relations; teacher training

teacher training, 8, 28–9, 45, 154, 191–2, 198–200, 243 n6; for college and university foreign-language departments, 163–4, 172, 175, 180–1, 197–8, 241 n23; for culture, 192; inservice, 196, 203–5; methods courses for, 200–3; preservice, 203–4; videotaping in, 202, 203

team teaching, at college level, 172

television, 76, 117, 137, 139, 171

terminal and continuing courses, 156–7, 186

Terrell, T.D., 224 n11; *see also* natural language learning

testing: accuracy and, 152; for achievement, 31; for aptitude, 4; criterion-referenced, 142–3, 147, 151; discrete-point, 150, 152–3; and diversified content, 147–8, 153, 158; fill-in-the-blank, 150; guidelines for assessment in, 17; in individualized programs, 145–7, 153; influence on teaching and learning of, 141–2, 149, 151–2, 163; of listening comprehension, 105–6; for minimal competency, 14, 15–16; multiple-choice, 150; norm-referenced, 143; for proficiency, 143–4, 151; of reading comprehension, 105–6; of speech, 208–11; in stimulus-response (S-R) learning, 71; student-centered, 142–5; task-oriented, 150–1; *see also* ACTFL Provisional Proficiency Guidelines

Thorndike, E.B., 64, 110

threshold level course, 18; *see also* basic course; Council of Europe approach; functional-notional approach

Toffler, A., 167–8

Torrey, J., 232 n22

Total Physical Response (TPR), 116, 136

TOTE model, 142

Trager, G.L., 223 n1

transfer: positive, 90; negative, 97

transformational-generative grammar, 63; see also Chomsky, N.; deep structure; hypothesis testing; language acquisition device (LAD); surface structure

translation and interpreting, 2–3, 20, 88, 160–1, 178, 239 n8

transposition (Gestalt), 65, 90

Tursi, J.A., 53

two levels of language control (Rivers), 149–50; manipulation in, 64, 65–6, 67; selection in, 63–4, 65, 67

two-stage approach, 187–9, 241–2 n8

two-year undergraduate institutions, foreign languages in 183–90, 206–7

unit-credit system *see* Council of Europe approach

universals of language, 88, 99

university foreign-language departments, *see* college and university foreign-language teaching

University of Illinois study (1973), *see* questionnaires, University of Illinois (1973)

Valdman, A., 239 n4

Valette, R.M., 141, 150

values clarification, 15, 27, 32–3, 33, 54, 158; at college level, 170, 175, 183

Veatch, J., 146

videocassettes and videotapes, *see* cassettes and tapes, video

Villani, S., 240 n13

visual aids, 66, 85, 127

vocabulary, 128, 147; activities for, 228 n10; in L_1 acquisition, 56–7; in L_2 acquisition, 57; learning of, 73, 74–5; in natural language learning, 6; and reading, 103–4; *see also* memorization; networks, conceptual

Wales, R.J., 229 n16

Weiby, M., 233 n2

Weingartner, C., 189

Weiss, L., 118

Wilson, J.A., 100

writing, 160; ACTFL guidelines for proficiency in, 216–20; activities for, 161–2; testing of, 150

writing system, *see* script, new